# ALL IN MY HEAD

# ALL IN MY HEAD

## The Autobiography

## Lar Corbett
### with Damian Lawlor

TRANSWORLD IRELAND

TRANSWORLD IRELAND
an imprint of The Random House Group Limited
20 Vauxhall Bridge Road, London SW1V 2SA
www.transworldbooks.co.uk

**ALL IN MY HEAD**
**A TRANSWORLD IRELAND BOOK: 9781848271470**

First published in 2012 by Transworld Ireland,
a division of Transworld Publishers
Transworld Ireland paperback edition published 2013

Copyright © Lar Corbett 2012

Lar Corbett has asserted his right under the Copyright, Designs
and Patents Act 1988 to be identified as the author of this work.

This book is a work of non-fiction.

A CIP catalogue record for this book
is available from the British Library.

Addresses for Random House Group Ltd companies outside the UK
can be found at: www.randomhouse.co.uk
The Random House Group Ltd Reg. No. 954009

The Random House Group Limited supports the Forest Stewardship Council® (FSC®), the
leading international forest-certification organisation. Our books carrying the FSC label are
printed on FSC®-certified paper. FSC is the only forest-certification scheme supported by
the leading environmental organisations, including Greenpeace. Our paper procurement
policy can be found at www.randomhouse.co.uk/environment

Typeset in Ehrhardt by
Kestrel Data, Exeter, Devon.
Printed and bound by
CPI Group (UK) Ltd, Croydon, CR0 4YY.

2 4 6 8 10 9 7 5 3 1

# Contents

# Prologue

I wake up with the torment of the day before still raging in my mind.

After just a few seconds I know I have never felt worse in my life.

Rubbing the sleep from my eyes I peer over at the bedside locker and grab my phone. It's a reflex action at this stage.

There's a stillness about the place. I live on the outskirts of Thurles town in a quiet estate populated mostly by young families. The people are decent, friends are close by, and every-one gets on.

But while the silence suits just fine I know it won't last long.

I debate whether to get up and at it or crawl back under the duvet. I want to stay in this room for as long as possible but I'm drawn to my iPhone. Anyone who has one, well the first thing they do when they wake up is lean over and check their Facebook page, their Twitter account, whatever. That seems to be the way it is these days.

My mobile lights up and goes searching for a reception bar. In those few seconds I feel like a lad in the dock waiting nervously for a jury to hand down its verdict.

If I'm honest, I already know my fate.

Kilkenny have just hammered us by 18 points in an All-Ireland semi-final. Bad enough to be involved in an all-time low like that but worse still to be cast as the villain in the entire production.

The phone starts beeping and it doesn't stop. As I connect with the outside world it feels like the whole place is ganging up against me.

Most days I use social media to plug events and promotions at my bar. I find the interaction intriguing and very effective. Now I see the other side of it. There's a torrent of abuse coming at me on various forums and it's thunderous.

*I highly recommend you keep the doors of your establishment firmly closed tonight . . . He is a disgrace to Tipp hurling and a disgrace to Thurles . . . He should have been pulled off . . . Lar is past it . . . That shit with Tommy Walsh is juvenile . . . Where's the good sportsmanship? . . . That's not how hurling works . . .*

– Facebook

*Were ye watching the match? Lar done his best my bollix. A fucking disgrace, he should never have come back. The famous LAR CORBETT.*

– Twitter

*Everyone has a bad game but to have a bad game you must play the game instead of chasing another man around the pitch because he said something to him, probably like he had money on himself not to score today. Like against Waterford???*

– GAA website

Yesterday, knowing I wouldn't be allowed to hurl the way I normally do, knowing that Kilkenny's corner-back, Jackie Tyrrell, would do everything in his power to take me out of the game – by pulling and dragging out of me – I took on a new role in the Tipperary team.

It was a decision made by myself, the management team and three other forwards, all of us aware that the Kilkenny backs were going to snuff me out of the game by whatever means possible.

The plan was basic enough. If I wasn't going to be let hit a ball, well then, I would still try to influence the game by distracting Tommy Walsh, Kilkenny's best defender. If Jackie wanted me out of the reckoning that was fine but why should he dictate?

We decided that my job was to tailgate Tommy for the day and try to nullify two of their best backs in the process. You can say what you want about that, call me what you like, but our plan was working.

We led at half-time by a point. I had been on the ball three times, set up a goal and almost created another. Walsh and Tyrrell hadn't a strike of note between them.

Yet my phone tells me there was a massive row at half-time in our dressing-room. There was no row. In fact we were buzzing.

Then we went out for the second half, they started running at us and we collapsed. Shipped three more goals. In a flash our high hopes were crumbling all around us. Looks like I'm left standing in the rubble.

The texts keep coming.

*Did you hear what Michael Duignan said about you on TV?*

I didn't.

Someone else gets in touch to say that over 700,000 people tuned into the game and most everyone would have been influenced by Duignan's comments. He said I was a disgrace, that I was out to get Tommy Walsh sent off. That's not my game, I don't think like that. I've never once gone out on the field with a thought like that in my head.

The beeps continue.

Did you hear what so-and-so wrote?

*Babs Keating says he will never go to watch Tipperary hurl again if you get another jersey.*

There are a few nice texts and messages too but they're almost lost in the storm. I won't lie to you, I feel isolated. It's devastating that people think it's all my fault.

Eventually I put the bloody phone down. I drag myself out of bed, hit the shower, and get ready to go to my bar to do a couple of jobs.

Opening the front door I take a deep breath and head toward my van. There's salt in the air.

It feels like I've been here before.

# 1

# Young, free and foolish

As a young lad I was all over the place, a disaster in school and lackadaisical about sport. In a county where hurling is king it was great pucking the ball around but when it came to playing games I wasn't much bothered.

Still, I suppose I can thank our neighbours the Meehans and the Craddocks for the fact I have a half-decent first touch – for years they endured the relentless rattling of the sliotar against the gable ends of their houses, next door to ours in Willowmere Drive.

Most evenings after school at Thurles CBS, their end walls were my goalposts and nets, even though I knew the vibrations were driving them nuts inside in their living-rooms, and I got many a telling-off. I didn't do it out of badness, it was just lack of thought.

They got their own back from time to time. Whenever the sliotar missed its target and went skimming over a wall it became the property of the householder and I knew I had a slim chance of getting it back.

Maybe if they had known I was a Tipp All-Ireland winner in the making they'd have been happier about having their evenings in front of the TV spoiled by the brat next door. But why would they suspect that? I played hardly any games. They must have asked themselves at times was I deliberately trying to annoy them.

That was me: a carefree contradiction. I played on and off for Dúrlas Óg. In 1996 we reached an under-14 Mid-Tipperary final, which should have been a big enough deal at the time. And yet it wasn't important enough to prevent me taking the day off and heading to Tramore. A few of my pals were bound for the beach – they weren't big into hurling – and I tagged along. I hardly gave the match a second thought.

When the team mentors called to the door, my long-suffering mother, Breda, had to tell them that I wasn't around.

So it would be no wonder if the Meehans and the Craddocks were confused. When out peppering the brickwork I was like Forrest Gump, new grips, the best sticks, all manic concentration and a fair bit of skill, and yet I might lack the motivation even to turn up for a big game. To this day that inconsistency is there in my life. Maybe it explains why my love affair with Tipp hurling has been such a stormy one.

I don't think I'll ever lose the will to hit a ball against the wall though; it's the thing I love most. When you're on your own doing something like that your mind is free and you can lose yourself in the drill. It's grand to be tearing around Croke Park or Semple Stadium, scoring goals and knocking over points, and the crowd roaring, but pucking a ball around is what I love most.

Our housing estate in Thurles was small and quiet and Pa Bourke was only down the road. Over the years we'd often tip over to the green in my estate and fire sliotars around. Wind, rain or hail. Tap, tap, tap. During the summer evenings the two of us would be out in our back yards, both peppering the walls with shots.

Even then Pa was better than me at trapping the ball – and he still is. That comes from practice.

When the new O'Neills sliotars were launched a few years back he asked John Hayes, the Tipp kitman, who is better known as Hotpoint, for a dozen. Pa ripped them apart, took out the black rubber core and started practising with that. From the other side of the green I could hear the ping those balls made, but I had been hearing similar noises from his house since he was a kid.

We mostly played a game we called 'cat', where if you dropped the ball once you picked up a C and the next time you got an A and so on. At the start I was beating him five-nil and ten-nil, but gradually he caught up. One day he had me on the rack and I pipped him only at the death. He missed out on the grand prize, which, by the way, was always the sliotar.

'Here, Pa,' I said, feeling sorry for him. 'You came close to beating me this time – you have it,' and I drove the ball toward his house. I was inside having my tea a while later when a knock came to the door. It was Pa.

'You can take the sliotar back,' he said, handing it over. 'I won't take it off you till I beat you fair and square.' And away he went.

'There's a bit of drive in that lad,' I thought, as he ambled down the path.

In the long run his determination paid off. I had to stop pucking around with him because his touch was just too good, and to have a lad seven years my junior beating me the whole time was wrecking my confidence. When I ran out at Páirc Uí Chaoimh for my Tipp senior debut in 2001 it was fitting that Pa represented the county in the Primary Schools game the same day.

Most of the Tipp senior hurlers have bulging trophy cabinets at home, having knocked off county titles at every grade all the way up along, but not me. I won only one juvenile medal – and that was at under-12 football with Dúrlas Óg.

We had a coach at the club, John Hickey, who was always encouraging me and looking out for my welfare – he's teaching in Clonmel now. He tried hard to get me involved more with hurling; whenever we met he'd stop and ask how I was getting on. He showed an interest but I didn't always reciprocate.

Back then I hung out with a different crowd – I won't call them a wrong crowd, but by the time I turned fifteen my mother didn't know the half of what I was up to, which was just as well. And people who saw me around the town back then would have been justified in thinking I wouldn't amount to much.

The lads I knocked around with were fond of a few cans of beer and a packet of cigarettes – and anything else that came their way. In fairness, they never caused any real trouble, and so I was content to tag along with them. We'd have a few cans and a few smokes before heading off to a disco. With a pack of ten in my jeans pocket and a bellyful of beer I'd be ready to go anywhere. I feared nothing.

One night I tipped over to The Ragg nightclub, cocky as you like about getting in even though I hadn't the root of a facial hair. Rody Lowry, a lad I knew, was on the door and we struck up a fine conversation while I queued. But when I got to the top of the queue he told me to feck off.

'Larry, I'm after refereeing an under-16 game only a little while ago and you were playing in it,' he said. 'How can I let you in? Come back to me in a few years' time and we'll have another look at your credentials.'

On weekend nights we might take off to Killough Quarry and set up a tent on the side of a hill close to the woods. That's where the boys would crack open a few cans. It was mighty fun while it lasted, though it's sad to say a few of them went down a rocky enough road since. I could have gone the same track myself, and

I'm grateful that hurling eventually intervened and I managed to take another direction.

I'd like to tell you that as I went through my teens I had a sudden change of heart – that I turned a new leaf and devoted myself to books and sport. Athletes often trace their success right back to their formative years and the way they listened to the wise counsel of mentors and applied themselves in school and training.

But you'd need several magnifying glasses to find any such pattern with me, because my indifference to hurling lasted until I was seventeen and my problems in school persisted to the end.

Before being called up to the county senior team in 2000 I can only clearly recall going to see Tipp in one championship match away from home, and that was in Cork in 1999, when Clare beat us after a replay. When I was nine my father, Eddie, brought me to games but I have little memory of those. Seemingly I would hop into the back of his van and he would sit me on his knee during the match. As I got older I didn't trouble the turnstiles too often because most of the time I was experimenting left, right and centre with a whole variety of things. Hurling was well down the pecking order and I didn't even finish out my underage career with Dúrlas Óg.

That chapter ended badly, in fact. We were playing a match when one of the selectors started shouting at me. When I shouted back, he got even angrier, pointed a flag at me – how dare I undermine him? – and threatened to get me thrown out of the club. Later in the dressing-room he had another pop at me. I thought it was unfair, so I just asked myself why I would bother even playing for the club when this fellow wanted me out.

In hindsight my grievances were with just one chap and I should have seen the bigger picture. Dúrlas Óg gave me my start in hurling and they taught me the basics. They are one of the

most successful clubs in the county and have helped out count-
less young lads. It just didn't work out for me. Mam dropped me
up to my first training session when I was five. She knew very
little about the technical side of the game but she wanted to give
me the best possible start and so I arrived with a 34-inch hurley
that reached from the ground to my neck. One of the Dúrlas Óg
lads laughed when he saw me.

'Come back in about five years and get a smaller hurley,' he
said.

I did go back but that disagreement with one selector remains
an unfortunate memory.

Any Thurles lad who moves on from Dúrlas Óg has a choice of
two adult clubs: Thurles Gaels and Thurles Sarsfields. I went
to the Sars and made their minor team at just fifteen. Playing
three years' minor club hurling in Tipperary is not bad going,
particularly when you haven't set the place alight from twelve to
sixteen. I suppose even though my busy social life was leading
me everywhere from the woods to the quarries to the back lanes
of Thurles, there must have been some deep-seated grá for hurling, because it kept dragging me back.

It had to compete with other sports too. I tried rugby, lining
out for Thurles at under-12 and under-14 and thinking I was
the next big thing when I scored a try and saw my name in the
*Tipperary Star* newspaper. I also played soccer with Peake Villa
at under-12, slotting in at left back for a full season.

Around that time I couldn't even make the Harty Cup team
for Thurles CBS. The Harty Cup is the premier competition for
Munster colleges hurling and it's a badge of honour for anyone to
play in it. But while Séamus Butler, Damien Young, John Lawlor
and other bright young lads about town were stars of that set-up,
I didn't even make the team in my final year. I had no complaints
either; I wasn't good enough.

To be fair to the teachers, you could hardly pick a lad for the Harty team when he would be in the bike shed puffing cigs at ten o'clock in the morning and there again at lunchtime. A lad who might turn up for training or might not.

My Leaving Cert results were average and there was no real prospect of a job so I started helping out in the family pub. I wasn't long into that job when I was asked back by the school to repeat the Leaving Cert. I knew they weren't inviting me back to prepare for a distinguished academic career in Trinity College Dublin. Essentially, I was brought back to play hurling. My guess is that the teachers saw me dossing around the town and felt it was better to have me in school in the faint hope that whatever little talent I had might one day blossom.

I argued that I was already getting plenty of further education from the daytime drinkers in our family's bar on Cathedral Street, which was where I got much of my early knowledge anyway. The folks had that pub for the bones of twenty years and while you would get a fair few drinkers in there, it would mostly be slow and steady – Guinness after Guinness. They'd be in for the chat as much as the black stuff.

I got to know all the regulars and got plenty of free advice – what they call life coaching now, I think. One old lad told me not to be wasting my time and exhausting my brain with book learning but to instead go out and buy as much land as I could.

'Why?' I enquired.

'Because God is not making it any more, son – 'twill be worth a fortune some day. Now, could you put a head on that like a good lad?'

Despite that nugget of wisdom, I eventually agreed to go back to school. Séamus Butler went back to repeat his Leaving Cert too and we would head up to the school, grab a cup of tea and have a chat, take a few classes and then tip off training. That was about the size of it.

The reformation was short-lived. The week after we lost the Harty Cup I left school again, this time for good.

There's no point in looking back with regret. Those wasted years can never be recovered or changed. But the one thing I will say is thank God for hurling, because without it I might still have a big, fat zero beside my name.

I was brutal in school, going out of my way to frustrate the teachers, was flirting with trouble around the town, and had no interest in taking on the family bar. In fact there were times when I wouldn't have been a pleasant fellow at all and I'm not proud of that. I'd like to think I'm a better person now. Let's just say I'm a very lucky man I got to play for Tipp. I'm also blessed that, no matter how many headaches I caused, Mam always stood by me, even when she didn't know what I had been up to. I hope I've repaid her trust over the years. I leaned on her pretty much all of the time.

I have a sister, Helen, two years younger than me and very close to my mother as well. I suppose Mam always spoiled the two of us and made sure we wanted for nothing. Nearly every family in Ireland could lay hands on the Bible and honestly testify that the mammy is the rock of the whole clan. And that's just how it is with us; my mother is the one who keeps it all going.

She stood up for me even when I acted like a muppet. There were times when I'd be gone all day and night and yet she wouldn't lay into me when I wandered in like an oul' stray cat. There was never any hassle. And it wasn't just me – she would be kind to everyone who crossed her path.

If I wanted a hurl she would get me one, even if I might not use it for months. If I asked for a helmet there was one put in front of me. I had a pair of boots whenever the old ones split. I was spoiled and I knew it.

It can't have been easy for her that I was sloppy in school and outside of it too. And if it was unpleasant for her to have to clean up my mess, I'd say it was a nightmare altogether for the school-teachers who had to endure a cocktail of disruption and apathy when they dealt with me.

I reckon my bad attitude was very much the result of brutal insecurity. I had huge problems with reading and writing and I suffered agonies in trying to avoid being found out and humiliated. And so I was the smart fellow down the back of the class with all the answers, letting on to be the clever man simply because really I knew very little of what was going on. I'd find a weak spot in a teacher and set about pressing that button for as long as I could get away with it.

I was compensating by acting the ape. My spelling was and still is atrocious – so bad that even the predictive texting on my phone can't make head or tail of what I'm trying to write. In fact I now suspect after all these years that I'm dyslexic, though I was never checked for the condition. And maybe it's something I should get checked out for.

In school, my biggest fear was that I'd be asked to write spellings on the board or read in front of the class. When I left school I thought all those worries were behind me. But there were scenarios in the Tipp team room over the years when I was asked to go to the white board and scribble down my thoughts in front of the whole squad, and I just couldn't do it. I'd panic and deflect the request, maybe asking Eoin Kelly to go up in my place. To this day it bothers me.

But in school I masked all that stuff and just concentrated on making life hell for teachers. Not surprisingly, I was never in much contact with them after leaving but I often imagined a few of them watching Tipperary games, spotting me and muttering, 'Ah, Corbett! That fella broke my heart.'

In most secondary schools around this county you can get away with blue murder in class if you're a good hurler. That's not right but it's just a fact of life. For most of my time in school I didn't even have that to lean on; I was regarded as a lad who could hurl and had ability but I definitely wouldn't have had any great reputation.

There was a turning point, however, and if I was to map it out it was winning a county minor title with Thurles Sarsfields in 1999 and then starting an apprenticeship as an electrician shortly after. I ended up working with two bosses for ten years and never once had an argument with either Tom McDonald or Ray Corbet, no relation. In later years when I was preparing for big games and needed time off work they never refused me. And during the height of the economic boom I often went to them and requested weekends off for training camps and matches and never came away disappointed. They were brilliant.

I worked hard too, especially for my electrical senior trade exams, which involved numeracy, calculus, formulas, all that sort of stuff. I hadn't applied myself to that in school so I sought grinds, took whatever help was available and ended up with 85 per cent in the exams. That showed I could achieve things if I put my mind to it.

Initially, though, I started my apprenticeship in and around Dublin and quickly learned a few facts of life. I was soon dispatched halfway between Dunshaughlin and Navan. They were building some sort of retreat centre costing megabucks and the company I was with won the contract.

I was taking in about £125 a week – it was still punts at the time – but because I was based outside Dublin I secured another £100 in travel money. I didn't even know how to wire a plug and I was making that much. Meanwhile, fully qualified and experienced electricians down home were pulling in barely £300.

One of the lads I worked with was Larry Breen and I was his gofer. I had to make him tea, fetch messages and that sort of stuff. After leaving that job I didn't hear from him for about four years. Then one day the phone rang.

'Was that you I just saw on telly, tearing around Croke Park for Tipperary?' the man at the other end of the line enquired.

'It might be,' I replied hesitantly. 'Who am I talking to?'

'It's Larry Breen. I didn't believe it when I saw you running so fast – I couldn't get you to move an inch when you were getting paid for it.'

Larry always looked after me. I remember him laughing when I went off and spent my princely wage on a new Honda Civic worth about £6,000. Well, Mam financed most of it and I paid her back over the years.

I was flying it. But then, about eight months into the apprenticeship, another rookie and I were summoned to the office and told one of us was needed in Baldonnel, where they were building a new hangar. Immediately we both copped there was a big catch – the £100 a week in travel money would be cut. That's £5,200 down the plughole over an entire year. We tossed a coin, I called heads and sure enough harps came up.

Without the travel perk I could no longer afford digs so I decided to drive to and from Thurles. After a few months of that I was getting car fever, so I pulled the plug (excuse the pun) and looked for something closer to home.

Part of the Dew Valley factory in Thurles had burned down and a company called King and Moffat got the contract to rewire it. I called to their office and told them I was looking for work, and they told me to start the following Monday. I stayed with them for a year before joining Tom and Ray.

If life was stabilising somewhat I was also starting to go places on the hurling field and the county minor title gave me a lot of confidence and fuelled my interest in the game a little more.

We won that championship in October 1999 and I enjoyed my

best season to date in the sport. I managed 1-6 against Killenaule in the minor semi-final and people were starting to take a bit of notice. The Sars senior selectors called me up to their squad and I was summoned for county minor trials too. Suddenly, after years of only partial interest, I was playing games, people were saying 'Well done' and I was doing something I had never done before – committing.

Slowly, my circle of friends evolved and over time I distanced myself from the boys of summer with their cans and cigs in favour of lads I was hurling with.

It was nice to be in the mix for the county minors. Growing up, I entertained the odd notion that I could replicate the moves of Nicky English or Pat Fox – the feints, the jinks, the shimmies – but I think the blunt reality is that Sars had to send three or four players for a try-out and I was probably only going to make up the numbers.

Paudie Butler, the manager at the time, didn't need long to make a decision anyway. He always tells it like it is. 'You only have one side,' he explained. 'If you want to play at the next level you must have two sides.'

They weren't going to call me back and I was sharply culled, the door shut with me on the outside looking in. I took it on the chin and agreed with Paudie on the spot. Off my left side there was absolutely nothing there. And even though I wasn't all that worried about not making the minors, I still realised it would do no harm to practise and improve my left. Funny how it goes: a little over a decade later I would score two goals in an All-Ireland senior final off that same side.

And so the Tipp minors went ahead without me. One Sunday I sat down to watch them play, still wondering if I could actually cut it at that level. I looked at a guy I knew very well on the Tipp team, a fella I'd always been very comfortable marking. Sitting on the couch I asked myself a question: 'Would you like to mark him, Lar?'

Dead right I would.

So although there was no door opening, I had a growing feeling I could survive at that level if the chance arose. And while the minors didn't see fit to call me in, I heard soon afterwards that Paddy McCormack and the Tipp under-21s had been eyeing me – but were put off because I hadn't made the cut at under-18.

I was at a fork in the road with both my life and hurling. I suppose in a way I was stuck in a rut. It was mildly frustrating, and I would at least have appreciated the chance to give it a shot at some level in the blue and gold. But friends were telling me to be patient. They reminded me that most lads who star for the county at minor or under-21 later fall away.

They were right. I wasn't beyond redemption.

# 2

# Out of the shadows

There were increasing signs that the wheel was about to turn.

Pat Joe Whelahan called me into the Thurles Sarsfields senior team in 1999 and shortly after drew me aside one evening to tell me I'd soon be playing at the highest level with Tipp.

'I sincerely doubt that,' I blurted. 'I'm barely on the Sars team.'

But Paddy Doyle, a selector with the club, seemed to feel the same and offered me plenty of encouragement. It was nice to hear people saying good things about you – that's not always the Irish way – although I just couldn't see a call-up in the pipeline. We had lost the 2000 county senior final to Toomevara and I was solid useless. That defeat took a lot out of me and I was going around half depressed for a few days until Mam greeted me in the pub one afternoon with a bit of news.

'I'm after getting a phone call from Jack Bergin, one of the Tipp selectors. He said if you're interested there's a county trial against Clare at the end of the week. You're to meet the bus at the Park Avenue hotel if you want to go along.'

I wondered was someone taking the piss, and I sort of convinced myself it had to be one of the lads. I just put it to the back of my mind.

As the weekend loomed, however, and my mother asked again if I was going, I began to have second thoughts. What if it was a genuine call and I was about to blow the opportunity to play for Tipp for even one game? I decided to show up and if there was a bus waiting, fine. If there wasn't I'd just be ready for one of the boys to hop out from behind a wall and fall around the place laughing.

Sure enough it was there when I arrived. The next job was deciding whether to go on board. I looked on as fellas hopped on but as it was a second-string outfit I recognised only a few faces and knew only one, Kieran Carroll, from Thurles – his brother Brendan had been in the county set-up. And so I decided to take the plunge.

As I walked down the aisle of the bus it was plain as day that apart from Kieran no-one had a notion who I was. The rest of them had various items of Tipp paraphernalia – tracksuit bottoms, a top, a gearbag – but I didn't even have a plastic bag you'd use for shopping. Nor did I own as much as a Tipperary flag, because I had never been involved with any county team.

Years later, my teammate John O'Brien confirmed what I had long suspected: the lads hadn't a clue who I was – all they saw was this skinny, gangly yoke shuffling down the bus with a beet-root face. Little did they know I was only waiting for someone to jump up and say, 'Sorry, lad, this is a team coach – Bus Éireann is down the road!'

Fortunately nobody did, and since the place beside Kieran was already taken, I dived into the nearest vacant seat. I found myself beside another chap who seemed as shy as myself because we exchanged only a few quiet words on the long road to Ennis. I think that lad was Pat Coman from Moycarkey-Borris, but I'm not certain; we never formally introduced ourselves.

When the bus arrived in Ennis, we hopped off and trooped into the dressing-room. Still not a word from anyone. By now I was starting to relax. If I was being set up, the pranksters would surely have broken cover by now. 'Surely none of my lads would have the creativity to carry the joke this far,' I reassured myself.

It turned out we were there for a Southeast League game. Nicky English came in and read out the teamsheet and there was my name in the first fifteen. I didn't know what to feel. I wasn't too nervous but I was still taken aback at being in the mix. Growing up, I had been kind of indifferent to the urge of playing for Tipp but when Hotpoint threw me my first jersey I must admit I felt a bit daunted as I clasped the blue and gold shirt in my hands.

I togged out quickly, said nothing to anyone, played without inhibitions and scored a goal and four points.

Midway through the first half a ball fell out of the sky. Brian Quinn, my marker, got the jump on me and the sliotar looked to be heading sweetly for his lámh, but I made a dart from behind and gathered above Brian's head. I stuck it over the bar for good measure.

At half-time when I went to take a leak Nicky told me to keep up the good work. I just couldn't believe that someone like him was praising me. On the way back from the toilet Kieran Carroll called me over. He had overheard Nicky and the boys talking and it was all good news.

'Larry, they have great time for you,' he said. 'They were raving about that high catch. I'd say you'll definitely be called back.'

Sure enough, Nicky must have been impressed, because he even referred to that little highlight in subsequent interviews – something to the effect that he hadn't seen a better piece of fielding.

If I were to look back now and recount everything I did in hurling at the top level I would have to admit that catch and score were what made me. No matter what I did later in the season Nicky never lost faith in me. More than that, his belief and backing were probably what kept me in the Tipp panel for four to five years after he stepped down, at a time when I couldn't hit a hayshed from the six-yard line.

Anyway, I had never felt hurling come as easy to me as it did that day in Ennis. The speed of the game was unreal, even though it was a meaningless tournament, and I just loved the quick and accurate passes from really skilful hurlers. It was a step up from club hurling but it seemed to suit me.

'This is right up my street,' I whispered to myself as I left the field. To make an immediate mark was smashing because I had wondered about my ability to reach another level.

I was drafted in again for the next match, against our old enemies, Cork. Back then there was no serious training before Christmas, just a succession of these tournament games. I landed two points off Mark Landers, who had previously been their captain, and that set me up nicely for the next day out, against Waterford. We played them in Clonmel and I managed 2-2.

Everything was working out well, and I think Mam was getting as much of a buzz as myself. She came to every game and thankfully she went back home with a smile on her face after most of them.

All the while, Nicky scarcely said two words to me. Himself, Jack Bergin and Ken Hogan would just say, 'Keep doing what you're doing.' Nicky is one of the sharpest men I know, and I think he understood pretty quickly that I was a kind of free spirit and it was better to let me at it.

I was officially embedded into the Tipperary senior squad in January 2001, and everything became a learning curve from there on in. We started training with a fitness test on New Year's Day at the Garda College in Templemore. It was serious stuff, but by all accounts the new programme was nothing compared to the hellish regime the team had undergone in Nicky's first two years in charge.

Clare had pipped Tipp in 1999, and though the lads won two championship games in 2000, they later lost to Cork in the Munster final and then Galway in the All-Ireland quarter-final.

At that stage Clare were by far the fittest team in the land but they had brilliant hurlers too and Nicky wanted his team to be right up there with them in every possible area. No matter what happened in 1999 he had decided Tipp wouldn't be beaten by fitter teams. Clare had needed a replay to win that 1999 tie, so Nicky raised the conditioning bar even higher in 2000. But then for 2001 he changed tack – no better man to do it – and thank heaven he did.

I think Nicky recognised you could go too far with the weights and circuits and cross-country runs. He also reckoned that even from a starting point of January the team would be as fit as a fiddle come the summer. Now he was looking for a bit of speed and touch. That seems to be why he saw a place for me in the set-up.

Having heard all about those early fitness sessions, I still can't say enough novenas in thanks that I was spared them. Legburning climbs up the Devil's Bit, boot camps away with the army, psychology sessions, diets you wouldn't endure in the holy season of Lent. It was rough stuff.

They even had training camps at Sunderland FC, where Nicky's friend Niall Quinn – a good hurler himself in his day – was a hero. In fairness, that was one part of the regime I would have signed up for.

As soon as I got to know a few of the lads on the Tipp panel I had to take fierce slagging about how I had conveniently jumped on the bandwagon just when things were getting cushy, whereas they'd had to suck up all kinds of torture and human-rights abuses over the previous two years. The Eugene O'Neill story in particular kept cropping up.

I know it only through hearsay but it has become part of the folklore of Tipp hurling. It seems the lads were in the middle of a punishing dietary regime, and players were dropping pounds at a frightening rate. After six weeks of chicken and no carbs the boys were leaner than greyhounds. But there was one exception – Eugene.

Teammates were baffled and management were growing suspicious. How could someone be showing so little effect from a regime that had everyone else looking mean and lean? The boys could only conclude that Eugene was dining out against the rules – he was at college at Cork IT from Monday to Friday and probably eating all the wrong foods.

Management decided to interview the suspect, and Ken was duly dispatched to order Eugene to report to the Park Avenue hotel immediately after training in Semple Stadium.

Upon arrival, Cappawhite's finest was ushered into a room with a table and three chairs, two of them behind the table and one for Eugene, in front. It was like an interrogation chamber. And Nicky was shining the torch at the prisoner.

'I won't beat around the bush, Eugene. The panel are breaking their holes here and everyone is down in weight, but you're not making any inroads. What's going on?'

'There's nothing going on, Nicky.'

'Eugene, don't try to pull the wool. Nearly every lad out there has lost half a stone. Some of the boys have lost well over a stone. Come on, spit it out!'

'For God's sake, Nicky, I have no problem at all.'

By now there was exasperation.

'Fuck it, Eugene, it doesn't make any sense. You can't be doing all that training and not losing weight. We're going to get to the bottom of this.'

'No, Nicky, I'm grand so I am.'

By now, the story goes, Nicky was close to losing the plot so he walked to the window to draw a few deep breaths.

Ken now took up the baton – but completely changed the tone of the interview: 'Look, Eugene, everyone has something going on in life. But if there's anything we can help you with, that's what we're here for. We're all in this together.'

A slight pause: 'I'm grand, Ken.'

'Whatever you say stays in here. Is there something we can help you with? Because there has to be a problem. Nicky and I will do everything to help, I promise you.'

There was another pregnant pause, longer this time. Sensing their man was about to crack, Nicky jumped in again.

'Anything, Eugene. We'll do anything we can to help.'

And then it all came out.

'Sausages, Nicky.'

'What?'

'Sausages!'

'What do you mean sausages?'

'I'm in college, Nicky. I come down in the morning for breakfast and the boys would have a few sausages in the pan for me. If I'm home during the day they might stick on another few. And sure I could have a few more in the evening. Sausages left, right and centre! They're feckin' killin' me.'

For once Nicky was almost lost for words.

'Are you serious? Ah for fuck's sake, Eugene!'

And out stormed Nicky as Ken tried to choke back the laughter.

Besides Sausagegate, there were lots of other stories. There were also plenty of characters to get acquainted with. But I decided to make haste slowly in getting to know who was who and how the set-up worked.

Jim Kilty arrived in as fitness coach and the boys said he brought more science to training. I reacted well to it all; I was enjoying hurling more than ever before. I was nineteen and fit as a fiddle. And I seemed suddenly to have developed blistering pace out of nowhere.

The start of the National League was delayed by an outbreak of foot-and-mouth disease but we finally got the campaign underway in Waterford. I had settled well enough into the team but I didn't hold any great hopes of making the cut for the championship. On the way into that first league game, however, my mother met Nicky and introduced herself. He shook Mam's hand and told her that if Tipp were in the All-Ireland final that coming September her son would be playing. Mam could hardly believe her ears.

Turns out Nicky wasn't codding. He was about to break with the judgement of every Tipperary underage manager of the previous six years and throw me straight into the senior team.

We enjoyed a good league campaign and ended up winning the competition.

People to this day maintain I'm not a league hurler and don't enjoy slogging it out when the ground is soft, but I played my part in that competition and scored 4-11 in six games, which is not bad for an unknown trying to carve a niche for himself on a quality team.

Unlike in my only previous final appearance of note, for the Sars in the 2000 county final, I didn't bomb when we met Clare in that league decider; I came out of it with four points. For the first time I could picture myself consistently performing at this level.

They say league hurling doesn't compare to championship, but I don't necessarily agree. You always go out to win, and the ball still arrives at about one hundred miles per hour. The only real differences between the league and championship are the hardness of the ground, a more do-or-die atmosphere and bigger crowds. I certainly felt the 2001 league was a good proving ground for me and was happy to take my first major medal to add to my under-12 football title and my minor championship.

Supporters were now stopping me on the streets of Thurles and asking how I was getting on. I wasn't a bit used to that but I enjoyed meeting people, chatting and feeding off the friendliness. I was getting nearly as much confidence from wellwishers as from the non-stop supply of quality sliotar being fired into the Tipp full-forward line.

During those early days Nicky kept a watchful eye but he continued mostly to just leave me be. He was living in Dublin but it was like he was watching us on Google Earth or something because he didn't miss a trick.

I was working in Tipp Town and used to tear there and back in my Honda Civic. I had just arrived home from work one evening and was settling down for the dinner when the phone rang. It was Nicky.

'Hey, Larry, slow down in that feckin' car! I hear you're bombing it up and down to Tipp Town. I don't want you going to Croke Park later in the year wearing a neck brace.'

'I'm not bombing anyone or anywhere, Nicky.'

'Larry, slow down!'

Over and out. Message received and understood.

There was another occasion when Nicky surely must have questioned my sanity. I was down in Ailbe Bonnar's pub for a bit of mouseracing. Now, if you've never come across this sport, you're missing out, because it's the best craic you'll probably ever have.

It's a simple enough concept: you put a perspex container up on the wall, equipped with stalls for the contestants and with a few devices hooked up to a TV set. Switch on the channel, put six mice into the perspex arena and throw a bit of Galtee cheese in front of them. The mice are in the traps (not the ones with springs on them) hidden behind a flap and when the flap comes up the mice leg it for the cheese.

A bookie was there to take bets, the punters had a few bob on the various traps, and everyone could participate as the proceedings were relayed to the widescreen TV. It would pass a right few hours, and you wouldn't even notice the time going.

At the time there was one particular brown lad that won everything (I suspect he crossed the border from Kilkenny) so the hope was always that you would draw his trap. Many's the time a mouse led out the posse and almost reached the line only to double back. And there was no good in saying you had him backed 'each way' – he had to breast the finishing tape.

Anyway, Nicky got wind of that as well, and even though I was drinking nothing stronger than Britvic, he reckoned I'd be better off passing my evenings some other way.

I often wondered who 'ratted' me out and have a sneaking suspicion it was Ailbe himself; he comes from one of the strongest hurling families in the county, his brothers Colm, Cormac and Conal all having won All-Irelands.

Again, the message from Nicky was short and to the point: 'Hey, Larry, just stay out of the pub!'

And so that was the end of my miceminding career. The man simply had certain standards and I wanted to meet them. That's the respect he demanded. He had an aura about him when he walked into a room. Still does.

I made my championship debut against Clare at Páirc Uí Chaoimh and sauntered into the corner to be met by an angry-looking Brian Quinn. I had scored for fun against him in the

Southeast League but it didn't look like he wanted an action replay this time around. He gave me a drive with the butt of the hurley to welcome me. He was wound up.

'You won't fucking do what you did in Ennis!' he roared.

Declan Ryan saw it and came over to say that if there was the slightest bit of hassle I should call on him. In the pre-match formalities Declan, Eoin Kelly and I had broken away from the rest of the team to line up as a full-forward unit and face the Blackrock end for 'Amhrán na bhFiann'.

Declan wrapped his arms around us, minding us. That year he was a real father figure, never giving out and always high-lighting the positive. But he couldn't entirely cushion me from the real world that day, and I found out all about championship hurling soon enough. From the throw-in, timber crashed and bodies clashed. There was a hiss of tension around the ground. You could nearly feel the heat coming in from the crowd on top of you. It was nerve-wracking. And I just didn't perform.

I think I got one lousy point from play but other than that I was a spectator. The whole affair passed me by and I was whipped off with fifteen minutes to go. I was lucky to last that long. Quinn was all over me and as I hadn't played minor or under-21 for Tipp I didn't really know what to expect from senior championship hurling or how to handle him.

Before the game Nicky had drilled it into me that I had to use my speed, play Quinn from the front and lose him on the turn, but as the game progressed, his experience began to tell and I was hanging behind him more and more. Nicky wasn't one bit happy and ran down to give me a piece of his mind.

'Hey, Larry, are you playing corner-forward or corner-back?'

Struggling with the occasion and physically and mentally tired, I didn't cop straightaway that the question was ironic. I thought hard for a couple of seconds.

'Corner-forward.'

24

Nicky looked at me hard and then just started laughing before walking away.

I wasn't the only one taken aback by the whole experience of a championship Sunday: inside the dressing-room lads were covered with cuts, welts and bruises. And yet we had to listen for days after to the Banner boys whingeing about the referee, Dickie Murphy.

They should have taken a look at the treatment that Mark O'Leary had received before the throw-in. Mark went to shake hands but his marker just hit him with the hurley across the paw. The two of them got yellow cards. Don't even ask me why Mark got booked.

Of course I knew this game would be fairly brutal and edgy, a street fight. I wasn't afraid of any of that. It's just that you can't always respond when you're in the middle of a battle like that even though you've tried to visualise what's coming.

Fifteen minutes after Mark's slap, Eoin Kelly got his official welcome to championship hurling. He was about to take off on a run when Seánie McMahon met him at full speed. Eoin wobbled. Then Ollie Baker caught him off guard with a signature shoulder. Eoin was flipped like a pancake.

I was about to go over and check for signs of life when he bounced to his feet and in the same movement tried to get his shot away. Eoin was stunned but he still got up and threw the sliotar in the air. His attitude was clear: if he managed to get the ball up the field it was good but if he got a skelp at a Clare lad as he drove it away so much the better. That was the day I first saw the cut of Kelly.

We got through by a point so my score was useful enough, I suppose, and I remember Nicky running onto the field at the final whistle with a big smile and the weight of the world lifted off his shoulders. He really looked like a man after being set free, which just showed the pressure he was under. As he dished out the bear hugs you could see the anxiety draining from his body. I was pure delighted for him, given the way he had looked after me.

Nicky never missed a trick with me that year. A few weeks before the Munster final, the Tipp under-21s were due out in the championship and I was picked for the team. I was worried; I had never been on a Tipp underage team and suddenly I was supposed to be a leader for the under-21s because I was a senior player. It looked like I was under pressure to go out and score six points to justify the hype around me.

Nicky must have sensed my unease, because he phoned before that game and said that unless I broke a leg I was on his team for the Munster final. That meant an awful lot. I played with the under-21s and sure enough I was rubbish, but Nicky was true to his word – I was in for the senior decider.

He just had this way with people and he didn't always have to talk to you either. Most of the time he'd just give me a grin as I got off the bus. That was enough.

Mind you, in the Munster final I was only marginally better for the seniors than I was for the under-21s. In fairness, it was a big leap considering I had been selling match programmes for Thurles Sarsfields just a year earlier. Yep, that's what I was doing for the 2000 provincial final between Tipp and Cork.

Usually, I worked at my parents' bar on the morning of a big match before moseying on down to the stadium to sell programmes. You could get a plum gig inside the ground or you could be unlucky and get marooned outside the ground with a hundred programmes. If the latter was the case the rule was that you couldn't come back inside until they were all sold. So you could be feckin' stranded out there for most of the afternoon. Years later, Eamon Corcoran asked me if I felt pressure before games.

'Pressure,' I replied, 'is standing outside the stadium on match day, hearing the national anthem, when you still have thirty programmes to sell.'

At the 2000 provincial final, however, I got the rub of the green and ended up selling inside. There it didn't matter how many you offloaded – you'd still get a flat fee of thirty pounds. I was able to wander down to the sideline, where the Barry's Tea hoarding was, and position myself there for the match. That's where I watched my clubmate Eddie Enright and the other boys walking around for the pre-match parade. It was some experience; by now my interest in hurling was picking up and I appreciated my vantage point.

Anyway, here I was a year later on the field, not with the programme sellers but in the dressing-room, right in the thick of things. Life is mad sometimes.

I scored a goal and a point but each came with an asterisk. For a start, I think the point was illegal. There were over 47,000 people in attendance and how the Limerick fans didn't cop it, me throwing up the sliotar and catching it again, I'll never know. The referee never saw it either, so I soloed on another ten yards and tipped it over the bar. Immediately I looked around like a bold child after breaking a window, waiting to be scolded, but it never happened.

I was on Stephen McDonagh, a fine hurler. My approach was that, good as Stephen had been, he was by now past his best and the legs were going so I would give him the runaround all day long. To no avail; I was confined in the full-forward line and he was well on top. His day must have been spoiled, though, when I plundered a goal that, like my point, could have been disallowed in many people's eyes.

Brian O'Meara aimed for a score but his effort rebounded off the post and directly into my path. I flicked the ball into the net like a tennis shot. There was a huge squabble over whether I was in the square and their players reckoned I had a foot inside the white line. It was a close call and the Limerick boys went mad, but while they had grievances with the referee, they missed so many chances they didn't deserve to win.

With five minutes left the scores were level and another cliff-hanger ensued. We hung on to win by two points, 2-16 to 1-17, and while I was poor enough for the second game on the trot, my scores had helped make the difference.

Overall I was left with a kind of bittersweet taste; I had definitely slipped a notch from the league, and for the second game in a row I was given the shepherd's crook. Yet I had a league medal and a Munster championship and we were into an All-Ireland semi-final.

As the victories were racked up, so too was the load of expectation on our shoulders, and to release a bit of pressure we went off to Wexford for a golfing weekend and a bit of team bonding. I had only ever dabbled in golf but most of the boys were deadly serious about it and had all the best of clobber and the right moves.

Me? I went down like Happy Gilmore with a bag that would fold into itself every time I stood it up. I had only seven clubs inside: a driver, a putter, four irons and a three wood. The clubs were all different brands and I'd say they hadn't seen daylight for thirty or forty years. The event was a Tipp Supporters Club classic and I was paired with a lovely man called Denis Finn, who encouraged me to take up golf because he thought I had an eye for it and a natural swing. I think he was shocked – though not half as much as I was – when I split the fairway with my first drive.

After the game we repaired to the nineteenth hole for a meal and enjoyed a free bar before we hit Wexford town. I had never received anything free since I stopped believing in Santa, and so I went mad, and I wasn't the only one. Lads would have one drink in their hand and one on the table and be ordering another. I was only nineteen and daft as a brush.

We went off to a nightclub before heading back to our digs, one of these nice houses on the grounds of the golf club. We were well on it and a few lads came into my place – it's always my place – to take out the clubs and start working on our approach shots. Of course we damaged the house in the process. After a few pints with the boys I actually thought I could get away with playing golf indoors.

When we woke up the following morning we genuinely thought we had been burgled – couldn't remember a thing. Then someone came in and assured us we had done the damage ourselves. I felt as low as I had ever done in my life.

One or two others arrived and we did a major clean-up. We packed several large black bin liners with debris, swept the floor clean, put tables and chairs back in place, straightened pictures and prepared to leave the accident scene.

Mark O'Leary arrived to drive us to the main hotel for breakfast, but as we pulled away, Nicky approached like a raging bull. Word of the vandalism had filtered back to management.

'What happened?' He was spitting fire.

Mark jumped in: 'Ah, I think a few of us got carried away last night, Nicky, but we've cleaned it up and we'll make sure to apologise and pay for the damage.'

Mark and I had only known each other seven months and he had absolutely nothing to do with the rampage. And yet here he was stepping into the breach, literally taking one for the team. I'll never forget him for that because I genuinely feared Nicky would throw me off the panel and with good reason.

Before he walked away Nicky poked his head in and stared hard at me in the back seat. He knew I had the potential for madness.

'I hope to fuck you had nothing to do with this, Larry.'

I was genuinely terrified.

'I did, Nicky, but I'll take my punishment on the chin. I'm sorry.'

It got much worse. It turned out the house belonged to my new golfing friend, Denis.

Mortified, I called Denis aside and apologised, begged him to send me the bill and guaranteed I would cover all costs. The bill never arrived. And for a few years afterwards Denis and I hooked up again on the golf course to play a round here and there. It said everything about the man.

I survived on the panel and despite being taken off two games in a row I made the team for the All-Ireland semi-final against Wexford. I was damn lucky to start.

We had that game wrapped up until Martin Storey came out of retirement and hit the pitch for the last few minutes to absolutely haunt us. I'll be straight – had that game gone on another thirty seconds we were dead in the water.

Without even touching the ball Storey was creating general mayhem in our full-back line. Meanwhile Larry O'Gorman was running the show out the field. The score was 1-16 to 2-8 with only five minutes left and we were cruising until Larry O grabbed a goal and Mitch Jordan and Adrian Fenlon pointed, leaving the scores tied up and us clutching the rosary beads. In the end the referee couldn't blow the whistle soon enough.

Still, once the shock of throwing away an All-Ireland semi-final had subsided, we knew we'd get a good second crack at it. The tide had turned on us in the last quarter of that game but the real worry was that we had switched off, too many of us waiting for someone else to spray a few points and make the match safe. I certainly wasn't one of those people you'd look to for leadership. I was marking Doc O'Connor and he beat me up and down the field. I was a passenger again and for the third time in a row I was taken off.

My confidence was dented but I still started in the replay the following Saturday afternoon. I'd say a few supporters couldn't understand how. I didn't know how to fix what was wrong; training was good, the drills were great and I was performing in practice. I was happy with my touch and my fitness was razor sharp. But come each match day I was subdued.

It was people like Tommy Dunne, Eoin Kelly and John Carroll, whose move from right half-back to centre-forward probably changed the course of our season, who had kept us in the hunt when Wexford came biting.

We went back to Dublin the Friday afternoon before the replay and later that evening Eoin and I went for a puck-around. We were staying at the Berkeley Court Hotel and started tipping a few balls at each other in the car park. Next thing the manager came hurrying out in a flap.

'Lads, please stop! There are cars here worth three hundred thousand pounds. You can't play hurling here.'

He was right. We looked around at all these Bentleys, BMWs and Jaguars. What had we been thinking? A broken windscreen or a panel-beating job on one of those could break the bank. We moved on down the road and as we passed Lansdowne Road we noticed the stadium gates were open, so we moseyed onto the outside pitch and pucked around there for about twenty minutes. Then I got an idea.

'Hey, wouldn't it be some craic to go onto the main pitch?'

Eoin reckoned there was no chance, but we walked around anyway until we found an opening to the terrace, hopped over a railing and made our way onto the main pitch. We stayed there for an hour, pucking from goal to goal in our Finches tracksuits. The pitch was set up for a soccer friendly between the Republic of Ireland and Croatia the following Wednesday and the surface was immaculate. We had a great time and no-one came near us.

With the Wexford rematch to come the following afternoon, Eoin and I surely made a bit of history by playing twice in Croke Park and once at Lansdowne Road in the same week.

As for that semi-final replay, well, it turned into a farce, if you ask me. It went down in history for the sending off of Brian O'Meara after he got involved in handbags with Liam Dunne. How Brian got the line is still beyond me. It was a crazy decision. He was my roommate and had offered me the double bed while he took the single the night before my championship debut in Cork. A real gent. He was forever giving me good advice and I felt awful for him that he would miss a final.

But I was soon able to console him at first hand because I was taken off at half-time and replaced by Eugene. It was a miserable, grey old day and I barely registered a shot in anger. I looked on then as Eugene, now fit as a flea, scored two goals and a point in the lashing rain of the second half. They were two right good goals as well. A week or two later he buried five goals in a challenge match. I felt there was no hope of starting the final. I just couldn't see it.

Tragically for Brian, attempts to get that red card overturned were rejected, and ultimately a harmless bit of pulling and dragging cost him his place in the All-Ireland final against Galway. I felt sick for the lad.

When the team was named I suspected the only reason I stayed on the starting fifteen was because he was suspended. Years later I asked Nicky would he have started me in the final had Brian been available and he said he would. But there's no way he could have.

Brian's red card and suspension were hugely controversial. There was talk of taking out an injunction to allow him play;

I think Nicky and himself spoke about it. Even journalists campaigned to get him off the hook. Most of the country was behind him. The whole thing could have distracted us only for the man himself drawing a line under it. He went to Croke Park to appeal his red card but it was to no avail and the red card stood.

Brian knew that was it, and though the man and his family were devastated he decided not to bring his appeal any further for fear it might not only upset our preparations but also put Nicky in an awkward spot when it came to picking the team. Instead, he drove us on with a few words here and there, and advised us on and off the pitch. He was the ultimate team player.

The build-up was pretty relaxed apart from that. Getting measured for a suit was brilliant because I think it was the first suit I ever had. I did one interview, along with Eddie Enright, to emphasise the Thurles Sars connection, but that was it. As I was new to the scene all that stuff was mostly left to other lads. On the street people wanted to talk and sure I loved that. In fact, the whole lead-up to the final was easy-going once I had an inkling I was going to start.

There was better to come: they named me at wing-forward, where I would have played a lot with Thurles Sarsfields. I felt much more comfortable there and resolved that come hell or high water I was going to throw off the shackles. I made a vow – knowing that if I played as poorly as in those recent games I'd only be taken off again. I just decided to run, run and then run some more. I would hook and block, get onto balls and make more runs. There was nothing to lose.

With no background at this level I had nothing to compare the final to, but the other lads were confident we'd beat Galway and that was enough for me.

Tommy Dunne laid down a marker with our first point on the

run from the left wing. That got us all going. Mark O'Leary's goal settled us down even further but the classic handpass from Declan Ryan was worth the admission fee alone.

At half-time I felt secure enough because I had done one or two things right and was well up to the pace of the game. For the first time in the championship I was out in space, able to cover ground and create room for others. I was liberated. I had felt locked up in the corner but out the field I had serious energy. We all had.

Galway were looking principally to Joe Rabbitte and Eugene Cloonan in attack, but Philly Maher and Paul Ormonde were flying it on them. Every time they got close to us on the score-board we would pull away. O'Leary scrambled another goal past the line and finished up with 2-1. I'm sure people imagine he'll dine out on that forever more but he's not that kind of lad. On that day, though, his tally was the most important contribution of the lot.

I managed two points in the second half and Mark's second goal really left us feeling we were on the way as it came from dire Galway defending. Still, we don't do things easy in Tipp and they came right back at us. Indeed, had Kevin Broderick not been called back by the ref after getting in behind David Kennedy, who was tripped, we would have been in big trouble. They came at us strongly near the end and piled attack upon attack. Inevitably there was controversy. Galway reckoned Broderick's disallowed goal in the dying minutes should have stood, and they had a beef with the ref over a few other decisions as well.

Yet I felt we always had the initiative and the momentum in that game, and we swapped skill for sweat and hung on to win by three points, 2-18 to 2-15. When the final whistle sounded O'Leary and I just threw our arms around each other. It had been ten years since Tipp last reached the summit, and to be honest I felt like a gatecrasher when I looked around afterwards and saw some of the great ex-players that hadn't an All-Ireland medal.

I was delighted for Tommy Dunne. He had poured his heart and soul into Tipp hurling. When he first came on the scene he went straight into an ageing team and it seemed like he had to play the role of a leader from day one. Before the final he gave an unreal speech in the dressing-room. I just sat there listening with the hairs standing up on the back of my neck as he talked about what it meant to be a Tipperary man in Croke Park. More important, he then went out onto the field and walked the walk. The first point he got settled us all down. Like some of the other lads he had the mental scars of many a summer war but he kept the faith and he deserved every bit of that 2001 success.

Me? I wasn't so sure. Not when I saw Brian O'Meara and Johnny Leahy in the dressing-room afterwards, fine hurlers who hadn't been out on the field with us, Brian ruled out and Johnny injured.

All the same I lapped it up for the next few weeks and enjoyed the celebrations and everything that went with them. What follows after an All-Ireland final merits special training all on its own. You have to embrace it and see what it means to people from your county. Whenever people took time to congratulate me I tried to chat away to them, ask them about themselves, and be mannerly.

Even though I was older than him I looked up to Eoin Kelly in that regard. On the field he was one of these lads you had heard about ten years previously. The whole county was talking about him on one occasion when Mullinahone played Nenagh Éire Óg in an under-14 county final at Holycross. Mullinahone scored 1-16 and Eoin got 1-15 despite having two lads on him.

I didn't really know how to conduct myself as a Tipp senior player so I watched how Eoin dealt with it. He gave people so much time and stayed level-headed and grounded despite everything. I tried to act like him because I felt it was the best way to conduct myself. The day you think you're someone in sport is the day you're starting to go soft.

It was soon back to work in Tipp Town. I still reckoned that after only five games, winning an All-Ireland was sort of unreal. Even getting an All-Star nomination surprised me. Fourteen Tipp players got proposed in total – the two Cappawhite lads, Eugene O'Neill and Tomás Costello, were the ones who lost out – and that banquet was another great night. It felt like a Tipp social event, although it probably wasn't quite the same without the two boys!

When the fuss died down I was able to look back on the year and assess how fortunate I was. Everyone said that the quality of Tipp's hurling was better in 2001 than in the previous two years and it's true that in training we had concentrated more on first touch and other hurling skills than gym work and the like.

To be blunt, I would say that's what kept me in the team. Plus maybe the memory of that catch I had made against Brian Quinn in Ennis, because people told me that was what persuaded Nicky, Ken and Jack Bergin that I might be the real deal.

It also helped that the whole focus in training had been on picking a teammate in a much better position and making clever use of the ball rather than pulling the trigger on sight and taking Hail Mary shots from way out the field. A lesson had been learned from the 2000 Munster final, when the lads had wasted a load of ball and clocked twelve wides in the first half alone.

But the team only needed time to develop naturally, and I just happened to arrive at the optimum time when players were becoming more familiar with their roles and tactical play. Sometimes it just goes like that, I guess.

The team holiday was announced and we were packed off

to South Africa for a few weeks with a few quid each from the county board. Not everyone was convinced I was going to make Cape Town though.

'No way are we bringing Larry to South Africa,' Nicky joked. 'Sure we couldn't even bring him to Wexford.'

I took it all on the chin. A year earlier I was selling match programmes but here I was now with an All-Ireland medal in my pocket.

It kind of suited to be the rabbit pulled out of the hat.

# 3

# Doyle on troubled waters

I can look back on 2002 with complete honesty and say I was the luckiest man alive to have stayed on the Tipp panel.

We hadn't put back-to-back All-Irelands together since 1964 and 1965, but as we headed into the 2002 campaign there was serious confidence we could bridge the gap. After all, we were on top of the world. Tommy Dunne had just picked up the Liam MacCarthy Cup and with it the 2001 Hurler of the Year award. Eoin Kelly had been named Young Hurler of the Year. We had ploughed through the whole season unbeaten, seventeen league and championship games in total. And we picked up seven All-Stars at the end of the year.

The blueprint for success was there, but typical Tipp of recent vintage, we couldn't refine or add to it the following season. We made the league semi-final and played six championship games but lost a Munster final to Waterford and an All-Ireland semi-final to Kilkenny. Those were two cruel losses. Waterford's off-the-cuff hurling in the Munster final severely derailed us, and try as we might, we never got back on track. A few weeks later, we put it up to Kilkenny but they knocked us out of the championship in the last four. It wasn't a desperately poor year's work but it wasn't great either considering where we had come from. I don't know why we in Tipperary seem to go soft after we win titles, but I suppose it's hard to find a chip on the shoulder when everyone is clapping you on the back.

We lost our hunger and without intending to we definitely mellowed in 2002. I can't exclude myself from that charge either. I had a shocking season.

Perhaps the writing was on the wall as far back as February when we played UCC in a challenge match. Coming into that game I was fully expecting to drive on for the season ahead. I was an All-Ireland winner and I was ready to go up to the next level. UCC were getting ready for the Fitzgibbon Cup and they had a strong team out. I knew it would be a good test but a lad from Kilkenny with a green and black helmet latched onto me and marked me out of the game. I can safely say I've never taken such a hiding in all my life. It got so bad that I was taken off before the game was even three-quarters over. I was like a dog walking off; I had never been burned so badly on the field. Even Nicky saw how down I was. He came straight over and put an arm around me.

'Hey, don't worry about it,' he said. 'That lad you're marking is going to become one of all the all-time greats. You won't be the last to be taken off him.'

I didn't think much about those words at the time but after the game I enquired from one of the UCC lads the name of my marker.

'Tommy Walsh,' came the reply. 'He's serious.'

Nicky wasn't far wrong.

Soon after that he put an arm around me again, this time following training one evening, and warned that a much bigger test of my credentials was coming down the tracks: 'Larry, the second year is going to be an awful lot harder than the first.'

He was dead right.

\*

My form was up and down during the league – I managed only 1-6 in the entire campaign, and three of those points were against Derry. I started just two of our six championship games and lasted the full seventy minutes in only one of them – the Munster final in Cork. Rather than build on the reputation I established in 2001 as a fast, opportunistic poacher of scores, I fed the perception that I wasn't to be relied upon. People began to remark that it was little wonder I had never played for Tipp at underage – I was only a flash in the pan. No-one said it to my face, but I heard it all on the bush telegraph.

I didn't realise exactly what was needed to win back-to-back titles. I eased up on the gym work and made fewer off-the-ball runs. I still didn't fully understand my role as an inside-forward, and as the belief waned I nearly stopped making runs for fear of missing the ball.

It wasn't so much a conscious decision to ease back, but maybe myself and a few others had been so happy to win an All-Ireland that we weren't as hungry to go again so soon. Brendan Cummins summed it up recently when he looked at a video of the 2002 Munster final, noticed he was out of shape and described himself as 'a big panda bear inside in the goal'. He was being ultra-self-critical, as usual, but if most players are honest I think they'll agree we could have been a lot sharper. We just didn't go the extra mile as we had done the previous season.

If 2001 had been a fairytale, 2002 brought me back to reality with a bang. Eoin Kelly almost single-handedly brought us past Clare and Limerick and into the Munster final against Waterford. In that final Benny Dunne scored 2-2 and still ended up on the losing team. I truly don't believe Waterford ever played as well again as they did that day – even in those unreal games against Cork in the mid-noughties.

Traditionally, the Waterford lads would huff and puff and try to intimidate you with the physical stuff but this batch were more stylists than sluggers and the crowd loved them. They told us afterwards that 85 per cent of McCarthy's training sessions had been conducted with hurley in hand and they were super-confident of winning.

That game was the making of the likes of Ken McGrath, John Mullane and Eoin Kelly, some of the most natural hurlers I had seen. All you need do with a bunch like that is tell them what time the match is on at and let them off. Call them in at half-time for a drop of water before sending them back out to do what they do best. I just wouldn't interfere with a group of hurlers of their quality.

They lit the place up that afternoon; they were flashing around, kissing their jerseys, cupping their ears and picking little rows with lads in the crowd. They were hugging each other one minute and looking demented the next. They seemed to have giants all over the field but none stood taller than Ken McGrath. Ken's shoulder was hanging off him but he still scored seven points off Philly Maher, David Kennedy and later on Eamon Corcoran as he moved between full- and centre-forward. That was the sheer madness of his talent.

It was their first provincial title since 1963. When the final whistle sounded they were all crying. I remember Nicky staying on the pitch for a fair while afterwards, congratulating them, and a few of us did the same even though it was devastating to lose.

By now I was seriously running out of excuses to stay on the team.

My hamstrings had been flaring up over the winter but in no way could I use that as an explanation. We beat Offaly in the qualifiers but I played no role. There was, though, some chance of redemption against Antrim in the All-Ireland quarter-final.

The result was in the balance until four minutes from time but coming off the bench I set up a goal and a point and scored a point myself. It was the first time since the 2001 All-Ireland final that I genuinely believed I had something to offer Tipperary hurling. In my own head I was constantly having to persuade myself that I belonged.

Still, we were back in an All-Ireland semi-final. And although we were well off the pace for the first half we kept plugging away and the scores were level ten times during the game. I came on for Benny near the end but contributed hardly anything. On the other side the turning point for Kilkenny came when they brought Jimmy Coogan on and he scored a goal and a point. DJ Carey made his comeback in that game after a year blighted with injuries and he killed us, setting up Coogan's goal and nailing a point that clinched it for Kilkenny.

We trooped into the dressing-room and that's where the silence hits you hardest. We did what we would have to do for the next six or seven years: batten down the hatches, lick our wounds and look for solace with our clubs.

Meanwhile, Nicky took stock of where he was at and word came through on 24 September that he was done. Only for his faith in me I might never have got to play for the county. He took me from nowhere and gave me a shot at the big time. I was sad to see him go.

After all his good work we should have been in a position to drive it on without him and stay near the winners' carousel. We had a young team and had won the game's ultimate honour. The likes of Kilkenny and Cork should have feared us for the bones of the next decade.

Instead, we looked on as Cork sorted out their player-welfare issues and sprinted off into the distance. And we let Waterford knock us aside as the second-best team in Munster. Within four years Wexford, who were going through a bad patch themselves, were beating us.

In the immediate aftermath of Nicky stepping down I was disappointed, but not too devastated. I resolved to push on with the rest of the lads under the new manager. Tipp are part of a core of historically successful hurling counties who never think of looking for a manager from outside their own ranks – and so we sat back to see who would get the nod from within.

It was only after several years that I came to fully appreciate what a massive loss Nicky was. To me and to Tipperary.

Barren times lay ahead.

John McIntyre was widely tipped to take the helm from Nicky in 2003, but instead it was Michael Doyle who came to speak to us on our first night back training. Early in his tenure word filtered through that Eddie Enright and Tomás Costello, lads who had won All-Ireland medals just two years earlier, had been dropped, and so there was a ripple of uncertainty almost from the start.

I have to say I was gutted for Eddie, who had been absolutely super to me in my early years with Tipp. Before my debut he came over and shook the hand off me: 'The best of luck, Lar! Keep going no matter what and don't change the way you're playing. You're flying it.'

Along with Eamon Corcoran, who was always there with advice, Eddie was a rock and I needed him in those early years because I hadn't played underage with the county and didn't really know the lie of the land.

Michael's first words to us did little to settle the nerves. Determination and passion written all over his face, he stood in the middle of the dressing-room at Dr Morris Park and let rip.

'I'm after getting a taste for blood, lads, and believe me I'm only getting going,' he roared.

Two of our stalwarts had already been ruled surplus to the

cause. And now the rest of us were being told by the new manager that our necks were on the chopping block. We looked at each other. Lads were dumbstruck, shaking their heads. So this was how things would be handled from now on. It was further proof, if we needed it, that with every passing season the all-conquering team of 2001 was becoming part of history.

I had little previous knowledge of Michael Doyle, but then I'm not one to devour videos of old games or read up on the past. I don't think I had ever laid eyes on Michael himself, even if he had Tipperary hurling royalty in his DNA. I really only knew that his father, John, was the most decorated hurler of all time.

When you met Michael outside of hurling he was as sound as a pound but as manager he terrified me. Apart from dropping Eddie and Tomás at the start he made other big calls, bringing in Ger 'Redser' O'Grady from my own club as well as promoting Colin Morrissey and Eamon Ryan after a trial game at Dr Morris Park.

He was different from Nicky; whereas Nicky had been quiet and low-key, it was clear Michael was coming into the job to stamp his mark and would be taking no prisoners. It was a totally unfamiliar approach for us and we were all under pressure as a result.

I soon became unsure about everything I was doing, whether in training or in matches – I seemed to be more concerned about not making a mistake than about creating chances or actually scoring.

Michael would arrive for training sessions and before he even got out of his car I was feeling nervous. And that was despite the fact he never took that many drills. Instead, Liam Sheedy came in as coach and took most of the work on the paddock, supervising ball-work and the like.

The third selector was Kevin Fox, Pat's brother, from Annacarty, and sure he was as fit as most of us. He would do most of the runs with us and, believe me, there's nothing more demoralising than having a selector beating you in a sprint.

Bringing in the likes of Redser, who had really come to prominence by scoring eight points in the 2000 Mid-Tipperary final, was one of his first acts, and another big move of Doyle's was to place Tommy Dunne at centre-back as the year progressed. To be fair to Michael, he was only playing the hand he had been dealt. This was Nicky's team, by and large – most of the best players in the county would already have been in the squad – and since our underage guys weren't setting the country alight, Michael didn't have too many other aces to play.

Putting Tommy at the heart of the defence probably worked in one way but it also left us devoid of leadership around the middle and in attack. I suppose we had sprung leaks in a few positions by the time Doyle came in.

That said, he was 100 per cent old school and we weren't weighed down with tactics and complicated game plans or anything like it. I know it's easy to have a go at a lad and waffle on about game plans. Like, what are they? Does every team really need a plan? I don't know, but at this level I would imagine so.

At that time teams were coming up with all sorts of new-fangled strategies and tactics, defensive and attacking. Cork had the short passing; their calling card was movement and off-the-ball running. Kilkenny were clogging opposition forward lines, blowing everyone out of it in the air. But Tipp just went out and hurled.

We were told to stay in our positions and as a result most of the forwards, with the exception of Eoin, were uneasy. The likes of Red and I would be looking to the sideline, waiting to be taken off if one or two balls went astray or were fumbled. Sad to say, then, that when the championship came around I was dormant inside in the corner, half afraid to come out and make a few runs.

*

The gas thing is we got off to an absolute flier in the league. I was bang in form myself after a dire 2002 and it probably helped that I had missed much of the heavy pre-season training because I was injured – I was fresh and right upon my return. In fact, my rhythm was so steady that I played in all our league games and managed 9-13 in the process. Now I look back, that's a fair answer to all those people who say I'm not a winter hurler, that I function only on hard ground. I've been hearing that all my life.

I scored 3-3 against Offaly in Nenagh and was delighted with it. Wexford were next up, and it was probably fitting that I scored 2-2 on my twenty-second birthday.

Red started full-forward against Wexford after being on the verge of a call-up for about three years. It never happened under Nicky and I knew he was very frustrated about being left in cold storage, but he kept saying to me, 'Larry, if it happened for you, it can still happen for me.'

He was right. Eventually, he got the nod and as a result he remained loyal to Michael. Outside the county not a huge amount was known about him but anyone around the club scene knew he was good enough.

I kept up my good form against Wexford and after two games I had 5-5 scored and became the league's top scorer. I suppose deep down I was waiting for Michael to offer a word of praise or encouragement but it didn't happen. Mostly what I recall is that he'd be on the sideline roaring at me for keeping only one hand on the hurl.

'Look at Larry with the one hand, the one hand!'

Wherever I was on the field I'd hear him shouting about it.

No matter, we ploughed on. We had good wins over Limerick and went down by only four points to Cork, who were brimful of confidence and intent a few months after their strike ended. Eoin

Kelly scored 3-5 that day and what he was doing even back then was unreal. I don't know how he handled the pressure because it seemed we had to turn to him at every opportunity.

We beat Derry well, scoring 4-19, but they clocked up 2-14 in reply, and that was worrying. I wasn't happy either that I managed only a point. Red told me on the way home he had been in Boston in 2001, watching the championship unfold with a group of Irish lads, and come September they were calling me 'One Point Larry'. I think Clinton Hennessy, the former Waterford goalie, was part of the gang that rechristened me. Thankfully, my averages had improved by the time I came up against Clinton in the 2011 Munster final.

Red was enjoying life with Tipp. We went to Nowlan Park for a group game and very few gave us any hope of winning, but he came out of there with 1-6 against Noel Hickey. The Cats didn't know how to handle him and Hickey was eventually taken off him and replaced by Philly Larkin, who had his own ideas on how to mark my teammate – aggressively.

Red was the talk of the GAA world. Tommy Dunne spoke to him in the dressing-room and advised him not to answer his phone to reporters in the coming days – adding that apart from everything else we had another big match to look forward to. Red is the type of lad who would have relished a big display like that so maybe Tommy was right, but sure you have to take those special days and appreciate them when they come.

That was obviously how Michael Doyle looked at it. 'Redser O'Grady, you will bask in the glory tonight,' he said before we boarded the bus.

Michael was genuinely delighted for Red and must also have felt great personal satisfaction now his investment had been vindicated.

At the same time I remember thinking how differently Nicky English would have reacted in similar situations. I recalled in particular when Eoin Kelly and I scored nine points from play between us in the 2001 league final and Nicky was asked to evaluate the 'input of your two young stars'. He just said we still had plenty to learn. He was keeping us grounded.

Of course Michael's pride was understandable and he only meant well, but it showed he had a different approach.

Red was proclaimed the new saviour of Tipperary hurling and it was serious pressure for a lad who had waited an eternity to play senior intercounty and had yet managed only a few games. We knew Kilkenny would reappear before long, their wounds healed, and I could imagine them waiting in the long grass, plotting revenge, with only one man in their crosshairs. There could be a mighty fall ahead. There has to be when you come out of nowhere and are suddenly written up as a world-beater.

Still, I was delighted Red was getting recognition. We've been good friends for ages. I can talk about only some of the stuff we got up to.

For three years on the trot we sold Christmas trees for a local businessman. We'd head off to the conifer forest at Kilcommon and buy sixty trees at a time. We'd put them in nets, drag them to the van and trailer and head back to our operational base in Thurles.

We went door to door – sure it's the only way to meet people – and charged an average thirty pounds per tree. The price could easily rise to thirty-five if we saw a few flash cars parked in the driveway or had to be buzzed through fancy gates to reach the hall door. We gave ourselves plenty of time to achieve our sales targets and knocked serious craic out of it.

On one doorstep where we made our pitch they said they were fixed up already but was there any chance we'd sign a couple of autographs.

I suppose the biggest coup we pulled off was when we were stuck with about fifty trees one Christmas Eve. I was seriously worried – what were we going to do with fifty trees just twelve hours before the big day? Fortunately Red, our stock-control man, wasn't for panicking.

'I have the perfect lad in mind,' he assured me. 'And he's a right diamond.'

Sure enough we somehow offloaded the fifty trees – at a knockdown price in fairness – to this poor oul' codger in the same line of business. I don't know how we managed it. But a lad who passed down by the place on St Stephen's Day reported that our friend still had most of what we'd sold him.

On another occasion we set up a tree in someone's living room only to be told by the client he wasn't going to pay the full asking price. 'Grand,' we said before going to the car and returning with the bushman. Your man asked what we were doing and we told him we were going to saw off about ten quid's worth and then we'd be evens.

Years later, after we won the 2010 All-Ireland final, we had another business brainwave. We would print off a few Christmas cards with a picture of my mug on the inside, wishing all and sundry a happy holiday. That winter, a YouTube video of a Tipp woman putting a 'Kilkenny cat' in the bin was all the rage and we decided to take advantage.

We should have been on *Dragons' Den* because the cards went down a treat. We put a cartoon image of the cat being binned into the heart of the card and lobbed in an image of myself offering the Yuletide message, and the shops lapped it up. When we got the cards printed in Kilkenny the printer suggested I was only going there to rub salt in the wounds, but I reassured him it was strictly business.

We printed off a stack of them and Red travelled the length and breadth of the county dressed in a flash suit and carrying a fancy invoice book. He looked the part and he absolutely stepped up to the mark.

He had a bit of craic along the way – whenever shopkeepers asked how quickly he could get the cards to them he assured them they'd be in the shops 'faster than Larry Corbett'. They obviously believed him, because he sold volumes and did a right good job. Red has a great head for ideas and he can see them through as well. I was well impressed with what he achieved.

While Red was out and about taking orders I was at home putting the cards into envelopes and sealing bags of various quantities. It was mind-numbing stuff and I soon had a pain in my neck and my back and my ass with it. But we were in the middle of a recession and money was tight – you have to find a way. Thankfully, and not for the first time, Mam lent a hand and shortened the road for me.

Strange as it may seem, the trickiest thing about that venture was finding a decent photo of myself that wasn't copyrighted by someone or other!

There were other similar business schemes about the place that Christmas but our cards were fairly well designed and, if I say so myself, smartly thought out, so we made a few quid to get us over the holidays and enjoyed every second of it.

While Red definitely has a nose – and the snazzy threads – for a business deal he was also fast making a name for himself in 2003 as a hurler after cleaning the best full-back in the country. We made the league final after a pretty decent campaign and sure enough Kilkenny were there, ready to cross swords again on the May Bank Holiday Monday. It turned out to be probably the most exciting hurling league final in history.

Ten goals were scored and it helped the entertainment value that the GAA were trying out a new O'Neills sliotar that absolutely zipped through the air. I'm not sure it helped either goalkeeper, though, because Brendan Cummins let in five goals and so did PJ Ryan. The truth is Brendan must have saved about seven more from going in. It was one of his best games between the posts – a pure exhibition.

It just didn't happen for Red this time, though. We wondered before the game if Michael would try him in the corner, take him out of the line of fire knowing Hickey wouldn't rest until he had his scalp taken, but instead he was directed into battle on the edge of the square and told to meet his foe head-on again. There was only one winner on this occasion. Red was replaced and Hickey came out well on top.

Ten minutes from time we were home and hosed – or so we thought – leading by 4-13 to 2-11, having dominated most of the second half. Then Charlie Carter came on and hit a goal. In fact, they fired 3-3 in the endgame, and to rub it in, Henry Shefflin tips up the field and actually kicks the winning point in injury time. I thought Kilkenny were supposed to have no footballers. We discovered otherwise and lost in an epic, 5-14 to 5-13.

That wasn't the end of the misery either. We lost our full-back Philly Maher and midfielder Noel Morris through injury and those losses would dog us for the rest of the summer.

It left us up championship creek without a paddle; the first round of the Munster campaign, against Clare, was looming ominously and here we were on our hunkers, out of puff and down on our luck.

We really were all over the place by now. Eamon Corcoran had somehow picked up a three-month ban for an incident in a league match against Galway. I say 'somehow' because there were no cameras to record the supposed misdemeanour and Kenneth Burke, the Galway player involved, spoke in Eamon's favour, confirming it was only 'a bit of pushing and shoving'.

More important, anyone with half a clue about hurling knew Eamon wasn't the type of player to go around hitting lads on or off the ball. He was a thoroughbred and a real sportsman, but the powers that be in Croke Park work in mysterious ways sometimes; they threw the book at him and we faced into the summer without one of our great warriors.

There was an addition to the squad, however. Denis Byrne completed a transfer from Kilkenny to Tipp, which is like someone from Muhammad Ali's camp joining Joe Frazier's entourage.

We were surprised when we heard the news, but Denis knew his time as a Kilkenny player was up, which he obviously thought was unjust. Only four years earlier he had been pipped for the 1999 Hurler of the Year award and I'd guess he was just frustrated at not being able to hurl at the highest level. And so he transferred to Mullinahone.

Almost automatically he joined the Tipp panel and played a part as a sub in that league match against Galway. None of the players would have said too much about the whole affair for a while until Tommy Dunne broke the ice. He called us into a huddle.

'Lads, from now on Denis is one of us. Treat him as such.'

It was all that needed to be said. There were no hidden agendas or barriers to be broken down, no smart comments or anything like that. Denis was welcomed into the fold for who he was. I know some people weren't happy with a Kilkenny man joining Tipp but it didn't bother me. The way I saw it, if we met Kilkenny down the road the transfer issue would only add a bit of bite to the game and that would drive hurling on in the public eye.

Denis looked nervous at the start but you could see straight away he was dead sound, a deep thinker who absolutely loved his hurling, and he soon found a bit of confidence as he tucked a few training sessions and league games under his belt. He would often phone Red looking to go for a puck-around and he was the first to turn up every single night of training.

Perhaps his only problem was that he was too anxious to perform for his new team. But that's a good complaint and he was in the mix from the start. And we were going to need all the leadership we could get, particularly against Clare because we were sitting ducks.

Typical Tipperary, we went off gazing too far into the future and we were caught cold. I think we just expected we would fire a few more goals, do what we had to do against an ageing Clare team and eventually get back to Croke Park to have another crack at Kilkenny. Instead, we went down to Páirc Uí Chaoimh and got the mother and father of all beatings, 2-17 to 0-14, from a team many had written off because they felt their best days were behind them.

It was such a drubbing that we were never really in the game. At half-time we were sitting down in the dressing-room, trailing by eight points, and no-one was even listening to what Michael and the boys were saying, which is wrong. There was a deafening silence for a few minutes before Conor Gleeson broke it.

'Tommy, we need you now,' he said. 'Say something!'

As usual it all fell on poor Tommy's shoulders. He was our go-to guy; the man who wanted to win more than anyone. He was a ferocious competitor who demanded 100 per cent from his teammates. A quiet and private chap by nature, he probably spoke more than anyone in the dressing-room, laid out the battle plans and then went out to lead the charge on the field. He commanded respect from everyone who ever togged out beside him. On this occasion, though, there was only so much even he could do.

'Look, lads, just keep taking your points. Don't get too excited yet and don't be rushing things.'

Everyone in the squad knew he was the nearest thing Tipp had to a Roy Keane figure but this time even Tommy was running out of answers.

We ran back on the field and the sliotar was thrown in and Clare gradually pulled further ahead. The fans were growing more restless by the minute. A Tipp supporter ran all the way down the steps from the rear of the stand until Michael was within earshot.

'Doyle, you bollocks, put on Mark O'Leary!'

Michael could have put on the pick of the Tipp team of the 1960s and it wouldn't have mattered. When the questions were posed we were all out of answers. The poison from Kilkenny's sting was still in our system, and sensing we were groggy, Clare delivered the knockout punches.

The wheels kind of came off after that. We were in bits. Lads got cranky and ratty with each other. On the bus to the team hotel after the game scarcely a word was uttered.

It seemed like the whole county turned on us too and those following two weeks were horrendous. Management called a meeting a few days after the hiding and we met at the Tipperary Institute. Liam Sheedy took the bull by the horns, went to the top of the room and started chalking stuff on a board.

We all knew Liam was ambitious and would have a big involvement with Tipp teams in the future. Right now he wanted answers and so we started fessing up. A few points stood out: we had been thinking ahead to another shot at Kilkenny when Clare should have been the sole focus; training was not good enough; we lacked a game plan.

It went on and on until nearly everyone had spoken but, unusually, Tommy hadn't. I noticed he was shifting in his chair, and just when the board was covered in scribbles and trigger words and mantras he spoke up. It was in character for Tommy to give a frank assessment of where we stood.

'There's one word you're missing there,' he said. 'Soft. We've gone soft.'

He spoke for a bit and went through everything, including people – and not just the players – being late for training. He brought out in the open a good many things that had been left unsaid, and soon a positive vibe was spreading through the room.

Then Michael spoke. I felt sorry for him and it didn't help that the whole county seemed to be spreading rumours about us. You couldn't walk down the street but Chinese whispers would start. I never heard so many lies in all my life and to be blunt all the stories I heard were horse manure.

There was supposed to be some sort of running feud between the Dunnes and the Kellys. There was talk that the dressing-room was in turmoil and lads had come to blows. It was all a heap of shite. There was stuff about players going head to head with Michael. Another myth. He was the manager; we mightn't always have agreed with his way of doing things but we got on with it.

We were lucky that the qualifiers allowed us to get back on the horse – and even luckier that we got Laois in the first round in a fixture that was never going to crash the Ticketmaster website. Had it been one of the top-tier counties I imagine we would have gone straight out of the championship, but we hammered them 3-28 to 13 points, which helped rebuild confidence.

We were anxious going out, none more so than Denis, who was making his championship debut for Tipp but responded with six points and a man-of-the-match display. For the first time you could tell he was really at home in the set-up and I was delighted for him. It was great to see a bit of buzz about the place again.

Unfortunately, I played only a run-on part because I had been made one of the scapegoats for the Clare debacle. After our final training session before the Laois game I saw the Mullinahone lads drive off in a car together, five of them, and all about to start for Tipp. I remember doing the sums and thinking that's a third of the starting team from the one club – it's no wonder places are at a premium. I was beginning to feel paranoid. Eyebrows are always raised when you have more than three or four players from the same club but you couldn't argue with the quality of personnel that Mullinahone were producing.

While I didn't start, I did come off the bench, however, to register my trademark point. Consistency in a world gone mad.

We beat Offaly and then faced Galway in Salthill, just one step away from an All-Ireland semi-final. To this day I don't know what it was about Tipp teams back then, but once we went ahead of a team we tended to self-destruct. On this occasion we went eight points up but they came back at us and we barely clung on by a point.

That was the day Eoin Kelly was taken off after being marked out of the game by Ollie Canning. Eoin joked in the dressing-room afterwards that he felt he had done fairly well, holding Ollie to just a point, but the truth is our heads dropped when we saw him being taken off. Surely to God he should have been moved somewhere else to try and get him into the game – Ollie was hardly going to follow him out to midfield.

Despite all that, we hung on by our fingernails and reached the All-Ireland semi-final, where Kilkenny were waiting for us. Again.

I'd like to say we went at the Cats with all guns blazing and took revenge for the league final smash and grab, but even though we started with a bang and led at the interval we were simply blown out of the water in the second half; we had no plan, no heart, nothing. We were completely exposed in the end. Every time a ball broke you could see the black and amber shirts descending on you like a plague.

Not that I saw many breaks. I was playing corner-forward and I might as well have been sitting in the stand. All over the pitch we were cruel. We collapsed in the second half. The exceptions were Eoin and Brendan Cummins – those two again. Brendan had what was probably the second-best game of his life (the league final having been the best). He made three first-class saves in one passage of play before Tommy Walsh finally stuck the ball past him. The pictures from that sequence showed Tommy leaping into the air in elation while Brendan lay desolate on the ground. I was horrified at that snapshot. Only for our man we could have conceded eight goals that day.

At the end of the match one of the Kilkenny players was walking off the field when he held his fists up to Denis Byrne in our dugout and started shouting abuse about him being a turncoat. I don't think Denis was too happy with that and neither were the other Tipp players. I don't blame them. After all, Kilkenny had decided they didn't want him so who could blame a lad for looking to play hurling at the top level somewhere else when he still had plenty to offer.

You might argue that we were not automatically a top-level team any more. It was certainly a sign of things that some of us went home that evening while more stayed in Dublin. There had been no massive split, but we were no longer the united camp we had been.

A trend had now been set. With the exception of the league final, Kilkenny weren't just beating Tipp teams across all levels, they were absolutely raking over us. They beat us by twelve points here; it had been fourteen the year before in the 2002 minor final. In 2004 they would demolish us by twenty-one points in the All-Ireland under-21 final. That was a disastrous sequence of results and a big change from the traditional balance of power between the two counties.

In years gone by, say the 1950s and 1960s, there was always a guarantee there would be blood, and usually Tipp would win. Red loves his hurling lore and statistics and he came across an expression I liked: 'Kilkenny for the hurlers, Tipperary for the men.'

That saying had little substance any more.

For the next few years we would kind of look down at ourselves. We were a team riddled with self-disgust.

I would say Michael knew his time was up. There was a cloud of negativity hovering over us and usually in that scenario it's the manager who gets it in the neck. Soon the call came from a few senior players to attend a meeting at Dundrum House, outside Cashel.

I'm not exactly sure how many turned up for that meeting but I can confirm the room was far from full; it was definitely not the whole panel in attendance. But even if they had been, I doubt the result would have been much different. Even if Michael had support from higher up, and assuming he actually wanted to stay in the job, there was so much general unrest in the team and among fans that his position was almost untenable.

The players were unanimous in wanting him out. A good few lads spoke up at the meeting and it was clear that everyone in the room wanted change. Afterwards one or two senior players got the blame for orchestrating the whole thing but that was wrong – the panel was united behind the decision. Mind you, I didn't have much to say at the meeting; I just sat back and watched things unfold. I was only twenty-two at the time so it wasn't my place to be rabbiting on. I was also aware that after lasting the full seventy minutes in only one of our five championship games I didn't carry much clout.

Michael may have expected more from me and was probably

disappointed I didn't deliver, but my issues with him weren't personal, they were to do with hurling. I felt he was always shouting at me and I was always wary of making mistakes. On top of that there was his running battle with me about the one-handed hurley grip. I tried to explain my style – that it came naturally to me to pick up the sliotar running at full tilt with just one hand on the stick – but he wouldn't have it. He even took the camán off me one day and showed me how to hold the feckin' thing. The point I was making was that I wouldn't give up my time any more just for some lad to roar and shout at me.

The following day, a couple of lads went to Michael and he resigned almost immediately. He said it was one thing taking abuse from the paying customers and enduring all sorts of personal stuff but when he didn't have the support of the senior players it was time to go.

We had all been taking flak since the Kilkenny fiasco but Michael was subjected to personal abuse from outside the squad – I gather there were angry or abusive letters sent to his home, which nobody should have to put up with. It was obvious, too, that he was extremely pissed off at how the rumour mill kept grinding away; the most recent talk was of a row between team and management at half-time of the semi-final. That had never happened. In a newspaper interview around that time he said he had never taken so much stick in all his life.

I genuinely felt sorry for him, because we had been hurling well for a time early in the season and at that stage quite a few people would have backed him to the end. I also admired his bravery for putting the hand up and taking the job so soon after Nicky had landed an All-Ireland. I have time for anyone who puts themselves out there and takes a risk in any walk of life.

That was another problem for Michael, though. He had taken over from a living legend, and when the season turned sour, and he wasn't on a pedestal as Nicky had been, he got much of the flak that probably could have been directed at us. The county board should have seen that and appointed a different manager. Unfortunately they didn't. There was no doubt that the players had gone soft and had let him down to some extent. All in all, hardly anyone in Tipp hurling came out of 2003 with their reputation enhanced.

# 4

# The lost years

The lowest point of my hurling life arrived in November 2005 when Dr Pat O'Neill walked into his consultation room in Dublin's Eccles Street carrying my MRI and CAT scans.

After struggling with my hamstrings for three years and clocking in with almost every chartered physio, and a few un-chartered ones, in East Munster and South Leinster I had managed to score an appointment with Dr Pat. He was one of the best physicians in the land, but boy did he stick a pin in my hopes of ever making a recovery.

I'll never forget the way the good doctor broke the news.

'We don't do miracles here,' he stated.

I was fair pissed off with that summing up and I just stared, speechless, at him. The show is over and I'm twenty-four years of age!

He scrutinised the scans and passed sentence: there was really nothing either of us could do to help my predicament. I had a lower-back stress fracture that was causing the hamstrings to tighten. I believed that I would have to give up playing at the highest level because an operation would be too risky. It seemed there were no exercises and no treatment he could recommend that would remedy my problem and ensure a prompt return to intercounty hurling. I took it from this that it was curtains as far as he was concerned.

After checking the hamstrings one last time he reiterated that I simply could not resume training and playing at full intensity. The prognosis seemed dire: I really believed that I would no longer be able to tog out for Tipp.

Only a few years earlier I had been fairly blasé about hurling but now it was being taken away from me I was in tatters. I refused to accept Dr Pat's conclusion. I have to say I was also unhappy with the bluntness of its delivery.

Eventually I found my voice: 'I didn't leave Thurles at seven this morning expecting you to work a miracle, Pat. But I did come up to find out what was wrong with me and be given some hope the problem could be treated.'

On the way home I phoned Therese Ryan, the physio from Thurles who had recommended Dr Pat. I thanked her again for all her help but added that the doc had been very pessimistic about my prospects of recovery and the whole process had left me fair depressed.

The county board paid for my CAT scans and the rest but when a separate bill for €150 arrived in the post – I'm not quite sure what for – I binned it.

The hamstring problems that arrived out of nowhere in the summer of 2002 were to dog me for five years. I still cannot fully explain their origin. I was never an Olympic sprinter in school but around the age of eighteen I suddenly developed a burst of speed I never had before. Maybe the hamstring issue was a side effect of a growth spurt, because the experts told me my speed off the mark was unusual in someone so tall. It seems it may have caused biomechanical stresses. In other words, there was some imbalance between muscular strength and a gangly frame.

During Michael Doyle's time in charge the hammers had started to give me woeful trouble – when he took over I missed almost three months' training, and I didn't start either the 2003 All-Ireland quarter-final, against Offaly, or the semi-final, against Kilkenny, because I wasn't right – and they only got worse over the next four years. Michael managed to get a few games out of me, but his successor, Ken Hogan, scarcely saw me in action at all.

Ken had been training teams since he was twenty-seven and held massive experience. This was his third stint being involved in senior management – he had served as a selector, first with Fr Tom Fogarty and then with Nicky – and so he was probably due a shot at the hot seat.

He also came into the job with an excellent pedigree after winning five Munster titles and two All-Irelands during his own playing career. But hand on heart I can say that his two seasons at the helm, 2004 and 2005, were lost years as far as I was concerned. With a constant stream of injuries affecting me I simply didn't feature.

In fairness, Ken promised he would do all he could to help me, and he did. He was a garda based at the training college in Templemore and he used his contacts to point me in various directions. But answers were hard to come by.

When we played Galway in the 2004 league I was taken off at half-time because I was solid useless. At one stage their corner-back raced onto breaking ball while I laboured behind like a lame nag. It looked like I wasn't even trying and the groans from the stands told me as much; the crowd felt I couldn't be arsed chasing a lost cause. But the reality was I couldn't move. It was then the truth hit me like a brick between the eyes: I was in serious bother.

Things got so bad that on Ken's watch I started just two championship matches and finished neither. You hardly need me to tell how frustrating that was. I think I managed 2-1 in the entire 2004 league and played in only three games. Worse still I didn't raise a flag in that year's championship.

A year later I made only one league appearance, against Kilkenny, scored 1-1 and then went missing for the rest of the competition when the injury flared up again. If I was a racehorse I would have been put down. I was depressed, I didn't want to be near teammates, and I knew some people thought I was playing the old soldier.

Every possible dark thought invaded my mind in that period. I contemplated walking away, going off to travel the world. I didn't want to see a hurling match.

The outlook brightened for a bit in the 2005 championship. I got some pitch time against Limerick in late May, scoring a point in both of our games with them, and in the Munster semi-final, against Clare in early June, I had a goal in the bag and another set up when I limped off well before half-time. Normal service was then restored. I saw the rest of the championship out as a bagman, carrying hurleys and running on to give the lads a swig of water. It was terrible.

Without being in love with myself, I genuinely felt I still could play a main role in packed theatres, but during those two years I scarcely got the chance to audition. The seasons and summers were passing me by and my career had stagnated. At least once a week I felt like flinging the hurl into a corner and just walking away. I've never been shot, thank God, but it felt like I took a bullet each time one of the hammers ripped.

During those few years, apart from providing business for almost every physio in Tipperary, I also went much further afield. The county board backed me all the way. They just asked for the bill and covered it. I reckon I underwent hundreds of sessions and cost the board about €50,000 for treatment.

Before seeing Therese, I attended Audrey Ryan's clinic, also in Thurles. I did everything I was told by the two ladies. Then after a few weeks of faithfully following orders I would return to training, keen to remind management I was still above ground but knowing deep down I wasn't fully right. The bloody thing would go again and either leg could be affected. It was only a question of which one went first.

In hindsight it seems crazy to have gone back training when all was not right but this is Tipperary hurling; the stakes are high. I was under pressure to get fit because I was no longer a regular on the team and needed to re-establish myself if I wasn't to fall entirely out of the loop.

I wanted to be right for my club too. Sarsfields won the county title in 2005, our first in thirty-one years, but I wasn't able to train more than six times all year. On county final day I struggled onto the pitch wrapped up in bandages like an Egyptian mummy. I didn't get near a sliotar, never mind puck one. The following day the team was celebrating when one of my friends, Pat Lawlor, let a shout at our coach, Ger Cunningham.

'Hey, Ger, the least you could have done was give Larry an oul' run after all he did for the club!'

Everyone laughed but the message hit home: I might have been on the field but in truth I was a spectator.

Do I take the blame? Yes. I wasn't listening properly to my own body. In my anxiety to find a cure I was going around meeting experts from all over. I took something positive from every one of them, but they often had conflicting ideas about how I should proceed. I should have stuck with one, kept the head down, taken a total break from the game for a year or two and then attempted a comeback.

Instead, I was trapped in a vicious cycle. I would tear a hamstring and need several weeks off. Another big match was always looming so I'd try to be back in four weeks instead of five. I'd pull the hammer again, do even more damage and miss out on another five weeks. One night, out of boredom, a friend of mine Googled me to see what people were saying in the chat-rooms. He hadn't even my surname fully spelt out when the word 'hamstring' popped up.

I could usually tell when trouble was coming. A week before a match I might get this unreal dart all the way up the back of my legs, right to the cheek of my buttock. The hammer would tighten like a guitar string being tuned and I'd get a dart of pain that no-one should be subjected to. The sensible thing would be to pull out of the session but for an intercounty GAA player that is the hardest thing to do – tell a manager you can't put it in. I worried that my teammates might feel I was shirking the hard slog. So more often than not I'd shut my mouth, try to stand out in training and put the hand up for a place on the team again. It had to stop.

In the winter of 2005 friends could see that Dr Pat's diagnosis was weighing heavily on my mind. Tommy Maher, one of my closest friends and soon to be best man at my wedding, is a great character for lifting spirits. He loves reading and had come across an article about Alistair Cragg, the South African-born distance runner now representing Ireland, and it seemed Cragg had overcome problems just like mine.

'Larry, this isn't the end,' Tommy said. 'If you have enough time or money anything can be done. We might not have the money, but we have plenty of time to sort this out.'

His words gave me a real boost just when I needed it. Encouraged, I decided to seek yet another opinion.

But first John O'Brien and I travelled to Dublin, to Hume Street Hospital, for laser treatment. It was all the rage back then and we went with high hopes. I have to say, however, that for all the good it did me I might as well have rubbed jam on the legs.

It didn't help John either. He was up for treatment on his legs too. The hospital waiting-room had a notice saying not only could you get your hamstrings done but you could also have your teeth cleaned on the premises. We later agreed we picked the wrong service and should have got our smiles brightened.

Another time I was referred for cryotherapy. It was the new big thing in sports conditioning and rehab, and I went to Wexford town, where Whites hotel had installed the technology. When you're going under for the third time you'll clutch at anything.

I didn't get any benefit from it at all. The best thing about it was I got to stay in a fine hotel room, eat lovely grub and relax. The chamber itself was a savage experience. You're in there for three minutes and the temperature drops to twelve degrees below zero, and though it's cruel while it lasts it didn't bother me – I knew plenty of others had survived in there and I'm not claustrophobic. I took the medicine at night-time and again in the morning but despite all the hype I'd heard about it I experienced absolutely no reaction, good, bad or indifferent.

Things took a turn for the better when I went to see Eamon Ó Muircheartaigh in Maynooth. He tested my hamstrings on a specialised machine and to my amazement said the results were highly impressive. Contrary to what I had been told elsewhere, Eamon believed I had the strongest set of hammers in Tipperary. Indeed, he told me only the Meath footballer Trevor Giles had scored better on the machine. That gave me a bit of confidence again.

Not everyone was convinced, though. Two comments in particular, one from someone inside the Tipp camp and another from a clubmate, were relayed back by friends. One said 'Lar has a hamstring in his head' and the other suggested I'd have been 'back quicker from a heart transplant than from those bloody hamstrings'.

*

During the times I was sidelined, a bunch of new lads got chances to impress. Noel Moloney, Tadhgie Slevin, Franny Devaney and Micheál Webster were brought in by Ken at various stages, but despite the infusion of new blood we started depending on Eoin Kelly way too much. He seemed to be hitting 2-8 or more in every game, and other lads, myself included when I did tog out, were too inclined to look to him for a spark rather than rubbing the sticks together themselves.

We didn't reach the final of either the 2004 or 2005 leagues, maybe because our game plan was essentially built around one man. We also ended up most of the time playing backs as forwards. You couldn't blame Ken for experimenting. The perception was we had no half-forward line worth talking about. He probably felt he had to do something.

Over the next few seasons Conor Gleeson, John Devane, Johnny Carroll, Diarmuid Fitzgerald, Benny Dunne, Shane Maher and Paul Ormonde, defenders the lot of them, gave service up front. In fairness, Carroll had plenty of aptitude for the task – I think he scored sixteen goals during his Tipp career, which was exceptional.

I somehow patched myself together, got back and managed the full seventy minutes against Limerick in the drawn 2005 Munster quarter-final and then lasted forty-four minutes in the replay. Those games were seriously intense and we only got past them after extra time in the replay.

All hell broke loose on the night we finally beat them, 2-13 to 0-18, on their home patch. We wanted to let the hair down knowing there were two weeks to spare before the semi-final with Clare. We got some grub after the game and most of us decided to stay in Limerick overnight. Everyone was on a high and in good form. We went into a lively bar and settled down for the night there. Well, that was the plan.

A group of lads came in wearing big Bob Marley wigs and

asked if we wanted to try them. Of course we did. It was all good fun; everyone was buzzing and it was great to unwind after the stress of two tight games.

I looked over my shoulder and saw Eamon Corcoran nearby. I called to him but he couldn't hear me above the din. I went over to him and started messing, just fooling around. He started laughing but unfortunately the bouncers didn't see the joke. In a flash there were five or six of them around me.

Feck this, I thought, the craic's too good here, I don't want to leave. So I wrapped my arms around a nearby pillar, hoping the heavies would have calmed down by the time they unwrapped me. Not for the first time, though, Lar's logic was a little off-centre and it had the opposite effect – the boys only got more agitated trying to bounce me off the premises. It wasn't pretty. I was out of line with my messing but it was only a bit of fun. I genuinely couldn't understand why the bouncers were making a big deal.

Eventually, I was shown outside and I wasn't a bit impressed. Red was chatting to a few people on the footpath, and like any good friend would, he came straight over to suss out the problem. I should have known what would happen next. He is the most loyal lad you'll ever meet and would do anything for me. He went to the bouncers looking to know why they had gone over the top. The exchange didn't go well. Let's just say Red held his own.

The bouncers weren't happy, but their eyes must have lit up when they saw a passing squad car indicate left and pull in at that precise moment. Didn't the gardaí throw the siren on for good measure? Talk about things getting totally out of hand!

Rattled, I decided to stay where I was and accept whatever came my way. After all, how much jail time could I get for acting the goat?

Red took a different course, however. Off he went, running like a half-forward cutting in from the wing, hungry for breaking ball. He turned on a sixpence, cut into a laneway and disappeared from view. I shook my head as four or five guards piled out of the car and, without giving me a second look, took off after Red, who having soon run out of puff – he was never the marathon type – had gone to ground.

He slid underneath a van that was parked up for the night and waited for the madness to subside. The boys in blue passed his bolthole a couple of times without spotting him, and Red felt confident it was just a matter of staying put for a few minutes before crying freedom again. Little did he know that some sleuth had started checking CCTV footage.

The search party returned to the bar while the security men rewound the cameras and spotted Red skulking under the van. Back went the guards with their flashlamps and chivvied him out.

Red was only doing me a favour, standing up for his friend, but he always seems to get it in the neck for doing stuff like that – over the years he's been blamed for everything from global warming to the collapse of the banks.

I tried to argue his case but he was taken away for the night by the cops and by the time we were reunited the following morning word of our misdemeanour had spread like wildfire. The phone lines at Tipp FM were hopping as people rang in to voice disgust at the hooliganism of the county hurlers on tour. That was bad enough, but my heart sank when I opened the *Irish Independent* a couple of days later and read a report of our night out.

In many ways Red took one for the team that night, but talk about hyping things up!

Red was duly suspended for one game. Ken said he was under fierce pressure to inflict a much tougher penalty, and in fairness they could have thrown him off the panel altogether because the whole thing had been blown out of proportion by the media and the phone lines were still buzzing. Maybe I'm being naive but my view is that we were amateur sportsmen letting off a bit of steam after a match and didn't deserve all that.

Despite all that fuss we beat Clare a couple of weeks later, even if it was my turn to get some comeuppance this time. I knew I wouldn't even last until half-time and the week of the game Ken actually stood up in the dressing-room to tell the lads as much.

Still, I had a goal in the bag and another one created for Micheál Webster – who went on to be man of the match – when my hammer downed tools with only twenty-five minutes on the clock.

Hurling folk are a hard audience, not easily drawn to sentiment, and I can still hear the collective groan when I pulled up.

Amid the general murmur and the bit of slagging the taunt from one Tipp fan rang out loud and clear: 'It's all in your fucking head, Corbett!'

What do you say to that?

People are entitled to their opinion because they pay good money for a ticket, but did they seriously think I would be hobbling off pitches every five or six weeks if I could help it? I blocked out the crowd, traipsed into the dressing-room and buried my head. I genuinely couldn't see a way back with all this going on.

My career was looking like a story already told.

# 5

# Running slowly off the ball

Two days after we beat Clare I went to see Gerard Hartmann in Limerick.

Hartmann is the former triathlete who has built a career as physical therapist to many of the world's greatest distance runners. He said everything he had heard about me suggested the injury was indeed all in my head, but after an hour's work he found there was a serious deficiency in my hamstring–quad strength ratio – it was only 30 per cent when it should have been 75 per cent.

Ger spoke to me in plain language and spelt out what was happening.

'None of this is in your head, Lar,' he reassured me. 'The hamstring is very weak, there is a serious tear and there's also a bleed and bruising around it. Don't mind what anyone has been saying to you. There's a serious problem here and it's stopping you from performing. I know how to fix it and if you let me, I'll help you.'

I felt like bursting into tears, and I'm sure Ger could see the relief on my face and a weight lifting from my shoulders. When everyone is telling you it's all in your head it's hard not to half believe it.

'Your confidence is shot and you appear to be totally confused about how to fix this problem,' Ger added. 'You're constantly stretching your hamstring. It's like a twig – it will snap if you keep at it. There's only one way to sort this out for once and for all – you need a complete break from hurling. Are you prepared to step away from the game for six months?'

I was rattled at the thought of missing half a year with club and county but deep down I knew something drastic had to be done. Ken and the lads wanted me available for selection there and then but Ger said there was nothing to be gained by that, in either the short or long term.

'I can patch you up and send you back out but it will tear and repair and then tear and repair again and you'll be caught in that vicious cycle for the rest of your career if that's what you want.'

After sleeping on it for twenty-four hours I went back to Ger's practice in Limerick and told him I was taking six months out of the game. He thanked me for the vote of confidence and said he would do all he could to get me back.

He told Ken I was out of commission till further notice, and that in itself helped. Until then I felt no-one believed how bad my problem was, and I was sick of going around trying to find answers, knowing people doubted me.

Ger started my recovery by giving me a ten-point stretching programme, which he called 'The Perfect Ten'. Not one of its components involved working my hammers directly. Instead, I was to work on my hips, glutes, core and lower back: all the surrounding areas. And I had to make sure I built up my strength and was properly hydrated before I went anywhere near him again.

'There's no point coming here pulling out of machines if your tissues and muscles are not properly hydrated,' he said. 'You'll only do more damage.'

The treatment was all hands on. No machine was ever

involved – there was no pressing a start button and heading away for half an hour. He'd be nearly sweating himself by the time he got finished. I would be in agony on the table – nearly crying at times – but he'd know to push things only so far. He brought me out to do shuttle runs and he could see my confidence was gone. I was decelerating into cones and easing around them when I should have been bursting through them. I think he saw straight away he'd have to work on my mind as much as my body.

Ger Keane, a pure gentleman from Kerry, was the right-hand man in the set-up and he was just as capable.

They not only worked hard; they lifted my mood too. Hartmann was a breath of fresh air in a season that was threatening to smother me. Every time I went to him I came away feeling better about myself. He was one of the few practitioners who didn't speak to me in Latin. I had enough problems getting the head around everyday words without trying to remember the difference between my adductor magnus, my gastrocnemius and my ischial tuberosity.

Ger would tell me the injury was not as bad as I feared. He kept saying I will get you right, I will get you back playing. There were no early-morning programmes or anything out of the ordinary – he just kept preaching the same things: I was going to improve my strength, flexibility and movement. He's a serious man, a charismatic sort of fella who's good at figuring out your mindset. The way he saw it, everyone who arrived at his clinic came in with a problem or an issue, and he was there to help. In many ways he's a psychologist or a counsellor. And that's where I probably benefited most. Every session with him lifted my confidence.

He's also a great talker, and there was always plenty to talk about. Sonia O'Sullivan was there one day when I arrived, Paula Radcliffe another. The walls were a picture gallery of superstars he had treated, Pádraig Harrington and the likes. I would throw a name into the mix and off Ger would go. I loved lying there and listening to his stories. Only for the pain I might have fallen asleep, I was so comfortable.

I followed his instructions to a T for six months. I had his stretching programme close at hand and I worked really hard on flexibility, just stretching gently with a rope. I kept fit by going on long walks and doing no more except building up muscle in the gym and repairing tissue by loosening and resting.

When I did get back right, Hartmann told me not to wait for the hammer to tighten up before paying him another call, so ahead of a game I might go down and be loosened out for an hour or so. At the end of every session his last words struck a chord: 'Remember, Lar, you're only with me for one hour. It's what you do in the other twenty-three that will make the difference.'

Meanwhile, I saw out the 2005 season as Tipp's new water-boy. As pissed off as I was, I had to look at things from Ken's perspective – we were into a Munster final against Cork and he could do with all hands on deck. He hardly needed me to be moping about the place, choking on my own misery. I had to remain upbeat for the team and hope that if we progressed I could again contribute something.

In Tipperary, hurling is the be all and end all, and while some folk had sympathy for me, the bottom line was I couldn't do a job for them any more. Plenty of people had given up on Lar Corbett and probably saw my injury as just another chapter in an endless tale of woe. They'd raise an eyebrow when they saw me passing. I knew they had their doubts about me.

I had absolutely no hope of making the Munster final, but Ken decided to keep everyone guessing and in the match pro-gramme he named me at number fifteen, despite the fact I had no chance of playing.

Evan Sweeney took my spot and I looked on as we went down

by five points in the end, 1-16 to 1-21. We were well off the pace and the longer the game went on the more it became a straight shootout between the entire Cork team and the Kelly brothers, Paul and Eoin, who between them fired thirteen points.

My sole input – having played in the championship just a few weeks earlier – was to stand behind the goals with a batch of hurleys and a supply of water. Some difference!

Still, I actually got a great kick out of it, particularly from watching Micheál Webster in action. Webby was still a novice at this level but had revelled in his first championship start against Clare, driving Brian Lohan demented with his antics and unorthodox style of play – one of the lads said it looked like Webby had woken a grumpy bear from hibernation. He got Davy Fitzgerald going too – though that wouldn't be the toughest job in hurling. There was pure chaos on the edge of the square that day.

But if marking Lohan was like entering the lion's den, taking on Diarmuid O'Sullivan, also known as 'The Rock', in Páirc Uí Chaoimh was hardly a day at the seaside either. From the start the two boys went at it. One minute they were snarling at each other, the next laughing at some shared joke. You'd look around and see Sully trying to undo the clasps of Webby's helmet; the next thing Webby would be patting Sully on the head. At times the crowd were more interested in their private tussle than in following the general play.

Messing aside, Webby had a big role to play for us. He's six foot four and could pluck a cloud from the sky, so we fed him with high balls at every opportunity. The Rock edged the opening exchanges, and every time he cleared a ball the Cork crowd on the Blackrock terrace were in full voice: 'Sully's gonna get you! Sully's gonna get you!'

Webby kept his composure, though, and soon got a paw to the sliotar, held on to it and charged toward goal. Sully hauled him down. Penalty! Off goes Webby prancing behind the Cork uprights with a hand cupping his ear, goading the Cork fans who moments earlier had been singing to him. This was premiership soccer stuff. Brilliant!

The Rock, his fuse well and truly lit by now, took after his tormentor behind the goal. They faced off again but our big fella was growing in confidence. When he won a free or set up a score he would tip over to rally our fans in the crowd. We lost the game but he was a hero that day. He gave us all a lift.

We were pitted against Galway in the All-Ireland quarter-final and in the days before that game Eoin and I discussed the different brands of sliotar then in circulation. Eoin said that if he got a twenty-metre free he wouldn't mind having an old O'Neills model to hand. The new O'Neills ball was pinging all over the place, and Eoin felt the older job would give him more traction to bury a shot from close range.

I decided if that was my only role I was going to do it properly; I promised Eoin I'd be there with the sliotar in question if needed. Sure enough we got a close-in free at a crucial stage in the game. I ran out with the towel and water bottle, and slipped him the secret weapon, which he stitched to the back of the net. In fact he hit that ball so hard it spun the hurley of one of the Galway defenders. I sound like a stuck record here but he got a goal and nine points of our 2-18 that day, exactly half the team's total.

And yet Galway beat us. Don't ask me how. We were five points up with twelve minutes left, and I suppose because Webby was in flying form the lads kept lobbing balls into him, looking for the killer goal when they should have been taking their points. Afterwards, people accused us of showboating, but I don't think cockiness was in our nature at all in those days.

The real turning point came when Damien Hayes stooped low, cut through our defence and buried a goal that turned the match in Galway's favour. When the inquests opened on TV, the clip of that goal was replayed time and again and some people chose to see it as proof we were a 'soft' team. It's easy to say that, but the truth is Damien has a low centre of gravity, is seriously strong, a real terrier, and just got the better of our defence in that crucial instance.

Still, there was massive frustration at blowing a game we should have won. I also felt desperately sorry for Tommy Dunne; it was his last game for Tipp and he ended up playing in the corner. True to form, he signed off with a goal but I felt it was a pity a player of his stature had just one All-Ireland medal to show for fourteen years of unreal service. It was a shocking return and, you could say, a terrible indictment of the rest of us.

We were supposed to be a serious hurling county but I was beginning to wonder about that perception. We had expired with a whimper yet again. I couldn't even look at the papers the next day – everything written about us seemed coated with a crust of disappointment.

A few weeks after our championship exit Ken called a meeting of the squad at Thurles Golf Club but it wasn't really a worthwhile exercise. The players had come under serious scrutiny for speaking out against Michael Doyle's methods just a couple of years earlier and I don't think many of them had the stomach to pipe up again, particularly when we ourselves were falling short. I was definitely underachieving, so how was I going to preach to anyone? I just kept my mouth shut.

Everyone else seemed to have the same idea and when Ken looked for a debrief all he got was the usual stuff Tipp players had been complaining about since 2002: the lack of a game plan and the shortage of tactical ideas.

We had seemed content to look to Eoin while the rest of us just plodded along. What Eoin achieved that year was off the chart – he posted 1–35 in just five games and had an All–Star award wrapped up by the time we lost the Munster final. He was carrying us, but such over-reliance wasn't healthy. The load would have to be shared if we were to ever win anything again.

There was also our tendency to play lads out of position. Why, for example, was a specialist half-back like Eamon Corcoran detailed to mark Joe Deane, the most gifted corner-forward in the game, for that Munster final? It was nearly the ruination of Eamon and he lost an awful lot of confidence over it.

Tipp fans were up in arms over our lack of progress but the players were so ticked off with how the seasons were panning out that we mostly kept our mouths shut. You'd pick up a newspaper and see John Devane, a defender, getting flak even though he was doing his best for the team by filling a gap in the half-forward line.

There were rumours that because Toomevara had so many players in the squad they must have too much political clout in the camp. What did people expect? They were winning county championships for fun, Tommy Dunne was the team's spiritual leader and Benny Dunne was captain in 2005. Of course there was going to be an influence.

Some valid observations were made, though. Eoin's impact aside, it was pretty shocking that a complete rookie became the focal point of our attack. Webby was in the door only a wet week when he was almost forced into a leadership role, going around encouraging the rest of us. He got an All–Star nomination for his efforts – that was something from the year, I guess.

Shortly after our summit meeting Ken went before the county board but he didn't get a third year. We were no closer to winning an All-Ireland and hadn't even reached a semi-final since 2003.

Ken was always good to me, though. He did all he could to get my hamstrings up to pace. And he defended me against criticism. In interviews he praised my contribution in the cameo against Clare and said he often wondered if I might have become the catalyst for success during his time in charge. If only they could have kept me on the field, he said. My thoughts exactly.

Before Ken's fate was even sealed the word was that Babs Keating wanted the job. Babs was one of Tipp's best ever hurlers and after winning two All-Ireland titles in his playing days he delivered another two titles as manager in 1989 and 1991. He won every award in the game, was a great footballer and had a huge personality. But I wasn't sure he rated me. He had referred to me in his newspaper columns as an 'up-and-down player' so I didn't know what to make of his return to the set-up. To be honest I didn't really care either. I had other things to worry about. Five years earlier I was on the threshold of a decent career but now I couldn't even finish out a match.

Babs was duly appointed and called the squad together. Some days I could hardly walk, never mind jog, so I wanted to get my body right and that was going to take time. I more or less kept away from the Tipp camp. I had a hamstring to get right or my career was going down the Swanee.

Soon, the rest of the boys began telling me of Babs's style of management, and especially his frequent harking back to the glory days of the 1960s, but I just zoned out. I had made a promise to myself and Ger Hartmann that I would get to the root of what was causing me to pull up whenever I broke into a sprint. And that meant rest.

After a few months of following Ger's systems I could see definite progress and I decided to take it to the next step. Thurles Sarsfields had just brought in the former Olympic sprinter Gary Ryan from Kilcommon to help our new coach, Ger Cunningham, and I got to know Gary pretty well and found I could trust him.

To pass the time while I was out of hurling I went out and

bought a racing bike, and Gary and I arranged to have private running sessions, and that pushed me further along the ladder to recovery.

I felt a connection with Gary from the start, probably because he had gone through an injury cycle much like mine and had still managed to compete in two Olympiads, in 1996 and 2000. He knew my career was in the balance but straightaway he put me at ease. Gary just had that belief that came from years spent searching for methods he could import to help his own situation.

'Relax,' he would say. 'Just do what I'm doing and you'll be fine. I'll get you right.'

There was no cockiness; he was just a grand, laid-back and intelligent chap who made me look at my approach in new ways. He pledged he would be one step ahead in every stage of my rehabilitation, and I decided there and then that if he told me to wrap my legs in seaweed I would do it.

While sticking to Ger's programme I started from scratch with Gary: a few long walks in the mornings, a bit of light jogging in the evenings and some shadow runs. I was shown how to warm up and how to stretch properly. I learned to speak up for myself too – if the club wanted me to do a session I refused. No matter what exercise I did – climbing stairs or walking down the road – I was to down tools the moment I felt a dart of pain.

Gary also pointed out the error of my ways in not ticking over during the off-season. Tipp would usually be done and dusted by July so – and it pains me to say that – I would go back to Sars and maybe finish up hurling altogether in September or October. Cue three months of R and R before going back with Tipp and ploughing straight into the heavy-legged training. Gary winced as I described the schedule and he advised that I tip away over winter and avoid unleashing hell on soft legs every January.

I was enjoying being left alone to train, and after six months, with the blessing of Ger and Gary, I rejoined the Sars, because they cut their cloth around me and knew I didn't need to be pushed – Tipp could wait for the time being.

Every single training session was a landmark for me but upon the slightest tweak or twinge I withdrew and never a word was said. I didn't feel the need to prove myself and actually enjoyed the plod of January and February, albeit at a much different pace from the rest of the lads.

The club saw the effort I was making and made me captain, an extra motivation. From a base of essentially crawling around the place I was back running freely within weeks, though full-on sprints were still out of the question.

Gary then re-examined my jogging style and reckoned I was too hunched over and was placing excess pressure on some muscles. He showed me how to straighten up and pointed out that the straighter my back, the fewer problems I would have.

What I did in training was every bit as important as in matches – that was the mantra. He asked me to take a longer running stride and insisted that even if I didn't always sustain the new approach on match days the benefits would come from applying it in training.

All aspects, from breathing exercises to core movements, were overhauled, and the new regime emphasised explosive bursts – through winter as well as spring – instead of long, slow runs. Stretching was no longer optional but mandatory; I was at it daily and sometimes hourly. It was a massive commitment but when I went weeks without a recurrence of injury I knew I was making progress.

The spring of 2006 arrived and I got back hurling. Nothing major, a few league games here and there with the club, but I was playing well. We went to Cork to play Killeagh in a challenge match and I got a rake of scores. The following week I got a phone call from one of Babs's selectors, Tom Barry, asking me to return to the Tipp fold.

I hadn't been as happy in years and didn't want to jeopardise everything; every gut instinct and all practical logic told me to stay put with Sars and Gary, to keep working with Ger. But I was also feeling more confident in mind and body than I had done in years, and this was Tipperary calling. And so my heart overruled and told me to go back.

I should have listened to my head.

# 6

# Dead only to wash them

Genuinely, I haven't a clue what to put in and what to leave out in describing the second coming of Babs Keating.

He was given a two-year term by the county board – and the one thing I can tell you is that we were a broken team by the time that term ended.

Eamon Corcoran phoned me after the new appointments were confirmed on the RTÉ *Six One* news – Babs was taking charge, and John Leahy and Tom Barry were to be his fellow selectors. The return of Babs was a big deal in the GAA world and hype was the order of the week. The man was a legend; the dogs in the street knew his pedigree as a player and manager.

Everyone in the county would have greatly respected John Leahy as a hurler too. But when Eamon phoned me it was specifically to get the inside track on Tom Barry, a fellow clubman at Thurles Sarsfields, where he had served as chairman for a few years.

I had to tell Eamon I couldn't be a huge help. I knew that Tom had played for Tipperary at various levels for ten years and I was able to confirm that he seemed a grand fellow – was well educated and had a good job – but kept to himself and in my experience never said much. I told Eamon that even though Tom was a great servant to our club I actually didn't know him well enough to offer an opinion and I didn't want to be speaking about the man when I didn't properly know him.

As the Babs era unfolded, however, the lads in the squad probably listened to Tom more than anyone else. When he made a point it was clear and insightful. I've often thought it would be fascinating to get his thoughts on the whole set-up during those two years because while he clearly had something to offer, quite a few of us were in no doubt he was in the right place at the wrong time.

You couldn't blame Tom for coming on board, though. The return of Babs had the whole country talking. He had brought home the All-Ireland in 1989 and 1991, and the county board were delighted to welcome him back. The sports media were thrilled too because he had a huge profile and a big personality; they looked forward to a share of colourful quotes – and in that they wouldn't be disappointed.

Everyone felt he would give the set-up a lift. Stories were retold of how he had established the Tipp Supporters Club in 1986 to fund the team's training and preparation. Around Thurles we were reminded of how he built a massive groundswell of support for Tipp in every corner of the land, but especially in Dublin. It was a legacy that continued to the present day. Back then, while other teams turned up in shellsuits or casual clobber, the Tipp players were got up in only the finest lounge suits, enjoyed luxury holidays and duly delivered the goods during his time in charge.

Although there was a sizeable generation gap between Babs and his new team we were at least going back to a proven winner. And at a time when we were struggling to win even one championship game at Croke Park that had to count for something.

\*

When the phone call came from Tom Barry I said I couldn't make a snap decision but would like to meet the three boys together and explain where I stood with injuries and my state of mind. I wanted to let them know what I had been through and get some assurance that if I went back they would trust me to call the injury whenever I began to struggle.

We met the first weekend in May, just a week before we played Limerick in the Munster championship. There was no way I could be involved in that opener, so I had already agreed to work on match day for my boss, Tom McDonnell, who had a holiday booked in Spain.

Tom had had the contract for Semple Stadium for close on twenty years and he had shown me where everything was. He also knew I wasn't on the panel but that I'd be there to watch the game anyway, and so he gave me the stadium shift for match day – just routine stuff, looking after the cabling, keeping an eye on the alarms, replacing fuses if needed, nothing too taxing.

Those plans were thrown into disarray, however, when I sat down with Babs, John and Tom. They wanted me back in harness straightaway.

'Sure I haven't even a bit of training done,' I protested. 'I can't just walk back onto the panel a few days before a championship match.'

Not to worry, they said, it was as much mind games as anything. I was to arrive into the dressing-room the following Sunday and tog out.

'We'll put you down on the match programme. It'll give everyone a lift,' Babs insisted. I was taken aback but replied that I'd do whatever was needed.

Nevertheless, I had given Tom my word I'd look after the electrics and I couldn't very well ruin his holiday. So a week later I went down to the stadium with a gear bag and then checked around inside the stadium to make sure all the electrician's tools were handy.

I walked around the dressing-room with my tracksuit on, going around, wishing teammates the best of luck and half checking the wiring at the same time.

I popped into the physio room to meet the rest of the lads, and who was up on the treatment table getting a rub, only minutes before the most important game of our season? Not John O'Brien or Red or some other lad nursing a niggle, but the bold Babs himself. I just smiled.

It was a tough game – playing Limerick always was in the mid-noughties – and everything was still up for grabs at half-time. That's when the fun started. In the dug-out my beeper went off. Hadn't the feckin' fire alarm gone off in the press box?

Up I tore to the press room to see what was happening. There I was in a Tipp tracksuit, sprinting up the steps of the Old Stand. I'd say every bit of good work I'd done with those bloody hamstrings was jeopardised in an instant. It got worse – people in the crowd saw me running and thought I was warming up.

'Best of luck, Larry!'

'Are you coming on, Lar?'

I just looked straight ahead, mortified, and hurried to the scene of the commotion, where the din was earsplitting. When I rushed into the press room wearing the tracksuit the journalists did a double-take. While I checked the fuse board and tightened a few connections they consulted the match programme – too puzzled to even ask what was going on. I keyed the code in and the alarm was silenced. Back to the dressing-room with me then, before the boys went back on the pitch.

We won by four points and as I slipped into the team's formal wear it struck me I must surely be the first intercounty player to appear on a match programme and work the day job at the actual match venue during the game!

The lads were still on a high when I turned up for training a few nights later. But the buzz didn't last long. Babs called us into a huddle and asked Eoin Kelly if he was prepared to take responsibility for a loose pull that had gone out over the end line – one that Babs felt could have been very costly to us.

Now, Eoin had scored fourteen of our 22-point total and I thought it was a ridiculous proposition. The lad had just put in possibly his best ever performance – even the Limerick supporters had applauded him at one stage. Eoin being Eoin, though, batted away the curve ball and just accepted full responsibility. Just a few days later, Babs told the press that Eoin now belonged in the pantheon of great Tipperary hurlers. Talk about mixed signals!

Despite the contradictions, I decided to reserve judgement on the management, mainly because I was happy with how they treated Red, who had been made captain. He was flying fit and gave everything for the cause that year. He even passed up a team holiday with Thurles Sarsfields to Lanzarote and instead focused on Tipp.

Red managed a point against Limerick but also hit seven wides – each one closer to the posts than the previous one. Rather than roasting him out of it, though, Babs brought him down to Semple the next day to help him refine his shooting. I thought that was a nice thing to do.

Red wasn't the only one in need of a hand. The 2006 league was pretty average for the team but the likes of Shane McGrath and Darragh Egan had come into the squad for the first time and Babs was looking to a few of the senior players, including myself, to help bring those lads along.

That was the plan anyway. The reality was that by the end

of the season we were a laughing stock and with every passing fixture the manager's public comments about us seemed to get more bizarre.

One of the worst things he came out with was the 'dead only to wash them' comment – his way of telling the media we were lifeless in losing to Galway in the league in March 2006. Admittedly it hadn't been one of our better days, but out went Babs to the media with the eye-catching quote:

'I saw the Galway fellas, shouting at each other from goalkeeper to corner-forward – our fellas are dead only to wash them. On the field they're not applying anything near what they're putting in at training. I can't understand it.'

That particular soundbite caused ructions and even a year later people were talking about it. Shortly before he stepped aside in 2007, Babs went on RTÉ's *Liveline* and that remark was resurrected (pun accidental). Babs seemed to feel he was being misquoted, but he was up against one reporter, Shane Brophy from the *Nenagh Guardian*, who stated he had Babs on tape saying those exact words and sent the tape to RTÉ. Talk about a mess!

It was a bit like the uproar that happened in Laois in 1996 and Offaly in 1998 when Babs was in charge in those counties. He had good initial success with Laois and brought them to a national league semi-final but they parted ways after he criticised the team for losing by twenty points to Offaly, the next county he would manage. He went into a strong dressing-room there, but after he described the players as 'sheep in a heap' following their 1998 Leinster final defeat to Kilkenny, they kicked up and there was a parting of ways.

Leaving aside such commotion and getting back to the only places that mattered – the training paddock and the field of play – I have to say the drills were poor and lacked intensity during his second stint in charge of Tipperary.

Actually, the best training session we had was the one Nicky English took before the 2006 Munster final. Nicky spent most of that session roaring and shouting at us – I think he was bemused at how laid-back the whole affair was. Maybe as players we have to take responsibility for lifting the tempo, but when you're constantly training in second or third gear it's not easy to suddenly go into turbo drive again. Slowly, you stop egging yourself on, never mind anyone else.

Brian Murray, an international middle-distance runner from Templederry who had been on a sports scholarship in the US, was drafted in as our trainer. He knew his stuff but was given responsibility by Babs for way too many hurling drills.

It wasn't fair – the players knew Brian was expert in his chosen field but we didn't think that ballwork, and all that goes with it, was his forte at intercounty senior level. That's not a criticism – it would be like asking a hurler to show sprinters the perfect technique for exploding out of the blocks.

A week before we played the Munster final we were doing a drill that Babs loved (Brian didn't take this one). It involved kicking the ball at each other – Babs reminded us that this skill could be required at any time during a match. We were at it a good few minutes when the management were called into the stand. I think they half forgot about us so we continued for the next ten minutes kicking sliotars at each other. A few kicks here and there never killed anyone but we nearly had broken toes by the time they arrived back and told us to stop.

All things considered, reaching the Munster final was a fair achievement. After the win over Limerick we beat Waterford 3-14 to 1-12 in Cork. That same week DJ Carey retired from intercounty hurling, and when the media needed a new hero they didn't have to look past Eoin, who nabbed 2-9 and practically secured another All-Star on the day – after just two games.

I took my seasonal bow, running on for the last nineteen minutes, and before long Diarmuid Fitzgerald set me up for a goal. I was happy enough to be back with the lads and happier still to be in the frame for a Munster final, but Waterford were poor on the day and missed a heap of chances.

Cork, though, were close enough to the peak of their powers and I don't know if we really expected to beat them. They were all precision and power, brimming with short passing and making clever runs, whereas we were way behind in terms of organisation. Still, they beat us by only a goal, 2-14 to 1-14.

That game was there for the taking; we missed a load of chances. Diarmuid Fitz had been converted from wing-back to full-forward and on another day he could have buried two goals. I came back to life with a goal and a point, but sure it wasn't worth a curse because we lost.

Babs told me I was marking Pat Mulcahy and my mission was to expose him for speed and make his life a misery. If I got an early slap off Pat I had to make sure and milk it, maybe even hit the ground and put him on the referee's radar. Babs added that he would be close by and that he'd look after me. Sure enough, not long after the ball was thrown in, he ambled around the sideline and appeared in my line of vision.

'What in the name of Jesus do I have to do here?' I wondered to myself. 'Does he want me to hit the deck already?'

But there wasn't even time to do that. Only three minutes had passed when the ball arrived between the two of us. I took it on, beat Pat and gave Dónal Óg Cusack the eye to his left but then struck it to his right and buried the first goal of the game.

The crowd went nuts but I still half feared I had done wrong in Babs's eyes. I ran back out to the corner and saw him trailing off to the dugout again. He had walked all the way around for nothing so it was just as well I managed to raise a green flag.

Even though we mostly matched them for intensity we weren't ready for Cork. But boy were they prepared for us. They cut off the supply lines to Eoin, knowing that if he was starved of oxygen we would flatline. They put a screen in front and stopped our backs from finding him. Eoin managed only a point from play and that was the end of any realistic hope we had of beating them.

A couple of days later Babs came out and said something to the effect that Eoin needed to get fitter and more aggressive if he wanted to rank alongside the hurling legends of South Tipperary, where Babs himself hailed from.

By now I couldn't help thinking the Thurles Sarsfields training was streets ahead of what we were doing with Tipp. There is something amiss when a club training session is more intense than one with a county team.

Ger Cunningham, who had coached Newtownshandrum before joining Sars, was on top of his game and made sure everything was like clockwork. For instance, we had five different puck-out tactics, different signals for each one; everyone knew who was on frees and sideline cuts and we all knew where they would drop. With Tipp it was way less organised.

One thing I will say for Babs: he was streetwise and fieldwise. Back then there used to be fierce messing with sliotars, and Babs knew Cork were up to all sorts of shenanigans.

For a start they would introduce their own favourite, the Cummins Allstar, into games at every opportunity. That was entirely legal, so fair play to them. The GAA hadn't yet standardised the official ball and on match days they would usually supply a choice of sliotars, say six O'Neills and six Allstars, and whereas most counties preferred the O'Neills model, the Cork boys swore by the Cummins version.

You can argue that it shouldn't matter a jot what sliotar is used, but there's actually quite a difference in the various moulds and Babs knew that the Cork boys would play much better with the Allstar, which was reckoned to travel fifteen yards further than the O'Neills.

He also knew that they wouldn't scruple at bending the rules, that the different options cleared the way for a share of skulduggery and that serious ball tampering wasn't out of the question.

Before that Munster final, he sauntered over to Dónal Óg's goal in front of the Town End terrace, where the Cork supporters were gathered, and brought the umpires' attention to the bag of sliotars in Cusack's goal. That caused a right fuss but it was an attempt by Babs to highlight what the cute hoors were trying to do.

They had it down to a fine art. This is the kind of stuff they would get up to: if Tipp got a close-in free, a Cork defender would spark a skirmish while another would swipe at the ball in mock disgust and fire it into their net. Away would fly the brand new O'Neills sliotar and out in its place would come some clunky oul' lopsided yoke from the 1970s, with no brand – a sliotar you'd hardly shift with a rocket launcher. Everything was about inches with them, and if changing a ball made life even 1 per cent more difficult for an opponent it was a job well done.

We learned mostly to negate their trickery but sometimes in the heat of battle we were caught on the hop. I'll go back to the 2005 game between us to give you an example. Well in advance of that clash they took one of their own balls, shaped it into an O'Neills sliotar, got a marker and wrote 'Tipp' on it. Sure enough we were awarded a penalty, and they worked their bit of hocus-pocus and lobbed the counterfeit missile out to Eoin. That ball probably had all the life drained from it – to borrow from Babs, it was 'dead only to wash it' – and I don't know if it made any difference, but the penalty was saved.

In contrast they served up nothing but the finest wine for themselves. All around the field they had lads – sleeper agents as we called them – in situ and rolling out different balls depending on who had been awarded a free.

It didn't always work for them. John Gardiner missed three long-range frees in that Munster final – and I mean long range. Even though the free was seventy or eighty yards out the field the ball flew high over the net and soared into the terrace, showing just how light those sliotars were. Either that or John was eating spinach by the bucketload.

But they were cute and they were sharp, Cusack was running the show, and yet at the end we were only a goal off the pace.

That sickened us even more because we were nowhere near right in those games, strategically or tactically. Had we been we might have taken them. Cork knew damn well that things weren't good in our camp, and in his autobiography Cusack wrote how they never feared playing Tipp and imagined we worried much more about them than they did about us. He was probably right.

They knew they had the jump on us because we had no real game plan while theirs was highly developed and rehearsed to a fine art. I looked out the field in envy as they launched attack after attack through their short-passing and running game. God, I would have loved to be part of that, tearing onto balls, dashing into space. Dónal Óg was the conductor and he had every one of them singing off the same hymn sheet. In contrast, we hit nothing but bum notes after losing that Munster final.

After that game, Babs spoke in the dressing-room and said we had to be at Dundrum House Hotel the next morning for a recovery session in the pool. Most of us went out that night for a few drinks and it was only when I woke up I remembered the pool session.

I phoned Babs and told him that Red and I couldn't make the pool because we had a funeral to attend. We went to that removal and when the rest of the boys finished in the pool they went out for a few beers anyway. Generally, if we are allowed go for a drink after a match I actually prefer to tip home on Sunday evenings because I'd be wrecked; the best craic is to be found on the Mondays when you've had a good night's sleep and can fully unwind.

But the postscript to that final is messy. Management told us to limit the socialising, but on Monday evening some of the lads went to Clonoulty for a pint and a few more went to Borrisoleigh. The boys in Borris were minding their business when a young lad with a hurley and sliotar entered the bar, saw our boys and asked for autographs. The lads chatted away and signed his hurl, and the youngster went back to the Borris field and told his friends how he had obtained the autographs. What the boys didn't know was that Brian Murray was taking the session in Borris that night. Word of their exploits reached Babs in Dublin and he wasn't happy.

Meanwhile, Red had been thinking about how poor we were against Cork and he wasn't happy either. He got it into his head to phone Babs. Tired and emotional – and resisting the pleadings of his pals and their efforts to wrest the phone from him – he did just that.

He had been a good leader, had trained well and put everything into the team but in the matter of a minute all that went up in smoke. Red left a pretty crude message for Babs, not complimentary at all at all, and hung up. He knew straightaway he shouldn't have done it – he hadn't been thinking straight – but the die was cast.

In team sport this sort of stuff can happen quite a bit but it's usually kept in-house. Not in Tipp, though. Babs phoned Red, called a meeting and said they were dropping him off the panel.

That was the end of Red's stint in the blue and gold. In a flash his intercounty career was done and dusted.

No-one in the county would have denied that Red was good enough for the Tipp set-up and everyone who knows him would testify that he has a heart of pure gold. Only a few months earlier he had been in the papers for the right reasons after a vandal had damaged a neighbour's window. Red had restrained the person responsible until the gardaí arrived.

But there was no reprieve here. Red was given his marching orders, and following a meeting he shook hands with Babs, John Leahy and John Costigan, the county board chairman, and wished them luck. He had been the first Thurles Sars man to captain Tipp since 1974 and now his dream was over. On his way out of the room and the team he loved, Red stopped. He just turned and said he hoped Tipp would win the All-Ireland.

The whole thing blew up and word of the infamous phone call reached the media. It should have been kept in-house but it turned into a circus. I couldn't help recalling the night I went nuts in Wexford and how Nicky dealt with that and kept it all under wraps. In total, five players were disciplined and I'm sure the Cork boys were choking on their own few pints that week, laughing at us as we self-destructed.

Red's phone was hopping as journalists hunted for quotes, but I couldn't give him much advice because I had my own issues. Sars were reigning county champions, which meant I was next in line for the Tipp captaincy. Tom Barry came to me at training and asked if I would take it on.

I asked Red what I should do and he gave it to me straight.

'Grab it, Larry. We're still in there with a shout. I'd love to see you going up the steps of the Hogan Stand in September.'

Red had seen his Tipp career end over a silly voicemail and was then hung out to dry in the media but here he was, wishing me well and telling me to take captaincy so that some good might come of his misfortune. He never got another chance with Tipp again and I don't think the punishment fitted the crime.

As I thought Red had been dealt with harshly, I should have said no. But I wasn't man enough to do that – the only small defence I can offer is that I also felt the squad was in enough turmoil – so I agreed to take it. And it's not every day you are asked to captain your county either, I suppose. In happier circumstances, though, it would have meant an awful lot more.

We were a disjointed lot by now and the few lads who hadn't been out socialising after the Cork game were thoroughly pissed off with the rest of us. One of them put it in plain terms: 'Ye are fucking around with our chances of winning a medal.'

It didn't help that the dirty linen was all being washed in public. The panel was now fragmented, and I should have asked them to give the captaincy to someone else – I can't say for sure but in the circumstances I doubt Sars would have minded. But for a quiet life, I just went along with it.

Tom Barry stayed in touch with Red, who decided to write to Babs and formally apologise. He got a lovely letter in reply. Babs reminded him how Cormac Bonnar once bounced back from being dropped off the Tipp panel to later win two All-Stars. He promised they would keep the door open for Red in the long term. Nothing ever came of it, but at least they got back in touch.

Red's Tipp career was over – several years before it should have been. He went from captaining the team against Cork in a Munster final to going off on holidays the week we played Waterford again, in the All-Ireland quarter-final in late July. In fact he landed back in Ireland just as the game ended and learned the result at a toll booth on the M50 in Dublin when he got chatting to a driver flying a Tipp flag.

On hearing we had lost, Red enquired, 'And how was Larry?'

The reply was blunt: 'Fucking useless.'

I wouldn't have argued.

# 7

# Curve balls and media sideshows

If 2006 ended on a downer, 2007 was a disaster almost from the start.

Long before the end of the year trust between players and management had broken down. The more Babs criticised us in public the more we became a shambles. Why we put up with it for so long is another story – one I'm still trying to figure out.

Unlike the Cork lads, who stood up for themselves on three different occasions, not one of us had the gumption to shout stop. I had been five or six years in the squad and should have said what I knew in my heart: 'Hey, lads, this is all bollocks! We're going nowhere.'

We actually kicked off the season reasonably well, winning the Waterford Crystal tournament and then beating Kilkenny, who were missing the likes of Henry Shefflin and Cha Fitzpatrick, in the league at Nowlan Park, but those were rare bright spots in an otherwise bleak landscape.

Even beating the Cats had its downside for me because I got the mother and father of all tongue-lashings when John Leahy ran toward me after just ten minutes and loudly tore strips off me for not getting into the game. When I was dragged off at half-time I should have told them what I thought – I had no problem being subbed but being roared at in full public view was out of order. Once more, though, I bit my tongue.

Despite those early victories, we didn't set the world alight that spring, and our cause wasn't helped when our full-back Philly Maher was let go from the panel in March. The reason given – he was 'putting too much butter on his spuds'. The pressure seemed to ratchet up by the week.

Limerick beat us in the league opener and the knives were out. Babs made six changes for Kilkenny, who were unbeaten in nineteen games. Somehow, we got the better of them and things settled down for a while again.

The roof nearly caved in, though, when we played Antrim in the rain, wind and mud at Templemore and fell five points behind. The shit was getting ready to hit the fan, but we turned it around and came out on top by six.

The night before that game, I had felt a pain in the right hamstring. In the past I would have played away and probably aggravated the injury but this time I decided I wasn't going to risk it; I phoned Babs to tell him I was pulling out of the game. He was at the Horse and Jockey hotel, and fair enough, he was probably eating, but I had barely got the words out when the call was abruptly terminated. I'd say if I was a reporter looking for an interview the conversation might not have ended so quickly.

Galway were next up and thousands turned up to watch us play at Pearse Stadium. It was an exciting, high-scoring game and we lost by four. A day later Babs told Tipp FM radio he wasn't going to stand idly by while Galway dished out the nasty stuff, borderline thuggery. His comments made national headlines and of course the Galway manager, Ger Loughnane – another character who doesn't mince words – had a cut back at us. Again we were getting attention we could have done without.

We went on to hammer Dublin, lost to Waterford in the league quarter-finals and were left with injuries to Eoin, Pa and Conor O'Mahony as the championship opener against Limerick loomed.

But apart from the weekly newspaper headlines, our team talks were getting more and more bizarre. Before a game Babs would call us into a circle and the talk might be about a round of golf he had played with Paul McGinley or Pádraig Harrington and how he had chipped in from well off the green. There may have been a message there, but I for one would go away still wondering what it was.

I know others were puzzled too, but we just got on with it, half amused at the craziness of it all. I suppose there was also the lingering thought that this was a legend talking and maybe there was method in the madness and in the long run things would come good.

When he'd stand up to give a team talk one of his favourite sayings was 'I'm here to preach the gospel, lads, come on board.' I think Babs thought we were all against him and he was trying to make us see the light.

Another episode stands out. It was a league match in Thurles, and a short while before throw-in Babs brought a group of kids to meet us – I think they were from a Dublin club. The concept was a great one – Babs was brilliant with kids and always had time for supporters – but this was some sight: lads stretching and togging out and psyching themselves up for battle, and all the time minding their step so they wouldn't fall over a child. You couldn't move inside the dressing-room.

I'm all for promoting the game but it should have taken place before a training session or the likes. We never knew what to expect.

\*

There were serious injuries in the camp coming up to the Limerick game but we got out of the Gaelic Grounds with a draw, 1-19 apiece. They lost Damien Reale to a red card early on but we still couldn't put them away and they equalised with the last puck of the game.

Not closing out that match was bad enough but comments by Babs in the papers the next day seriously pissed people off.

'Coming down here was going to be a real testing ground for them,' he said. 'If they were men they'd have come through it. Some did and some didn't.'

Again management were let off the hook. And that even though we got little or no input from the dugout about making best use of the extra man. The only tactical move I recall is that, for no obvious reason, Eoin was relieved of the free-taking. Babs argued later that they were trying to spare his leg – he was only back from injury and they didn't want him running all over the field. If I was in charge I'd have wheeled Eoin around the Gaelic Grounds all day to take frees, simply because he was the best in the country at it.

The former Limerick manager Tom Ryan then weighed in with a boot, saying Babs was over the hill. Rather than ignore the jibe, which would have been the sensible thing to do, Babs upped the ante on Tipp FM the following week: 'To me Tom Ryan is an arsehole and always has been an arsehole.'

It was getting to be a pantomime. A report in the *Irish Times* summed it up, describing Babs as a 'quote machine' who attracted microphones like a giant, magnetic force field. Babs continued to speak on reflex for the rest of the season, but the players needed the media attention like a hole in the head.

We thought we had the replay against Limerick, in Semple Stadium, sewn up; we pulled ten points clear and should have easily seen the game out. We could blame the set-up and the background noise all we wanted but as a team we took our foot off the pedal, and Andrew O'Shaughnessy pointed in the last second to level the scores.

If that was dramatic – and in fairness the media labelled it one of the best games in history – what had happened in the preceding twenty-four hours was sensational altogether.

On the eve of the game we heard Brendan Cummins had been dropped and his place given to Gerry Kennedy, who had impressed with the Tipp under-21s. Gerry had loads of promise but it was incredible he was going to oust Brendan, still for most people the best keeper in the game.

The reason given was that Babs and the boys were unhappy with Brendan's puck-outs. And so for the first time in twelve years this goalkeeping superstar was starting a championship match on the bench. That's hard enough to take but it seems he was told only a couple of hours before the match, which was to throw in at seven o'clock. He didn't take it well and no reasonable person would blame him.

When we eventually got past the shock of Brendan getting the bullet we also wondered why it hadn't been done earlier in the week so that everyone – especially Gerry – would have had time to focus. But Babs liked doing things at the last minute and that sometimes included team selection.

As well as worrying about another heavy tussle with Limerick we now had to fret about fielding a rookie goalkeeper in a high-tempo match; we worried about how Gerry would manage in the heat of championship.

As it turned out – with encouragement from Brendan, who went on the field and warmed up with him – Gerry did really well and even saved a penalty after twenty-seven minutes.

Afterwards, I found out from a friend who had been stewarding on the sideline that I had been lucky to survive a cull myself.

Seemingly the boys had been on the point of subbing me after only seven minutes. All my friend could hear was Johnny Leahy roaring: 'Take him off! Take him off!'

On the sideline lads shout stuff like that in the heat of the moment but it was just as well they held fire because I got three points. Eventually, though, they got their wish and after sixty minutes I was replaced. We braced ourselves as this one went into extra time as well. And you couldn't make this up – they brought me back on after eighty minutes!

At the end of the extra time we headed into the dressing-room, level again but effectively half beaten after losing a ten-point lead and not looking forward to a close encounter of the third kind, which was down for Limerick the following weekend. We were cramped, dehydrated and pissed off that we had missed two chances to put them away.

The mood wasn't much better in the stands, where some of the supporters were venting anger against Babs. He also had to deal with some 'fan' texting him abuse during games.

We headed away from the cauldron of Semple Stadium to kick-start our recovery, part of which entailed fielding questions from journalists sniffing a story in the days after the game. Some of us had to publicly dismiss talk of unrest in the squad.

You could tell that people outside of the county were laughing at us now, lapping up our weekly sideshows. One joke going the rounds was that the Tipp hurlers were out walking greyhounds – so they could learn to hold on to a lead. There was another one. What's the difference between the Tipp hurlers and a heavy drinker? The drinker wouldn't leave ten points behind.

With the whole country talking about the Tipp–Limerick saga a crowd of 31,000 turned up for the third game. And finally, after a marathon tussle spanning three games, four hours and two extra-time periods, Limerick came out on top. We managed two goals but hit only thirteen points and they deserved their three-point win, after yet more extra time.

Even epics have endings and, sadly, ours was not in the Hollywood vein. We were shattered and down on our luck after three exhausting games. I remember sitting in the dressing-room and hearing the whoops and screams of the Limerick players as they ran back into their quarters to celebrate. The silence was deafening in our place.

Limerick had a Munster final to look forward to whereas we were confined to destiny's waiting-room, the qualifiers, and a date with Offaly in just six days' time. All we wanted to do was get out of the Gaelic Grounds but for a good twenty minutes no-one moved. We knew we would have to regroup mentally and physically but the road ahead was surely too potholed. Our camp was crumbling.

Just six days after our loss to Limerick, Offaly missed a gift-wrapped opportunity to beat us. We fielded an entirely new half-forward line and were level eight times in total. They went five points up within eight minutes of the restart and should then have delivered the knockout blow. Instead they kept conceding frees and Eoin rattled over six in a row to keep us in touch. They also hit seventeen wides and it was only when I got in for a goal with the last puck of the game that we were safe.

We were blessed to hang on. And if justice had been done, John McIntyre, the Offaly manager, would have been knocking on our door at the finish not to congratulate but to commiserate.

Still, if you knew what happened before the game you might have made allowances for us. I arrived at Dr Morris Park for the warm-up and I genuinely hadn't a clue if I was playing or not. I asked Benny Dunne if he knew the team, but he said he didn't.

'It's a fucking terror, isn't it?' I said.

After warming up we went to the dressing-room, where five

of us, including John Carroll, Benny and myself, were immediately hauled into the shower room by the management. They told us we were dropped. This was just minutes before throw-in.

'Lads, we won't be starting ye today, just to let ye know.'

Benny didn't take it well. 'This is an absolute joke!' he said. 'I pulled into Dr Morris Park an hour ago and Lar asked me if I knew the team. I knew it because I'd heard it this morning, but I didn't have the heart to tell him he wasn't playing. It's a joke!'

Someone else mentioned that Micheál Ó Muircheartaigh had been told the line-up before the players, which was an even bigger laugh.

John and Benny walked out of the shower room and I followed them. My only regret is that before leaving I didn't turn on the cold showers and give the boys a good hosing.

As we left the shower room five more lads were called in there. This time Pa Bourke came out with his jaw down to his knees because he was unexpectedly starting. I was delighted for him but I could see he wasn't ready at all. I could also see that he was down for me because I had been dropped.

'Pa, do me one favour,' I said. 'The throw-in is almost here. Forget about whatever you think is going on here and keep your mind and head clear. You have to be selfish for the next seventy minutes. Don't mind any of the stuff that's after going on here – we'll sort it out tonight. Remember why you're here and just go out and hurl. You can only control things that affect you.'

I looked over at Liam Cahill, who had been recalled to the team after a few years off it. He had been back training with us only a wet week and he was starting too. It was obvious he had been caught on the hop as well.

If Babs wanted to make a point about being unhappy with some of his players he had done so, but it didn't work out for him – Liam, Pa and Diarmuid Fitzgerald were taken off at half-time and John Carroll, Benny and I were sent on. We barely survived.

Another four – Liam, Pa, James Woodlock and Shane McGrath – were dropped for the Dublin game, our fifth championship match in four weeks. For the second time in a fortnight we came from behind to win.

Eoin was again left off the frees – Willie Ryan took over the duties and we had enough about us to get out of Parnell Park with a win.

A bit of respite, then, and at last some light at the end of the tunnel, because even if we lost to Cork we were still in the championship courtesy of the new round-robin system.

To this day a good few of us remain convinced the management fully expected us to lose. We knew that if we lost to the Rebels we'd meet Waterford in the All-Ireland quarter-final two weeks later. But if we won we'd play Wexford just eight days later. Those were the two scenarios.

Babs and co. must have been full sure Cork would beat us because they said they were considering organising a bus to bring us to Wexford on a two-day training camp the following week. The players just looked at each other. Tom Barry quickly copped it and twice interjected to remind everyone these were provisional plans. All the same we couldn't believe what we were hearing.

Around that time I was quoted in the media insisting that the players were fully behind Babs, that there was no disharmony at all. I did that for one reason: I was playing for Tipp and I wanted an All-Ireland medal. Babs was the manager and he would ultimately shape us up for a fall or a tilt at the title. I sensed we were drifting further away from that target so I spoke out in an attempt to get us back on course. I wasn't getting any closer to the goal of winning another medal and that's why I made those comments. They may have been misleading, but that was my only motivation; it wasn't to keep Babs happy. I wanted another medal, and to that end a contented and harmonious panel was the very least we required, and so I tried to dispel the storm clouds that were gathering around us.

We beat Cork – how, I'll never know. Eoin was injured. It was a Saturday evening game and I suppose a crowd of fifteen thousand is lost in Semple so the atmosphere wasn't what you'd expect – it kind of felt like a league fixture at the start, though it improved as the game went on. Half of Thurles came up to the stadium at half-time when they saw we were in with a shout.

They were slipping a bit at the time and everything just clicked for us. Willie Ryan got two unreal goals. I hit three points and so did Benny. Our backs were brilliant. We heard the crowd chanting: 'Tipp! Tipp! Tipp!' and it drove us on. We went six points ahead. Webby was killing them in the full-forward line and for the first time in a Tipp shirt I just decided to do my own thing. I rambled out from corner-forward a few times to get ball and managed to tip over the few points.

We caught them on the hop and the legend of Babs Keating only grew again. This was the first time since 1991 we had taken Cork in the championship. Back then Babs was also in charge. To many people in the county Babs will always be a hero, so credit where it's due. For the rest of us, the players, it was our first championship win against the Rebels. In fact, some of us had never beaten them at any level.

We rolled on, somehow still on the championship trail. The wagon may have been rattling and the wheels ready to come off but Babs would lead us into an All-Ireland quarter-final, and as players who had achieved nothing for the bones of seven years – and had been blamed for getting rid of Michael Doyle – we were hardly in the best position to be bitching.

We no longer needed to after the Wexford game. That was

another one we just threw away and the result effectively sealed the fate of Babs and the two boys.

They hadn't helped themselves. Just as things were settling down again and we were getting on with preparing for the Yellowbellies they pulled another rabbit out of the hat by dropping Eoin. They protested to all and sundry that he wasn't fit and had a dead leg, but Eoin had spoken to the contrary in the press – and sure he was first sub on the day. In my eyes fitness wasn't an issue at all.

There were all sorts of theories going around as to why Babs had dropped Brendan Cummins – his own clubman – earlier in the summer. I don't think Babs was happy that Brendan was pucking the ball out the way he wanted and he decided to act. Now Eoin, our best player, was also being left out because Babs didn't feel he was fit enough. After being left on the bench for seventy minutes against Cork, he had been taken aside in training before the Wexford game and told to focus on practising 21-yard frees. Then he finds out he isn't even starting. Nuts.

I won't say it caused ructions in the dressing-room – we had taken so much craziness by now that we were almost punch-drunk – but when your best player is left on the bench, morale is hardly going to be raised, particularly when every GAA reporter in the land is peering in through the windows.

I can't speak for Eoin in terms of how disappointed he was but he's one of the best fellas around to take the positive out of everything, even when the ball is not breaking for him. I always phoned him when things weren't going well for me because he's brilliant to bolster your confidence.

I looked over at him as we got ready to take on Wexford and there he was, still focused and able to go around and talk to lads. That's a mark of him. With the sewage hitting the fan all around him he never said a word out of turn and just got on with things.

Brendan was still missing, and Shane McGrath, a real find for us at midfield and a player Babs himself discovered, got the bullet, so we faced Wexford in Croke Park minus three of our best players.

All this upheaval was bad enough, but worse was that the Wexford manager, John Meyler, was turning it into ammunition; he had his troops well fired up after telling them: 'Tipp think they can leave three of their best players on the bench and still beat us.'

In fairness, we were doing our own motivation work. Babs asked us to go home and paint a big banner – 'Tipperary, 2007 All-Ireland champions' – and put it over a wall or on the mantel-piece. We could have rewritten the Book of Kells and it wouldn't have made a difference that year.

Sure enough Eoin was on the field after just twenty-seven minutes, replacing Darragh Egan. I felt we were by far the better team and, although we could never really close the door on Wexford, we were comfortable.

I was doing fine myself; I had managed a goal and a point before the break, and when John Leahy approached me in the dressing-room I assumed he was about to pat me on the back and tell me I was flying it. Instead, he let me have it again over a couple of mistakes. I was never as gobsmacked in all my life.

We blew it in the end, but in hindsight losing was the best thing that ever happened. They had lots of goal chances but near the end we were still a couple of points ahead when Wexford got a 21-yard free halfway between the sideline and the median of the pitch. Trying to waste a bit of time, Eamon Corcoran walked across the ball – and the referee instantly picked it up and replaced it dead centre in front of the goal.

Damien Fitzhenry picked up his stick, ambled forward and stitched the sliotar to our net.

Had the ball not been moved we probably would have saved

the shot and in the light of our win over Cork and qualification for an All-Ireland semi-final Babs and the boys might have been handed another year in charge. I also suspect they wouldn't have recalled Brendan, Eoin or myself to the set-up – we might have been retired.

That was the end of it, thank God. All we were doing in 2006 and 2007 was turning up and fulfilling fixtures. If the GAA said we had a match on a certain day against Cork or Kilkenny we would go in hope only.

The whole country raved about those three games with Limerick, how heart-stopping they were and the tremendous good they did for hurling. But, truthfully, if we were firing on all cylinders we shouldn't even have needed a second match to get past them.

For sure, those games were nip and tuck, full of excitement and tension, and they did light up the hurling world, but we were a man up in the first and ten points up in the second and we couldn't close the deal.

We have to look at ourselves and take responsibility but the proof is in the pudding for me – just a year or two later we were going into those same matches fully believing we would win and most of the time we did just that.

I decided to take stock. From 2003 to 2007 we were going up to Croke Park and getting one game a year there – it just felt like we were going up to play, lose and then have a night on the town. That was what our hurling careers were amounting to.

I tried to help the new lads on the team each time we visited Croker but I'd be so nervous myself I wouldn't be of great assistance. It was always daunting enough going into the dressing-room, not having been there for twelve months. In contrast, from 2008 to 2011 we were constantly there, we all had our own seats in the room and we were all much more relaxed. We knew the lie of the land and it made such a difference.

It's easy to take potshots at Babs and the boys but I'm not doing it for the sake of it. Rather than just have a go at someone I'd like to think I've spelt out the stuff that was happening from a player's perspective.

Babs had lots of good points – he could be great company, and when Joe Deane was ill he asked every one of us to sign a card and posted it to him. And I know Babs would argue that we, the players, let him down. In the heel of the hunt, I suppose you have to draw your own conclusions.

But if you think I'm being harsh you should remember that after Babs stepped down and resumed his newspaper columns he let us have it at every opportunity. A verbal gunslinger with both barrels aimed squarely at the Tipp team. Here are a few examples of what he said.

1 June 2010, *TV3*

Take the goal that Lar Corbett missed on Sunday (against Cork in the Munster championship). We missed three of them in last year's All-Ireland final because those guys did not take on board the advice they were given.

If Pat Fox or Nicky English got the opportunity that Lar Corbett got on Sunday it would have been a definite green flag. If Fox or English got the opportunity to score three goals like last year's All-Ireland they would be goals and we wouldn't be making heroes out of goalkeepers like PJ Ryan or Dónal Óg Cusack. This is where the team is lacking.

5 September 2011, *Irish Sun*

In 2007 I was in charge of a Tipperary team that lost to Wexford in an All-Ireland quarter-final. I felt that Eoin

Kelly, Lar Corbett and John O'Brien all failed me against a moderate Wexford team. I get no satisfaction out of saying that but unfortunately they failed to deliver again yesterday.

He had plenty of other pops too – he once said Tipp had been waiting eight years to get a great performance out of me and years before that he reckoned I was a player 'who will always blow hot and cold'. When I withdrew from the squad in 2012 he delivered a nice parting shot by saying I had been 'up and down' for ten years with my form.

Perhaps the most bizarre comments, however, came the week after we lost to Wexford. His theory was that we were too well educated.

2 August 2007, RTÉ's *Road to Croker*
I felt that less-educated guys had a greater ability to retain the bit of advice you gave. Nothing happened in that game against Wexford that we didn't work on since last November. You ask yourself, are you wasting your time? Do they listen any more?

One thing I'm comfortable with is that I gave Eoin advice last April, advice that his fitness programme wasn't what we felt it should be. I advised him that it's horrible to wake up further down the road and think you could have done better when you were a player.

Babs was right: he used to give us advice. I remember before we played Waterford he told Eamon Corcoran to watch out for Dan Shanahan because he was 'dangerous'. But he never told Eamon how to handle him – no game plan or tactical instructions.

Big Dan duly went to town on us and afterwards Babs said to Eamon, 'Didn't I tell you to watch out for him?'

Maybe it was that failure to communicate that left us so far apart – Babs felt that by giving general instructions he was doing enough, whereas modern-day players like to be told specifics.

Being honest, I used to enjoy reading his columns after he left the job. If I had bought the *Irish Sun* and found he was praising me or the team it would actually have broken my heart. If he had described me as one of the best forwards he had seen, for instance, I don't know how I would have reacted. When I was constantly being knocked I learned how to deal with it.

The criticism didn't bother me at all because I lost respect for his opinion, but some of the things he said were below the belt. There is no way your former team should be getting lashed out of it in newspaper columns. It got so bad that our sports psychologist, Caroline Currid, eventually compiled a bunch of his columns and quotes and we posted them on the walls for match-day motivation. It's sad to say his words were all over our dressing-room wall before the 2010 All-Ireland final.

I suppose one thing I admire about Babs, apart from the fact he served Tipp in a number of roles over the bones of fifty years, is that he always speaks his mind and stands over what he says. His columns are highly entertaining and I know plenty of people around Thurles read them and look forward to them. And the fact he knocked us so much actually took some of the pressure off us in the end.

Last year, I was invited onto a *Late Late Show* special for Micheál Ó Muircheartaigh, who described the 2010 All-Ireland final as the greatest he commentated upon. I was in RTÉ's green room when Babs walked in and straightaway he owned the place. He's great at meeting people and holding court and he made his way around shaking hands with almost everyone. I say 'almost everyone' because he didn't come near me. I didn't go near him either, but surely he could have come over and congratulated a fellow Tipp man on winning an All-Ireland. I would have shaken his hand too.

I stood back and thought about all he had done for Tipp hurling. He was a brilliant player, one of our most skilful, and a manager who led us to two All-Ireland titles and five Munster championships. I wondered what he did, where he went, on the night we won the 2010 All-Ireland. Did he come to the banquet?

Even after the stuff he wrote, someone like Babs Keating should always be remembered in Tipp folklore. But I just pray that in maybe thirty years' time, when I'm long gone out of the game, I can go to some young lad and say, 'Hey, that's one fantastic team ye have and I'm delighted for ye.'

We're all Tipp people at the end of the day.

# 8

# Sars in my eyes

When I think of Thurles Sarsfields the first person that comes into my head is Declan Ryan. Not the last Tipp manager, but the club's best supporter.

Big Deccie, as he is more commonly known, is the top man around here. He puts a smile on your face each time you meet him.

Before games he sometimes leads us from the dressing-room out onto the field at a half-gallop, he eats the wine gums and Jaffa Cakes at half-time, sticks his head in front of the TG4 cameras on match days – that kind of thing.

Across all grades Big Deccie hops in for the team photos, stands in the middle of the back row, puts his arms around the four players to his left and right and gives one big squeeze.

Ger Cunningham, when he was in charge, used to get him to take the warm-up now and again. Deccie would blow the whistle, tell us to jog to the far sideline and then shout, 'Come back to me, lads!' Then he'd hand the whistle back to Ger and say, 'They're ready to go now, gaffer.' The whole process took about forty seconds but it was priceless.

Characters like big Deccie are what make a club special.

Everyone wants to win but the atmosphere and goodwill generated by the real personalities like this fella are key ingredients in a club.

There are loads of other characters around the club and among their finest qualities is the ability to tell it as it is. In local parlance this searingly honest approach is known as 'cutting to the bone'.

In the bar of our social centre, at the back of the old stand near Semple Stadium, there is a round table in the middle of the room. This is where lads gather to thrash out sport's burning issues, where debate rages hot and heavy and all the answers carry the ring of authority. It has come to be known as the 'Critics' Table' and Michael Hanrahan has lately been the ad-hoc chairman of the proceedings.

It's no-holds-barred, straight-up, passionate stuff where reputations are left at the door and a keen wit is the key to survival. George Hook, Eamon Dunphy and Pat Spillane would struggle here – they'd probably be considered wafflers.

Approaching the Critics' Table I have often felt I needed a helmet even more than on the field of play. The good thing is, though, that you'll always leave it with a smile on your face. And if you can manage a good parting shot as you bail out it's a bonus.

However, it hasn't always been a bundle of laughs for me and Thurles Sars. Everyone around the town knows I'm a bit of a free spirit, fairly laid-back about most things. On the hurling field it's not all that different – I don't go bulling into fifty-fifty tackles, nor do I go up for a ball with my hurley flailing in the air. I'm fond of space, short passing and running free. Babs didn't like that and a good few in Thurles Sarsfields were not mad about it either.

We have a rich history here. Thurles is a town where the gable ends of houses are covered with murals of our heroes past and present; images of Jimmy Doyle and Tony Wall decorate the streetscapes. Our clubhouse walls are adorned with painted portraits of our All-Ireland-winning captains.

The GAA was founded in this town and Sarsfields are by far the most successful hurling club within the county. We have thirty-one Tipp senior titles. You can still meet several of the generation that racked up five in a row from 1961 to 1965. Some of them had already done the five in a row from 1955 to 1959. Talk about hard acts to follow!

I have to admit, though, that I'm not steeped in the lore and statistics of that era, and maybe that goes against me.

I think it does. If you follow Tipp hurling you'll have surely heard that the relationship between me and the club is a fraught one. That's the general perception anyway: I turn up when I feel like it; I'm always injured; I have no time for the winter tread-mill; I never get the same quality of scores for the Sars as for Tipperary.

The consolation is that when I hear intercounty forwards from other counties talk of their clubs it's often like déjà vu. At least I'm not the only one taking flak.

I have to say the above criticisms are nearly all rubbish and they don't greatly bother me – it's just something I have to live with. If you ask me where it comes from, I'm not sure, but if you bear with me I can throw out a few suggestions.

Jimmy Doyle played the 1961 All-Ireland final with a broken ankle. He received six painkilling injections before, during and after that game. Jimmy is our best ever player, probably Tipp's greatest and arguably the most skilful the game has ever seen. His reputation as an ironman was assured after that.

Me? I missed the bones of five years' regular action because of persistent hamstring troubles and half the older generation at the club reckon it was all in my head. Bullshit.

The fact I'm not John Mullane or Davy Fitz – I don't always

**Above left**: With Fergus Dowd and the 34-inch hurley Mam gave me on my first day with Dúrlas Óg.

**Above right**: Visiting Santa with my sister, Helen.

**Left**: With my pet dog Spot.

**Above**: I was forever practising my first touch against the wall opposite our family home.

**Below**: Looking on from my desk at Scoil Ailbhe, Thurles, as my classmates hold the Liam McCarthy Cup aloft in 1991. It was a happy day ten years later when I finally got to hold the cup myself.

**Above**: Receiving the cup for the Thurles Street Leagues in 1997 from Dick Callian.

**Below**: Heading to a game. (*Left to right*) Myself, Eamon Corcoran, Noel Morris, Eddie Enright, my uncle Fr. Larry, and (*in front*) my cousin Ciaran Roft.

**Above**: Sarsfields versus Ballingarry, with Connie Maher on the sideline, getting his point across again.

**Below**: Ger 'Redser' O'Grady celebrating Thurles Sarsfields' victory in the 2005 county final with his daughter Lorna on his shoulders. That first win since 1974 meant a lot to everyone involved with Sars as the crowd (*opposite*) shows.

**Above**: The Thurles Sarsfields team from the early noughties.

**Centre**: Declan Ryan: Sarsfields' best supporter.

**Above**: Taking instruction from Nicky English who gave me my chance in the 2001 championship.

**Below**: Arms around the man: (*left to right*) Eoin Kelly, Declan Ryan and myself on my championship debut against Clare.

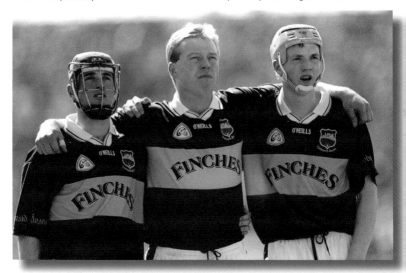

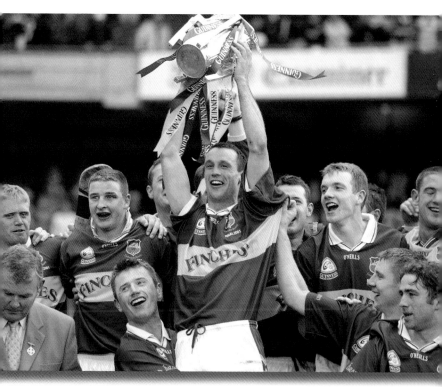

**Above**: Celebrating the 2001 All Ireland victory over Galway. (*Left to right*) Eugene O'Neill, Seán McCague, John Carroll, David Kennedy, Tommy Dunne, myself, Philip Maher, Mark O'Leary and Darragh Rabbitte.

**Below**: A family welcome for Liam McCarthy. (*Left to right*) My Mam Breda, my sister Helen, my Dad Eddie and myself.

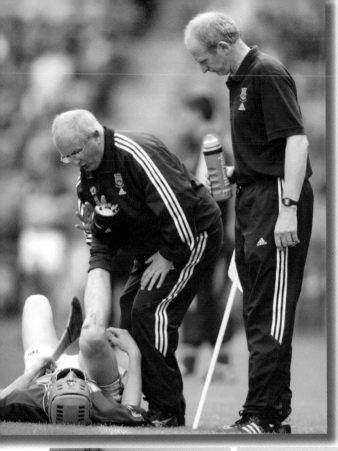

**Left**: I was cursed with hamstring problems for years. Here receiving treatment from Jim Kilty and John 'Hotpoint' Hayes in 2003.

**Below**: Celebrating victory in the 2008 National Hurling League with my team mate and friend Eoin Kelly.

show my emotions – doesn't mean I don't care. I'm proud of my club and was always passionate playing for them. I did miss a lot of regular action over the years but I was always mad to get out and play. Making the Sars minor team and then breaking through into the senior team in 2000 was the making of me. The Sars lads really helped shape my hurling career and showed me what was possible with hard work and training. And I wanted to be out playing alongside them as we tried to break through at senior level.

Until I learned how best to manage my body, though, I missed a lot of games for club and county. This hurt me more than anyone. Some of my best years were spent talking to doctors and physios but insult was added to injury when I heard of people from my own club questioning my commitment. Thankfully, this criticism comes from a minority. From the majority all I get is support and encouragement.

There were times when it seemed Sars would never get over the line and win a county senior final. I bawled my eyes out with pure disappointment after we lost to Toomevara in the 2000 decider. If my knockers saw the state I was in back then they might be slower to question my commitment. I was the youngest on the team, there were twelve thousand supporters watching closely and it was all too much. We went down by five and the pain of it all only hit me in the dressing-room afterwards.

I hadn't cried at a hurling match before and haven't since, but I had 3-10 to my name leading up to that final and had bagged 1-3 in the Mid-Tipp decider, so expectations were high that I'd crack off a few more fireworks on the big day – my club form at the time was what got me that first chance with Tipp. But there were no pyrotechnics that afternoon, and at the end I let it all out – the emotion just hit me.

Terrified the rest of the lads would see me whingeing, I bolted from the dressing-room and took off down the tunnel sobbing like a baby – straight into the path of the victorious Toome players arriving back in.

I kept going until I felt a hand on my shoulder. Paddy McCormack senior, one of our great clubmen, had spotted me leaving the room and sprinted after me. I was only nineteen and didn't know what I was at, but Paddy told me it was okay and led me to a quiet corner until I composed myself.

That 2000 championship campaign might never have taken off. We trailed to Holycross in the Mid-Tipp semi-final and went down to fourteen men for the second half. But after a serious fight-back Brendan Carroll scored a last-minute goal to clinch a win in added time. If Brendan hadn't hit that score I might never have been called up to the Tipp team. That's how fine the line is between success and failure. The Sars lads are the ones I owe a debt of gratitude to. The begrudgers and knockers? Well, you just have to leave them go.

My time with Dúrlas Óg had ended in frustration in my last year at under-16, but I always felt pretty comfortable with Sars, even if some of the managers and selectors struggled to figure me out.

I made my adult debut in 1998 at seventeen and got five points in an intermediate match against Moycarkey-Borris. Only a few other lads from the side who played the 2001 county final are still playing, so for someone who supposedly doesn't give a second thought to his club, fourteen years is a long time to stay plodding away all the same.

In that period I played every minute of eight county finals and was the only one to do so. We won three, which is not too bad. Yet when I withdrew from hurling at the start of this year one of our club stalwarts put the boot in: 'Well, he'll be no loss to the

Sars anyway.' Those boys talk the same way they hurled – very direct!

Around the same time I passed another former hurler on the street and the friend I was with saw him glance at me and throw his eyes to the heavens. Does it trouble me? It does and it doesn't.

Every club misses the services of its county players. The problem is that even when intercounty lads get a two-week break they're often told to wrap themselves in cotton wool. They have day jobs and are constantly training with the county team. Sometimes it looks like they don't care about the club. I think forwards get it in the neck more than backs; if you're not lighting up the scoreboard questions are quickly asked.

All I can say is that I apply the exact same methods hurling for Thurles as I do for Tipp. I check that my gear, grips and hurleys are ready. Truth be told I get more nervous playing for the club than for Tipp. I get jittery before games and often fumble a few balls.

With our rich pedigree, expectations are always high around here. It took the present generation a long time to break the duck of landing another county title so maybe patience was wearing thin. The 1974 win, our last senior championship before the most recent run, had become the bear on our back. When Jimmy Doyle lifted the Dan Breen Cup he hardly envisaged such a long wait before we'd see it again.

People were frustrated that having been on top we then went so long, 1974 to 2005, without winning a county final. Along with a few others I became a scapegoat for the lack of success. And once an opinion is formed of you inside a club it spreads quickly. Soon every hurler on the ditch 'knows' that I view Sars as an afterthought.

I seldom hear at first hand what's being said; it's usually relayed back through a friend or a clubmate. If people did accuse me to my face I could assure them I never once went out and said, 'I'll play a stinker for the Sars today. I'll doss away in the corner and let the other lads break their balls.'

At least the lads at the Critics' Table give you feedback to your face and you know those lads genuinely want you to do well. I can handle that a lot better than the whispering and the conversations that stop when you pass.

I've been lucky enough to win county minor, under-21 and three senior titles with the Sars, and while I mightn't have always set the world alight I've not done too badly. I don't really like replaying games and quoting stats and even though I nearly feel compelled to bury, once and for all, this fiction that I don't produce it for the club, it's a road I won't go down.

People have their minds made up, and I'll probably never change that. It's a bit like some of the other horse manure going around, such as Tipp having no half-forward line for ten years after Declan Ryan left. I'd say thirty different players must have togged out in that particular department since then. They can't all have been useless. It's a lazy line.

Many people in Sars have time for me and that's good enough. From Tommy Barrett, the former Tipp secretary and one of our mainstays, who is never short of a few nice words, to several of my best mates who are still heavily involved.

People ask why I don't go for my own scores more often when I'm on club duty – they feel I pass the ball around way too much. Again, I don't feel I have anything to justify but the honest answer is I'm actually happier when someone else scores. I like taking the right options, and if a score results I'm as happy to lay the sliotar off as to go for personal glory.

There's another factor. I always played further out the field with Sars and maybe that's why I didn't get so many scores. Being honest, I often moseyed along out the field to get on the ball – in that sense I always found it easier to play with Tipp because the ball would come to you at speed. If people want to judge me because of that it's up to them.

There are issues I have to accept. I missed the bones of four years when the hammers just weren't right, and maybe that's where the myth of Lar the Loafer was born. More than once I missed a league game with Sars but played for Tipp the following weekend because I was under huge pressure to keep my place. The whole town would then be on my back. But there were times when I played for Sars and missed league matches with Tipp and nothing was said about it. I had to learn to manage what I could and couldn't do in terms of number of training sessions and games. When I tried to be all things to all people I ended up out of action for both teams. Considering the improvement in my form over recent years, I think it's fair to say the more measured approach has worked for me.

In 2006, for instance, I didn't go near the Tipp camp until May and then I had people slating me for letting down the county. You can't win. Either way I was only trying to protect the legs and prioritise games as they came.

We've had our share of heartache at the club. Losing that 2000 final to Toomevara was like losing an All-Ireland final. It wasn't much better in 2001 and the misery continued in 2002 when we reached another decider against Mullinahone, who beat us in the county final replay. Back we came to reach another final in 2003, scored 3-16 against Toome and still lost. They were at the height of their powers but I was sick of the sight of their green and gold shirts and was starting to think we were stuck in Groundhog Day.

By the time we reached the 2005 final – our fifth in six years – we were called bottlers and had become the butt of gags. There was talk of a Chinese restaurant sponsoring us – we'd have the logo 'Win Wan Soon' on our shirts. People reckoned we hadn't the stomach for battle. 'Typical town team,' they would say, but they were wrong.

After losing one of those county finals Red, Tommy Maher and I were out early on the Monday morning. We were settling in for the long haul, if you know what I mean, when Ann Maher, the wife of Connie, a teammate, hurried into the bar nearly in tears. She said Connie hadn't come home the night before. We tried to look concerned – said we hoped he was all right and that nothing had happened to him – but we were only making the right noises because we weren't in the slightest bit worried.

The poor woman was obviously starting to fear the worst: 'He's not answering his phone. It's not ringing. I hope he didn't hurt himself or do anything stupid.'

That was a conversation stopper and it got our attention. I thought the poor woman was going to have a meltdown. How do you reassure her?

Red had an idea. 'Ah look,' he said, 'Connie hurled bad yesterday but he wasn't that bad.'

With that she burst out laughing and out came Connie from the corner of the lounge. They had us going.

After Nenagh Éire Óg's win in 1995, rural clubs had dominated the Tipp landscape from the mid-nineties to the mid-noughties, but we were closing in on them all the time with our young team. Bringing in Ger Cunningham, who had led Newtownshandrum to the 2004 All-Ireland final, was like placing the final piece in the jigsaw. He had a short-passing template with Newtown, and while we didn't copy it exactly, we did take a lot from it. To be fair I don't think he ever mentioned Newtown's success at all – he was only concerned with helping us break the hoodoo.

Eventually the wheel turned. We buried the Toome curse in the 2005 county quarter-final with five points to spare. That in itself was like winning a championship, but we put the foot further to the floor by winning our semi and setting up a decider with Drom & Inch.

It was Drom's first time in the final, but after the agony we had gone through there was no way we were going to take them lightly. But we were nervous – it was a greasy, slippy old day and we had it all to lose. Thanks mainly to Wayne Cully and Red, we beat our country neighbours – another five-point margin – to end the thirty-one-year wait for Dan Breen.

Red was captain, and funny how it goes, the sliotar just ended up at his feet as the final whistle sounded. He fell to his knees and lifted his face to the sky as half of Thurles descended on him. It seemed like ten thousand of the thirteen thousand in attendance were from the town, and when Red finally escaped their clutches he marched up the steps – with his daughter Lorna for company – and delivered the mother and father of all speeches.

After those four successive lost finals from 2000 to 2003 we had been consumed by this competition and Red let the emotion rip.

'The famine is over!' he roared, a loaded reference to Richie Stakelum and his famous 1987 Munster final speech for Tipp, which wasn't lost on the crowd – they let out an almighty roar.

On the field and on the steps below, grown men wept as he namechecked their fathers and brothers and cousins – many of them long gone to the great hurling fields above – and wondered how proud they would all be. I think he mentioned every soul, every Sarsfields Gael resting in St Patrick's Cemetery. No-one was left out.

Red reckons he's not a speechmaker, but that day he captured the mood perfectly and it was all off the cuff. Most lads can read off a page but these rousing words came straight from the heart and everyone warmed to that. Red went down in local legend that day, if he wasn't already there, for the quality of that address.

The Sars social centre was rocking that night, the Critics' Table was 99 per cent happy with the display – an all-time high – and the place ran out of beer. A deputation was dispatched on a mercy mission to borrow from other publicans downtown, so you can picture the scene. The first win after thirty-one long years was always going to be special and the place was in a fair mess.

The following day we rang to know what time we should head up for the après match and watch the match video. Andy Ryan was above cleaning up and answered, 'We have thirty-one years of shite to clean up – we'll let ye know!'

The Monday night turned out as good as the one before – but when I saw some of the bigger-boned members crowd-surfing in the hall I decided it was time to head home.

Amid all the euphoria, I still wished I had been able to contribute more. And that I wasn't half crocked all the time. I had barely trained with the team that year and my sole contribution was to make a couple of hand passes, which in fairness led to a goal and a point. I couldn't care less who got the scores. The jokes could stop now. I didn't so much mind the sledging – some of it was funny – but I was thrilled we had shed the tag of having loads of skill but lacking heart.

Ger Cunningham had adapted our strategy for every game. The Toome game we probably had no right to win. I had been sent off in the Mid-Tipp final and was suspended. Pat Lawlor, now a mainstay of the Sars team, had a broken hand. We were vulnerable, so Ger decided to rejig our system and play John Lawlor, Pat's brother, as a sweeper. We refined our possession game – a short-passing style designed to move Toome all over the park. Ger and his selectors, Ger Corbett and Tommy Maher, encouraged the forwards to keep them guessing for the entire sixty minutes.

When the curtain fell on the 2005 season I met with those three lads to review the year. I remarked that it had been a great year for the club but not as good for me personally. They didn't agree and replied that I got vital scores in the Mid-Tipp final replay and county semi-final and had made an impact further out the field as the county final neared its end. They said having me on the field, even short of full fitness, often tied up our opponents' best defender and forced their half-backs to sit deeper.

This showed me that the people close to the team, who were tuned into every match, could see I was trying to pull my weight. Just because I hadn't 3-3 on the score board wasn't the end of the world. I could still make a contribution.

We had won five Mid-Tipp titles by then so all we needed was a push to get over the winning line in the county and Ger gave us exactly that. Tactics, enjoyable training, great drills, puck-out and sideline-cut strategies, different plays for long-range frees.

Ger was with us for three years until he took time out after six full seasons without a break. We'll never forget the impact he made. He was one class coach; he changed our mentality and every player on the pitch knew his role. We've won two more Tipp titles since then, in 2009 and 2010, and while it may not match the golden run of yore, at least it now feels like our generation have made some contribution to the Sars legacy.

The 2000 county final apart, my biggest disappointment in a blue shirt was the 2010 Munster final, which we lost by the odd point in seventeen, to De La Salle Waterford. The game was played on a bitterly cold November day and Páirc Uí Chaoimh was frozen solid. We were five down at the break but we shot ourselves in the foot by hitting seventeen wides. It still kills me. I thought we had the more skilful hurlers but you can't argue with what DLS achieved.

That might have been my chance of a Munster club medal gone out the window but I still feel that if we get our act together, with the young lads on our team – the likes of Paudie Maher, Pa, Michael Cahill and Denis Maher – we could yet have our day in the sun.

Even if we don't, the likes of Big Deccie and the boys at the Critics' Table will always be glad to see me coming – and will more than likely put a smile on my face with one of their classic digs.

# 9

# The dream team

Near the end of 2007, Liam Sheedy, Eamon O'Shea and Mick Ryan were appointed to take command of the ship, our fifth management team in six years. To tell the truth I was growing weary of being recycled and reprocessed; my form in the blue and gold was hit and miss and so dark was my mood that my first meeting with the three boys was a disaster.

We met in October, in the McEvoy room of the Anner Hotel. They had hand-picked six senior players they saw as potential leaders of the revival and were meeting us one by one to present their vision.

I didn't feel up to the task; I was still physically drained from constantly battling with the hamstrings and emotionally drained from the rollercoaster of the previous few years. For a change, my mind and body were in harmony but it wasn't a perfect one – I was running on empty.

Nonetheless I went to the meeting, sat down in front of the boys, and told them I wasn't going to return until the new year. It wasn't what they wanted to hear.

Mick Ryan, in particular, was raging. A well-respected lad from Upperchurch, and an All-Ireland winner back in 1991, he had given massive playing service to Tipp and always in a quiet, unassuming way. He was pretty animated now, though.

'Tommy Walsh was training Christmas Day last year,' Mick said, looking me hard in the eye. I didn't reply. At that moment I didn't give a shite if Tommy was in a sled mushing reindeer on Christmas Day. It was no concern of mine.

Silence then for a few seconds until Liam put his plans on the table – and in fairness they looked impressive. But I was weary from the whole scene: managers coming and going like shuttle buses, trouble in the camp every season.

I put all that across to the lads and though the meeting lasted forty-five minutes it kind of went nowhere. They wanted me back straightaway, but my experience and gut instinct told me there was no point in returning, getting flogged and being on the physio's table till April or May, miles off the pace. Not after what I had gone through with Ger Hartmann and Gary Ryan. That was a vicious circle I had no intention of repeating.

I stood up to leave the room and the boys didn't stand with me so I didn't shake their hands. That bothered me as soon as I got outside the door – small things like that always do. I met Eoin downtown and asked him if he had shaken hands before leaving and he had. The following day I met Eamon Corcoran, asked the same question and got the same answer. I knew I was on a bad footing straight away.

That night I couldn't rest easy. The new coach, Eamon O'Shea, in particular had me intrigued. Only once throughout the whole meeting did he speak and that was right at the end. And then he caught me on the hop: 'Tell us what you want and we will sort it out.'

I couldn't recall the last time anyone said that to me. Usually you were being barked at: 'Not another injury, Lar!'

This lad spent the whole meeting taking notes and studying me. Straightaway I knew he was different.

\*

The weeks passed and I stayed away from the panel while the others took fitness tests and were given gym programmes. In late November I got a call to meet Liam in Nenagh but the outcome was the same.

'Liam, I can't go back until I get myself tuned in,' I said. 'I'm all over the place at the moment.'

He asked had I a plan and I mentioned going back to Hartmann and taking a few months away, this time to get my head right after a relentless few years of failure.

'Larry, if you're not prepared to come back soon this could be the end of your career,' he warned.

'Liam, if that's the case I'll just have to accept it and I know it's not your fault,' I replied. 'But it's the way things are. I'm just sick and tired of everything and I have to be able to function properly before I can do a job for anyone else.'

This time we shook hands, but as I pulled out of Nenagh I started getting emotional. The uneasy feeling hit me that I was burning too many bridges. Heading down Kenyon Street and out the Thurles road the eyes were stinging. I was facing into an uncertain Christmas.

Over the next few weeks the spirits lifted, though. I popped into Hartmann regularly and again he did as much work on my head as on my legs. That lad would power a small country with his energy and if you have someone telling you positive things for two hours a day it eventually rubs off.

In the evenings I'd wrap up well and head out on the bike, just shaking off the cobwebs and gulping in the cold, pure air; it was just something different. Soon I was off doing three-kilometre runs. The odd morning I'd beat the sliotar off the wall just to see how the touch was and keep the eye in. Maybe six or seven weeks passed and gradually the appetite returned.

Meanwhile, reports from the camp were unfailingly positive; by all accounts the new management had lifted things massively. For the first time in six years I didn't hear bitching or whinge-ing. I began to ask myself if I'd like a slice of that.

On New Year's Eve I raised a glass and bade 2007 farewell. A couple of days later I knew I was ready to recommit whole-heartedly – if called on.

Out of the blue, that first week in January, Liam phoned again. I sensed it wasn't going to be a lengthy chat by the tone of Liam's voice: 'Larry, are you ready to come back and give one hundred per cent for the county?'

I had some roadwork done; the legs were getting stronger again; Hartmann's healing hands and the positive vibes from teammates had worked the oracle. It had taken three months to freshen me up but the appetite was back and it was the right call.

'Liam, I'm one hundred per cent ready to play for you and Tipperary,' I replied.

That was it. 'See you Tuesday night,' he said and before I got to ask him what time the line went dead. He never once held that twelve-week sabbatical against me.

I returned a few nights later and you didn't have to be Jessica Fletcher to know things were now way more conducive to success. It seemed all our planets were finally aligned: we had Sheedy, the ultimate man-manager; O'Shea, the next big thing in coaching circles; Ryan, a rock of a third selector; John Casey, a brilliant physio; and Cian O'Neill, described by the former Kerry footballer Mickey Ned O'Sullivan as 'the best young trainer in Ireland'.

The trusted backroom lieutenants stayed in the trenches too – our kitman, Hotpoint; our masseur, Mick Clohessy; the doc, Peter Murchan – and everyone was working in tandem. Within weeks I knew the bar hadn't been raised as high since Nicky's time.

This is how it worked. Sheedy was the organiser-in-chief, the motivator and facilitator. Ours was like a rugby set-up – he made good backroom appointments and created an atmosphere where success might follow; brimming with passion, energy and positivity, he put aside his ego and backed everyone to get on with their jobs.

O'Shea was the tactician and he had some sort of magnetic quality about him. A tall, skinny fella from Cloughjordan, he looked at life from a viewpoint all his own.

We knew nothing about him. Some of the lads Googled him and learned he had won an All-Ireland club title with Kilruane MacDonaghs and hurled in the championship for both Tipp and Dublin. I asked a few people in the know about him and they said his sporting pedigree was only trotting behind his academic achievements. A professor of economics at NUIG, he was by all accounts one of the most respected in Europe in his field. He had fourteen books written and thirty-nine theses published. This lad was serious.

It was a stroke of genius by Sheedy to twig straightaway the connection between O'Shea and myself. He basically let us off. Eamon tapped into my mindset, one of the few to have managed that, and proceeded to teach me how to play the game properly. Coming from an intercounty hurler who was twenty-seven at the time that must sound awful – but it's the truth.

After the journey with the three boys had ended in 2010 All-Ireland glory we went on a team holiday to Jamaica. I remember standing at the back of the plane with Eamon as he recalled how they had taken over a team broken down physically and psychologically, and how they had to build us up again.

That stuck with me because besides being the best coach around he could be a psychologist; he lifts you with every sentence. He instilled such belief in me that my own family remarked how different I was in the three years he spent with the squad.

His style and tactics helped me achieve on the field things I never thought possible. In turn that later gave me the impetus to get off the dole and start up my own business. No way in the world would any of that have happened without his influence. He knew exactly what buttons to press to motivate me. But he was adaptable; he might help another player with an entirely different approach.

He would come into training with a blank canvas until he gauged our mood. His training drills evolved on the hoof. As he put it, 'What's the point in having my mind made up if your bodies are telling me you want something different? I have to look at you guys, start you off and then decide where to bring you.'

He'd mosey up to you, stare at you intensely, say something entirely unexpected and then move on to the next person. During one training session he sidled over to me but said nothing, just looked me up and down for several seconds.

'What's up?' I asked.

'Nothing, Lar, I just wanted to see if you're right,' he replied and gave me two thumbs up before walking away.

He would talk in this measured, calm tone but you sensed he had a multitude of ideas and several timetables of drills bouncing around in his head.

Before we played Laois in a league game in late March 2008, he reminded me not to be afraid of half-chances – if I got five pots at goal from thirty yards I was to go for them no matter how many I missed.

'I won't judge you for it,' he said. 'But I might judge you if you don't go for it. So take a chance and don't be looking to the sideline if it doesn't work out.'

Eamon saw something in me few others had seen. I was handed a free role for Tipperary and I found the best form of my career. I had hardly struck a ball in four or five years and I didn't really understand the game until I met Eamon. I had been hurling eight years for Tipperary and still hadn't a handle on how to play corner-forward. Eamon challenged me in a way no-one else had done, yet all the while he was building my fragile confidence.

We played Offaly in the 2010 qualifiers shortly after losing to Cork and there was a gale blowing around us. I was struggling because my mind was in overdrive; I barely hit a ball in the first half. He came straight over to me at the break: 'It's all in your head, Lar. Stop thinking. Hurling is instinctive. Just play the breaks.'

He was right – I was always thinking too much.

Movement was his calling card, creating space, making runs and seeing things no-one else would visualise.

We played Wexford in a challenge match in 2008 and I watched him head across the 21-yard line, pausing only to look back at the goal. Then he walked to the sideline and looked back to the posts again before walking into the middle of the field and doing the same thing. I was riveted – in his own mind he was already making space for us before a ball had been thrown in.

I often saw Eamon as a conductor in charge of an orchestra. Only an expert would know if one of the violins was out of tune or one of the horns had hit a false note, and he was like that. My mind was blown every time I spoke with him. I used to go away from meetings or training sessions and spend hours thinking about stuff he had said or done. Or I'd phone people on the way home, bouncing ideas off them because my mind was so full of stuff. When he looked at you, he looked you in the eye and it was obvious the only thing he wanted was for you to do well. I had that connection with no-one else.

It wasn't just the players who were fascinated by Eamon – I often looked at Mick and Liam when he spoke and it seemed they too were hanging on his every word.

And when Liam spoke it was the same. Silence.

Ryan was the quiet man of the three but as the months passed he too turned out to be a pillar of strength for everyone, players and mentors. If you wanted to know the truth about yourself Mick was your man. Black and white, he'd give the truth out to you, no bother.

Here are a few insights into how things changed under the new regime.

For years we would tip over to the Anner Hotel, push a few weights, then head for the jacuzzi and swimming pool. It was pansy stuff. In between reps and bench presses punters might come over and ask how you were shaping up for the game at the weekend – then get you to sign an autograph for a son or daughter.

For any intercounty player in any public gym across the land it's the same drill. I was doing little or nothing in there and I wasn't the only one.

That didn't cut the mustard any more. We enlisted at Tom Kenneally's gym, Mountain Fitness, halfway up the Devil's Bit. It was raw stuff. No frills. Character building. Tom had his gym suitably chilly and we all wrapped up in warm clothing, not that you kept it on too long because he'd soon have a personal trainer on your case. But who was the first person you'd see when you arrived? Sheedy.

If he wasn't there at the start he'd mosey in halfway through the session after visiting the Limerick-based lads at the UL gym or the South Tipp boys working out at the Hotel Minella in Clonmel. That was some driving from Portroe and it was the first time we'd seen a manager regularly turn up for weights sessions.

Sheedy was putting in as much effort as the players. Before we started the 2008 league the boys were doing laps around the field in Borrisoleigh – I was still in rehab. It was a filthy night, wind howling and rain lashing down. As they slogged away in the pitch dark, fighting the elements and their own minds, they noticed a car parked on the bank. As they approached there was a quick flash of lights. Sheedy. Letting them know he was in their corner.

That flash of lights gave them some lift and had long-term benefits. He had a young family and could have been at home by a warm fire, but he was with the team. If we eventually reached a Munster final and Sheedy entered the dressing-room full of passion, laying down the law, we would lap up every word because he'd been with us every step of the way.

Besides giving me free rein to follow my instincts, Liam and Eamon took another significant weight off my shoulders: they never once set a quota for scores. My confidence had been ebbing away with every season; I had developed a chronic fear that if I didn't raise a flag within the first half hour the substitution slip would be out. Sometimes the higher up the ladder you go the less secure you become.

Until they came on the scene I'd feel the need to go and hit some lad a jostle and drive him out over the sideline, or waste energy by sprinting after a beaten docket of a ball I had absolutely no hope of winning. And that's not my game at all.

From the start Sheedy demanded a greater work-rate of me. He wasn't happy with that aspect of my game at all and broke it down simply.

'Two blocks, two hooks, Larry.'

Before every game he'd saunter over to me, hands in pockets, and repeat that mantra: 'Two blocks, two hooks.'

I became obsessed with it.

We were playing a challenge match in 2010 and I tore after an opposing midfielder who was just about to try for a long-distance point. I didn't hook him but I did manage the faintest of touches on his stick as he hit the ball. It stuttered wide.

I was like a maniac after the game to find out if Sheedy was chalking me down for the block.

'Well, are you giving it to me?'

'Giving you what, Larry?'

'That hook!' I shouted.

Sheedy was just as thick: 'Jeez, I don't know.'

'You fucking are!' I roared as I jumped onto the bus.

We had won by twenty points. I'd say the boys from the other team who were looking on thought I'd lost the plot.

For years I was under pressure to get scores and it weighed me down. I felt if I didn't grab a point or a goal I'd be hauled off. Under the boys that pressure was lifted. Nothing mattered to them: only movement and work-rate.

Everything changed – even puck-out strategies. Eamon gave ownership to the goalkeepers, Brendan Cummins and Darren Gleeson, and put the onus back on them to send the type of ball he wanted into the forwards. I'm guessing here, but I suspect he told them not to be afraid of varying it – that they would get another chance to rectify things if they made a mistake. The lads instantly responded.

The introduction of John Casey to the set-up was a good illustration of how thorough was the new approach. He was brought in from Munster rugby, one of the best professionals in the business.

John was a massive help to me. If I was injured he told Liam and was confident enough to stand his ground. If I was gone for Saturday and Sunday I was gone – there was no rushing back and Casey had the balls to stand over that. Suddenly, after all those years of fretting about being considered a slacker, that weight was lifted. I wasn't going around, sneaking in physio sessions here and there. I fully trusted John, and after the foundations I had set with Ger Hartmann I continued to do the right things and build from there. As time went on my chronic hamstring problems, the injuries that threatened to end my career, faded into the background and to the back of my mind. That was some turnaround. I could now focus on hurling knowing I was finally 100 per cent right.

Pretty soon I could see Sheedy was going to make a leader out of me whether I liked it or not. Before a 2009 championship match I was getting physio with John Casey and missed a training session. The boss wasn't happy and phoned me that night; the man could ring you at eight in the morning or twelve midnight.

'You never came up to Dr Morris Park, Larry. It's not good enough,' he said. 'You're a leader and if you can't train you bring something else to the table and offer it to the lads. I want you up there with us even if it means giving out water. If the lads do just one thing right in training I want you driving them on.'

I told Liam I wouldn't even go to a Thurles Sars match if I wasn't playing for fear I'd be in the way but he wasn't having it.

'Hold on a minute, Larry, you're meant to be a leader. Start acting like one. Don't be selfish. Give back something, anything.'

It was perhaps the biggest lesson I ever got in hurling. I genuinely did want to give something back; I just was never sure how to go about it. Liam laid it on the line and his influence was telling.

He still influences me. In fact, you can judge my career by my pre-Sheedy stats. Before I played the 2006 Munster final I had started only five of Tipp's previous thirty-five competitive games. But under his watch I started and finished every championship match, bar Limerick in 2009, when they brought me off the field to my first standing ovation after scoring three goals. From 2001 to 2006 I scored only 4-14 in championship but after the lads took over I racked up 19-32 in just three years. To this day, every time I see Liam I want to go and talk to him. I love being in his company.

There were games when I barely touched the sliotar and still the two boys would find the positives. You know those games where you make twenty runs and not one ball breaks? Instead, your man gets it, drives it the length of the field and leaves you looking like a headless chicken.

That was my game now, throwing the dice. Putting down a punt and waiting to see if it paid off. I loved running onto break- ing ball with one hand on the hurley, just waiting for a spill or a hop. If the break came for me I was off and flying; if it didn't I was left grasping thin air.

Sometimes I wouldn't hit a ball for forty minutes and I'd look off the pace and out of touch. Another coaching team might give me the shepherd's crook, but not Liam or Eamon. I remember the early stages of the 2009 All-Ireland semi-final against Limerick when nothing seemed to be happening for me. If I had ducks they'd have drowned.

At half-time I still hadn't scored. Eamon came running over and singled me out, an index finger furiously jabbing the sky. I braced myself for a bollocking.

'Larry, those runs you're making are absolutely perfect,' he roared. 'Absolutely perfect.'

For a second I wondered was he pulling the piss. But he wasn't.

'I'm telling you, those runs are top class,' he added, the finger still making the point. 'You're only an inch away from every- thing falling into place. Keep at it and it will happen. I'm telling you that ball will break.'

It did. I got three goals and a point in the second half. And I walked off the pitch, apologising to Liam because I hadn't made a hook or a block.

A few weeks after we won the 2010 All-Ireland, I was surfing the web when I came across a hurling-stats website that fully brought home to me what the management were all about: I managed three goals in an All-Ireland final; three goals in the 2009 All-Ireland semi-final against Limerick; twelve champion-ship goals in just two years. All from new targets that had been set for me, none of which mentioned raising flags.

Within weeks of the lads taking over, the camp was more upbeat than it had been for years, and everywhere we looked we found reasons for optimism.

On the way home from that challenge match against Wexford in 2008, Eoin Kelly started talking about the young lads coming through. Liam had led Tipp to the 2006 minor championship and a year later Declan Ryan and Tommy Dunne earned back-to-back successes. The future was bright.

'Do you see those lads?' Eoin asked, pointing to some of them. 'They're winners – they've almost forgotten how to lose. We'll row in behind them because they're winners and we're not. We won in 2001 but these lads don't care – they're coming out with two All-Ireland minors and they'll do the job again at under-21. They're coming like express trains and they want to drive on. We'll do nothing except slip in behind them.'

It sounded good to me.

# 10

# Close but no cigar

Just as I was preparing to fade into the background and let the young lads lead the way I remembered what Nicky English had said to me at Eamon Corcoran's wedding a couple of years previously.

It was a brilliant day. Eamon and his wife, Deirdre, are great people and hugely popular, so there was a lovely mix of people and a grand atmosphere. Still, the occasion didn't necessarily mean that Nicky was going to get all mushy with me. He sat me down and gave it out straight.

'Larry, it's time to shit or get off the pot!' he said.

I was a little surprised but I didn't take offence and I didn't need to ask what he meant either. I'd always listen to Nicky because he'd have my best interests at heart – and I knew that on this occasion he was only saying what probably everyone else in the county was thinking.

From 2002 until 2007 any Tipp manager could have ordered me to walk the plank and I would have struggled to put the case for my defence.

Nicky was right – it was now or never. I had been only fluting about, nabbing a few points and the odd goal. Liam and the boys, meanwhile, were looking at a rich crop of emerging talent, All-Ireland winners ready to be added to the senior mix – mostly quiet young lads but dripping with silverware and ruthless, too. I could let them do the hard work and cling on to their coat-tails but the chat with Nicky was a timely reminder that if I didn't step up a couple of gears those boys would soon be looking at me in the rear-view mirror.

On Nicky's watch we had gone through 2001 unbeaten, and in Liam's debut season we played almost the same hand of cards. We marched undefeated right up to the All-Ireland semi-final, having won the Waterford Crystal league and the Munster final.

Our one loss all year was to Waterford. We went into that game a little rusty, maybe a touch over-confident. Before the throw-in their boys softened us up with a few digs, and as soon as the game started they drew our half-back line out of position, exposed our full-back line and racked up six points inside the first ten minutes. We were chasing our tail after that.

Up to then I had been having a good year; I had scored 5-10 in the league, and after we beat Ger Loughnane's Galway in the final Eamon said to me, 'Larry, if you don't hit a ball for the rest of the year I don't care.'

'Huh?'

'Seriously, you're after scoring enough for your county. You don't need to prove anything to us or the supporters. I don't care if you never score another goal.'

That was the pressure instantly off my shoulders. Away he went to work his unique brand of psychology on someone else.

With Galway accounted for we travelled to Dublin and stayed overnight at the Louis Fitzgerald Hotel, on the Naas road, before flying the next day to Browns' training camp in Portugal. Over there we trained up to three times a day, ate together, hit the gym and, I suppose you could say, bonded. By the time we came back we were ready for Cork and up for the fight of winning on Leeside for the first time since 1923.

I tried to visualise what it would be like beating Cork in the Páirc, but hard as I tried I just wasn't able to imagine it. It was as if they held the Indian sign over us.

And yet you could tell they were unsettled in the days before that game when Seán Óg Ó hAilpín came out and said certain careers were on the line. We knew then they were feeling tension on their pressure points. Sometimes you have to up the ante to get a performance – the way Ronan O'Gara sometimes does if he feels Munster or Ireland are in trouble or a bit casual before a game – but this time they could have hyped it to the heavens; we had the measure of them.

When the final whistle blew and we had won by six points I fell to my knees. Another memory of playing Cork worth holding on to. This time they were the ones in the mire.

I found it hard to fathom that they left Joe Deane on the bench, and harder still to understand why he was only the third forward introduced. Even in the autumn of his career, with the couch and slippers beckoning, there was no way Joe was the ninth-best forward in Cork. When he entered the fray he could actually have scored three points in five minutes but because they so desperately needed a goal it was pointless tipping the ball over the bar.

I don't know what was going on down there but I met Joe a while after that game and told him they could have taken us had he been on the field earlier. The type of bloke he was, he didn't make an issue of it.

Despite Cork's deficiencies that day, there's no denying we were a good team on a roll. Sheedy had the engine purring nicely and the road in front was inviting. Off-the-ball running was our strength and we blew several teams away in 2008. Three years later, in August 2011, *Newstalk* held a pre-All-Ireland roadshow at my bar and invited Dónal Óg Cusack along. He made particular reference to our movement on the day we broke the hoodoo.

'Lar, I'm not trying to find your trade secrets,' he said. 'But the way your six forwards move off the ball, it doesn't seem like there's any method or regulation to it – ye just seem to run everywhere and anywhere.'

'Dónal, I'm not trying to hide anything either,' I replied. 'But that's exactly what we do; we just move – there are no rules any more.'

Cork gunned down in Cork – another box ticked, another piece of the jigsaw in place, and you could see the bigger picture taking shape.

We didn't fear Clare in the Munster final, but we did fear ourselves. Most of us were still affected by years of failure and didn't fully trust ourselves to go out and get the job done. We were concerned we might not kill Clare off – going soft is something almost every Tipp team over the past twenty years has let seep into its mindset at some stage. We weren't far wrong either – it took us a fair while to get going before goals from John O'Brien and Séamus Callanan steadied the ship.

It was Séamie's first year with the team and I have never seen better footwork from a Tipp player. He got a goal and three points that afternoon, and though the world and its mother love to criticise him from time to time, I think he will develop into a massive player for the county if his talents are utilised properly.

I remember Liam brought eight of us to Nenagh for an extra training session once. He put Darren Gleeson, our sub-goalkeeper, between the posts. Darren is good enough to make any other team in the land and has been unfortunate to have Brendan Cummins ahead of him. Brendan has been part of the furniture for fifteen years, breaking Christy Ring's record of sixty-five championship appearances and holding off eleven sub-keepers during his time. But Darren would be right up there in terms of ability. We queued up to pepper shots at him from outside the 21-yard line and he batted them away for sport. Except when it came to Séamie's turn.

Each time he pulled the trigger Darren would be left wrong-footed. Séamie would feint to the right and Darren would shift his feet to take off in that direction. But the ball would end up in the opposite corner. It was incredible to see.

'Séamie, how are you doing that?' I enquired.

'Ah, simple game, Lar, simple game,' he replied with a smile, not offering the remotest insight.

After the session I collared Darren.

'Darren, will you explain to me, how is he doing that?'

'Larry, I haven't a clue. He's sending me left – his wrists and feet are pointing that way and the ball takes off left. But he's putting some sort of fade on it and suddenly it takes off right. He just varies it then for the next shot. I don't know how he's doing it.'

Séamie walked past and twigged we were talking about him.

'Lads, I'm telling ye, it's a simple game,' he laughed, chuffed as he headed for the showers.

There's no doubting he has a bit of cockiness and I love that because he can back it up. In his first six championship games he managed five goals, which is some shooting.

He has taken flak for inconsistency but I see a lot of myself in him. He probably feels he has to score a goal and a couple of points every game to stay on the team. With a bit of experience and the right approach that mindset will change. And when he gets settled he will be the one ghosting in for more goals like the crucial one he pinched for us against Galway in the 2010 All-Ireland quarter-final.

Séamus missed the 2012 league with an injury but it might not have been the worst thing in the world. A guy like him comes into his own only when the ground hardens. O'Shea always put it nicely for me whenever I was cleaned out in a league match: 'Larry, the back man has you till April.'

He was right. I often felt hurlers should retreat indoors in winter; the game gets bogged down in the mud and rain. But once the sun comes out and the ground is aired I'd fancy my chances against anyone. Maybe Séamie is the same.

Clare made life difficult for us early on. Colin Lynch still ruled the roost for them at midfield and Niall Gilligan managed nine points, but they eventually ran out of ideas, and after making hard work of it we took our first Munster title since 2001, winning by 2–21 to 0–19.

It was great to get our hands on some medals again, but while we had a good night we didn't go overboard. So solid were the foundations that we now expected to beat these teams. And we wanted more.

Along the way a potential diplomatic incident was neatly avoided, mind you. The rulebook dictated that the county champions could nominate the Tipp captain the following season. Naturally, they always chose their own. Loughmore-Castleiney, the reigning champs, duly proposed Paul Ormonde, who had been a great servant over the years. Now, though, he was struggling to get his place on the Tipp team and didn't make the championship cut. So the management chose Eoin Kelly to lead us.

Normally such a call would have been the signal for civil war to erupt. In 1988, Pa O'Neill from Cappawhite was dropped for the All-Ireland final and the captaincy handed to Nicky, who got a heap of abusive phone calls and letters for his troubles. The following year Pat McGrath was nominated as skipper but also lost his place, this time before the Munster final, and was replaced as captain by Bobby Ryan.

In total, three Tipp captains were dropped in the white heat of the championship during that era – Michael O'Meara was the other to lose out before the 1993 All-Ireland semi-final against Galway – and it caused howls of protest in various quarters. In fact the good people of Cappawhite and Loughmore still mention it from time to time.

With Paul being appointed captain but confined to the sidelines, we could have witnessed pitched battles in the streets and fields, but the lads in charge handled the situation with kid gloves. All interested parties were consulted, and both Eoin and Paul went up to accept the cups after the league and Munster victories. It can't have been easy for Paul, a great defender in his day, to look on from the sidelines, but he bit the bullet and just tried to win his place back.

Thankfully, that captaincy rule was scrapped. These days the Tipp management are allowed to choose the leader strictly on personal merit and job qualifications. They went for Eoin and all of what went with the job is grist to the mill for him. Eoin takes it in his stride and still manages to go out and play at his brilliant best.

Anyway, delivering victory speeches from the Hogan Stand wasn't something we had to worry about at the tail-end of 2008. Waterford had shown Justin McCarthy the door and they were all out to prove a point in that semi-final. They had their homework done and on the day Davy Fitz ended up winning the tactical bragging rights.

We were down by six points to no score and I was badly frustrated. Demented at having not even touched the ball I saw Eoin Murphy chasing the sliotar toward the sideline and decided now was the time to make a statement, do something to lift the team and get the crowd behind us. So off I took on a twenty-yard sprint and zeroed in on the yellow helmet. I would hit Eoin with the kitchen sink and clean him straight off the pitch – they'd be digging him out of the ad hoarding till further orders. If that didn't lift the boys, nothing would.

What I didn't know at the time was that just nine months earlier Eoin had won the RTÉ show *Celebrity Jigs and Reels*. When he saw the human missile arriving he did a nifty soft-shoe shuffle and skipped out of the way. Onward I went like an express train out of control and smashed into an unfortunate steward minding his own business. I flattened the poor divil and ended up on the floor looking like a complete ape. It was that kind of day.

Kilkenny went on to hammer Waterford in the final but I think they might have had a tougher test against us. It's easy to say that, though, isn't it?

A few weeks after our capitulation to Waterford, Sheedy called me to Nenagh for another one-on-one meeting and as usual he didn't beat around the bush: 'Larry, you were one of the best hurlers in Ireland during the league and Munster championship. You were on your way to an All-Star. But what happened to you against Waterford?'

After more than playing my part all year, I had managed only a point in the All-Ireland semi-final.

'Liam, I was full-forward for most of the year but I didn't score a goal in the championship, nor did I set one up. I know that has to change and it will. Next year.'

I left his office vowing I wouldn't let the man down again. Just twelve months earlier I had hummed and hawed about coming back but this time there was no doubt in my mind. The set-up was simply too good to be missing.

We were coming. It was only a matter of time.

# 11

# The last fifteen minutes

With six minutes to go in the 2009 All-Ireland final Jackie Tyrrell hit me a dig.

'Well, do you want it? Do you really fucking want it?'

We had been level on the scoreboard eleven times since throw-in, but Kilkenny had just edged four points clear – don't ask me how. Three times we had been clean through on goal, but each time we pulled the trigger the bullet missed its target. How Séamie Callanan's shot was saved I'll never know and twice I thought Eoin had scored – in the forty-fourth and fifty-sixth minutes – but their goalkeeper PJ Ryan defied all logic that afternoon.

The Cats were hanging on the ropes but still we couldn't find the knockout blow and there was no way they would throw in the towel. Instead they landed the sucker punch, when Richie Power hit the deck and the referee spread his arms wide and walked to the penalty spot. Diarmuid Kirwan is a good ref but in my view there is no way that was a penalty – before falling, Richie had taken more steps than Michael Flatley.

Brendan raced from his goal, pleading with Kirwan to watch the big-screen replay. The ref turned a deaf ear, and Shefflin stepped up and smashed the ball inside Brendan's left-hand post. Of course, he might well have done the same thing from a 21-yard free anyway – we'll never know.

As we tried to regroup they followed up almost immediately with a second sucker punch when Martin Comerford ghosted in for another goal. Before the ball landed in Comerford's hands Paul Curran's jersey had been tugged as he rose to cut out their attack. That didn't help our case but I can look further back the field to where the move started. I should have done more to force Michael Kavanagh out over the sideline. I should have been over to him quicker and been stronger in the tackle. Instead, Kavanagh slid close to the line but kept his upper body and the sliotar inside the field of play and then hopped up to deliver the ball long. Eoin Larkin grabbed it and fed Comerford. Bang. A small intervention on my part could have changed that game.

Instead, with only six minutes left it was our turn to hang on the ropes and Jackie knew it. That was when he put the hard question to me: 'Do you want it?'

I tried to be clever and play mind games with him. I still thought we could snatch the game – we had played some brilliant hurling and I reckoned if they dropped their guard at all we could hit them with the killer blow at the end. I had no doubt we were still in the hunt so I tried to get into Jackie's head. Maybe I was naive.

'No, I don't want it,' I replied, trying to throw him off course.

Jackie looked at me as if I had two heads. Of course I wanted to win the final but we were in a desperate situation and desperate situations demand desperate measures. I tried to confuse him.

The grand plan didn't exactly work – off he tore down the field to fire an insurance point at the other end. When the final whistle blew he celebrated with teammates before coming over to shake my hand. I'd say he was still trying to make sense of what I said. Sure it was worth a try.

*

I was sickened. In terms of my own form, the 2009 season had been the best of my career, and the final had turned out to be an epic; pundits were saying it would go down as the best All-Ireland final in history. We weren't even off the field when we started hearing the hype. To me, though, those superlatives counted for nothing. It didn't matter a curse that I had played well or that we pushed Kilkenny harder than they had been pushed in years. We still lost.

We can blame the referee all we want – and in fairness he gave us plenty of ammunition. Apart from the penalty I'd have serious issues about a free being awarded against Paudie Maher and then play being waved on when Jackie bulldozed Séamie Callanan with a charge to the chest.

But I have to be realistic too – we can't look past those wasted goal chances. Each time we got into the red zone PJ Ryan spread his body like a blanket and smothered our efforts. After his third miracle save – this time from Eoin – I just went over and patted him on the arse. Fair play to him, he was having the best day of his life. I had to acknowledge it.

Before that game people questioned PJ's credentials even though it was his third season as number one. He definitely went to another level that day – he basically stopped us from winning an All-Ireland. We were rampant at times: Paudie Maher had Shefflin living off frees; Derek Lyng, Richie Hogan and Aidan Fogarty were all replaced. We played brilliantly – the only thing we neglected was the small matter of getting the ball past PJ.

Because of his heroics I had to settle for points but I was happy to grab four of them – even if I was jostled and dragged and thrown around like a rag doll by the Kilkenny defence before I got my shot away for the first one. Pundits had questioned my ability to perform on the big stage so it was good to prove myself.

In general, our forward line silenced a few critics too. For years we were flaked over not winning ball in the air, but in the second half we collected twelve of their thirteen puck-outs. Our work-rate had improved too; I found myself tracking back and making tackles forty yards from our goal. It was that type of game.

Soon afterwards I found myself trying to escape this cloud of compassion gathering around the gallant losers. People meant well as they lined up to praise our contribution to a thrilling final; they reckoned we were the moral victors. We were in our holes. Liam Sheedy, thankfully, didn't think so anyway.

'No medals, lads, and unfortunately that's what it's all about,' he said through gritted teeth. 'You can forget this notion that we are winners. We won nothing. Kilkenny went home with the cup. We lost and don't let anyone try and soften the blow. Bottle it and come back next year.'

Otherwise it had been another decent spell. I racked up 9-11 in the championship and was a contender for Hurler of the Year, but none of that matters to me – I was more interested in the progress of our rising stars, youngsters who seemed to me natural-born winners and our best hope of another All-Ireland title.

Five of them were blooded en route to the 2009 final, and most of those had won minor titles in 2006 or 2007. A fair chunk of that group would go on to win an under-21 title in 2010, but while seeing them excel at underage was brilliant you never really knew how they would progress at senior level. For instance, Pa Bourke had been man of the match in the 2006 minor final but it took another six years for him to get regular game time.

Yet, I had a good feeling about them. Pa, the three Mahers, Michael Cahill and Noel McGrath. I remember one afternoon talking to Paudie Maher's uncle, Maurice McCormack, at the Dew Valley factory, and he enquired how the nephew was doing. I told him that even though Paudie was on the panel only a few months he was already doing things differently from everyone else and I dreaded marking him in training. You just couldn't get the better of him. Lads were ducking and diving trying to avoid marking him. When you did get past him he'd block you down a second or two later, always going directly for the sliotar and not your hurley.

Though he was only a kid, Paudie was regularly detailed to shadow the best forwards in the land, and even in those early days he did well on Shefflin whenever they clashed.

Brendan Maher isn't related to Paudie, but they play as if they were brothers, schooled in the same pure hurling philosophy – great position and touch, great vision, brilliant in the air.

Bonner Maher, another non-relative, is different again. I didn't really spot the full scope of his qualities until we played Laois in a challenge match in Portlaoise. Within thirty minutes he put two goals on a plate for me and showed exactly what he brought to the table.

The Bonner is really only interested in playing for the team. It probably took until 2010 to see the best of him but if you were to pin the word 'work-rate' on a dressing-room wall you'd have his picture underneath it.

His game-breaking style was badly needed because we had too many forwards out of the one mould. The Bonner is an alternative type but the undercard suits him – he always puts in a selfless shift, flinging himself into rucks and mauls to get hands on the ball so he can feed teammates – and without him the other Tipp forwards struggle.

Noel McGrath, meanwhile, has had the country raving about him since he was fourteen. Fortunately, management found a way to ease him in, not by holding him back but by giving him the freedom of the pitch and letting him be himself. He was allowed to express himself from the start.

I quickly developed an understanding with Noel. As soon as

the ball even looked like heading in his direction I was off and running. If a score wasn't on for him he'd find me in space. It's difficult to defend against that because it's so instinctive.

Before the 2009 final, for example, everyone expected me to ramble down into the number fifteen position and try to expose the Kilkenny backs with my speed, but I had no intention of that. I went out the field and roamed free. It was drilled into us not to let the defender know who he was picking up. We even considered having our six forwards pitch a tent around the centre-forward mark until the ball was thrown in and then disperse from there.

John O'Brien, Eoin and I constantly switched from full- to corner-forward anyway and once I was in the corner I'd trail off out the pitch knowing we had the edge of the square manned at all times. If the likes of Noel made a fifty-yard run I'd let him in for a breather while I went out and took his man.

It took opponents a while to cop what we were doing – you could look down on the field and see six Tipp forwards in their positions and then look back two minutes later and see the same six positions filled. If you looked more carefully, though, you might have noticed that all six of us were in different spots.

As Liam and the boys put their stamp on team affairs these were the things rubbing off on us. Before big matches I was often asked who I was marking. I'd kick for touch and throw out a name or two but deep down I was thinking, and I don't mean to sound arrogant, 'Hey, I'm the forward here; I'm marking no-one. Let them mark me.' That was some turnaround from the fragile and brittle Lar Corbett of the previous six seasons.

There was method behind the idea of constantly shuffling the forwards. It was to try and steal an early goal and immediately sow uncertainty in the opposition. I think it worked: we scored thirty-four championship goals under Sheedy in just fourteen games.

*

It was a massive setback to lose the All-Ireland. We were two years on the go with the boys and hadn't yet cracked the code, but at least we had a league and two Munster titles on the sideboard.

I suppose winning the 2009 provincial final in Thurles was some consolation. I had grown up watching the likes of Cork come to Thurles, win a Munster final at Semple Stadium and then parade down the town as conquering heroes, all dressed in uniform, soaking up the atmosphere and mingling with fans – often in my parents' pub and I behind the bar – before returning home. I had always wanted to do that.

I finally got to sample the Munster final atmosphere as a winner when we beat Waterford on my own doorstep and I decided I was going to soak up every second of it.

We showered and togged off, and I walked – or floated – down the town, in my Tipp gear, chatting to anyone who bothered to stop. We went into the Square and stayed there for an hour enjoying the buzz before moving on to Mackey's pub and then over to the Park Avenue hotel, run by the former Tipp captain Declan Carr. It was the experience of a lifetime.

That October at the All-Stars my old sparring partner Jackie Tyrrell approached me. Like most everyone else at the Citywest Hotel he'd had a few beers.

'You're some gas man, Lar. Do you remember what you said to me with a few minutes left in the final?'

'I do,' I replied.

'What did you say?'

I repeated the exact words I had used on the field: 'No, I don't want it.'

He looked at me, shook his head again and walked off, still perplexed.

I didn't even bother trying to explain.

*

You have to admire those Kilkenny boys, particularly their ability to come back year after year and keep winning. We never managed to do that but every year they stay the course. It's an easy job to motivate that team because they're all singing off the one hymn sheet. I doubt they really respected us over the past ten years but why would they? When you've won what they've won you don't need to respect anyone.

People have them down as hurling fanatics who can't have a bit of craic but they've had some right characters too. Martin Comerford, or 'Gorta' as he is known, was one of them.

At the end of 2009 we were on the All-Stars tour in Buenos Aires when he came onto the bus following an official banquet. We were heading into the city and spirits were high. Comerford saw us clustered at the end of the bus and I'm not sure if he grabbed the microphone on the dashboard. If he didn't he started shouting down to us.

'Where are the Tipp lads? There ye are! Jesus, ye're gas lads!'

'Why's that, Gorta?' one of the boys shouted back.

'Ye're gas lads. We tried to tell ye, tried to warn ye.'

'Warn us about what?'

'The last fifteen minutes! We tried to tell ye how important the last fifteen minutes were. We tried it time and again but ye wouldn't listen. We even put Henry Shefflin on the telly with a bottle of Lucozade Sport for eight months to remind ye how important the last fifteen were. Nah, ye wouldn't listen! Ye're gas men.'

In fairness it was a classic. All we could do was laugh.

There was some consolation to be found on home ground – Thurles Sars went on to win the 2009 county championship and it was something at the end of a disappointing year. But the hangover from losing to Kilkenny stayed with me for a long while.

The holidays approached and I prepared to take a few weeks

off and relax after a busy year. There was no doubt we were getting closer but after our underage success we now needed to come good where it really counted. We spent the winter licking our wounds. It was becoming an obsession now to get back and have another crack at them. We were all thinking about redemption. Non-stop.

On Christmas Eve I walked down toward Liberty Square to do a bit of last-minute shopping. Well, to be honest, I headed down to start the shopping. My mobile buzzed; it was Eamon.

'Lar, just to let you know that we're really looking forward to working with you next year. You played a huge part in the team in 2009 and you'll have an even bigger role to play next year. Happy Christmas to you and your family!'

I had been feeling a bit down since September but that phone call gave me an almighty lift. I wanted to tog out there and then.

# 12

# Second heaven

Welcome to hell by the Lee. It's 30 May 2010, and the Christmas cheer I got from Eamon's phone call has long since disappeared. Instead, I'm sitting in a dingy dressing-room at Páirc Uí Chaoimh after the biggest hiding a Tipp side has taken from Cork in sixty-eight years.

We were supposed to tear them apart. Our young, pacy team, full of hungry cubs with All-Ireland minor medals against a creaking team weary from a decade of epic battles on the field and political arm-wrestles off it. But it didn't happen. We lost by ten points and there could be no complaints – we hardly put up a fight.

This is a crap place to be. When you lose, even small things annoy you and right now what's bugging me is Páirc Uí Chaoimh and everything about it. The dressing-rooms, no more than twelve feet wide by eighteen feet long, are the worst I've changed in as a Tipp player, and I can't think of any worse at club level either. Imagine thirty players and another fifteen backroom boys trying to operate in a shoebox and you get the general picture.

It's a kip – dark and airless and smelly – and the heat is killing. For lack of space, some of the lads had to tog out in the toilets.

For the same reason Mick Clohessy had to put up his massage tables in the shower area.

I go to take a leak and see that some of the boys have dropped clothes on the floor and the floor is wet – piss has overflowed the urinals and is seeping into tops and leggings. Somebody's good shirt is a casualty – but I don't have the heart to alert its owner.

We shower and that's an experience in itself. There are two settings – ice cold and boiling hot. Either way no-one lasts more than thirty seconds under the water and we re-emerge, shampoo suds everywhere, to put our official gear back on. Some of the lads have to change again within minutes because the sweat is pumping out of them and their clothes are soaked.

We have just played in front of over thirty thousand people, but we have changed in a makeshift bunker that has been falling down for ten years and we walk back out the tunnel with our clothes sodden. It just doesn't add up. Meanwhile, up the corridor the Cork lads change in a lovely, spacious room with a gym inside. They could knock a wall in this chamber of horrors to make life easier for us, the opposition, but I reckon we'd be waiting a while for that to happen!

Of course, we can't entirely blame the stadium for the fact that none of us have played anywhere near the standard required. If you ask me we were peering too far down the road, planning our ambush of Kilkenny. Sure the whole country was looking forward to it after the excitement of 2009. Cork? We'd deal with them.

But we didn't. They went with the long ball every time and landed it straight down on top of Aisake Ó hAilpín, all six foot six of him. He unsettled us from the start and we never really recovered. We lost eleven puck-outs in a row, for God's sake.

I have never been as disappointed. We've spent the past two years building under Liam Sheedy and apart from the 2009

All-Ireland defeat we've hardly taken a wrong turn. But today threatens to derail the whole thing. All that good work will be undone if we can't get back on the horse.

My phone beeps on the way to the hotel. A text from a friend: *Hey, Lar, ye can still play a serious role in the championship. Don't give up.*

I save that message, knowing I'll need to reference it again before long.

We arrive at the team hotel but I'm too sick to eat anything – I just want to get home.

The next day the flak starts. The papers, noting that we've been ripped apart by an older team, question our character and our credentials.

Poor old Paudie gets the worst of it.

Earlier in the league he had tried to mark Aisake on the edge of the square but with high balls raining in he struggled. It worked so well for Cork that Denis Walsh – obviously looking ahead a few weeks to the championship and keen to keep his powder dry – moved Aisake out the field after about twenty-five minutes of that league game. He knew if he left Aisake on Paudie much longer there was no way Tipp would start Paudie at full-back come the big day.

In fairness to Aisake, all his numbers came up in Páirc Uí Chaoimh – he set up two goals and scored another. But now the talk was that he had cleaned Paudie, who took a whole pile of unfair and uninformed criticism. A closer look shows that Aisake caught about three balls, and it was more to do with the fact he's a human skyscraper than any fault of Paudie, who was moved to the wing before the break and went on to play a steady game.

But that's the way hurling is – the day after Cork beat us Aisake went from 150-1 to 20-1 for the 2010 Hurler of the Year award while Paudie was written off. Talk about overreacting!

I was more worried at how we had lost yet another game we were supposed to win. How many times did a Tipp team experience that feeling over the years? We seem to get complacent.

Maybe it was always going to be one of those days. I had a great goal chance early on. I broke through and was one on one with Cusack, but in letting fly I felt Eoin Cadogan's hurl scrape mine and the shot went harmlessly wide. From there Cork got the run on us and never looked back.

I have to admit I was scandalous in policing their puck-outs. I was mostly deployed in the corner with John O outside me on the wing. It had been drilled into us to cut out their short pucks, a trademark of Dónal Óg's. For one puck-out I noticed he was eyeing the left wing, so I drifted out just a touch, leaving that vital few feet between myself and John Gardiner, whereupon Dónal Óg halted his run-up and just batted the ball to Gardiner, who launched it high and handsome straight into Aisake's breadbasket at the other end.

Dónal Óg caught out myself and John O a few times during that game. I don't mind anyone catching me out once but being a repeat offender annoyed the hell out of me and to this day John O and I are still squabbling over who was supposed to pick up who.

But I don't think it matters – Cusack would have landed the ball on a sixpence that day no matter where he was aiming for. With him pulling the strings at one end, and Aisake causing us jitters at the other, everything rolled nicely for Cork.

We weren't buried yet, though. Deep down we sensed we still had plenty in the tank. Before we left Cork, Sheedy came to us and insisted we would be back. But he asked us to remember this day. 'Throw it in the filing cabinet,' he said. 'We'll need to pull it out again before the year is out.'

*

A meeting was called for the Horse and Jockey hotel the following Tuesday night. There we went through everything with a fine comb, pored over the evidence forensically and then scratched it from the record.

The good thing about the meeting at the Jockey was that Liam put us all in a circle – there was no such thing as the management on top, looking down on us.

Our doctor, Peter Murchan, was clearly upset by the result and did most of the talking early on. Until Declan Fanning stood up.

'Lads, I haven't been doing the gym work every Wednesday and Friday and that's one thing I'll have to change,' he said.

That was the tone set. There would be no blame game or recriminations. Rather than shine the spotlight on management or another player Dec listed three areas he himself could improve in. Everyone took his lead. Talk is cheap but one by one the boys stood up and said what they needed to do.

Brian O'Meara from Kilruane MacDonaghs made an important contribution. 'Buggy', as we call him, was on the panel only a wet week but had started against Cork on Eoin Cadogan. When he offered a friendly pre-match handshake to Eoin he got buried with a shoulder for his troubles and ended up on his arse.

It was still the talk of the squad a few days later and sensing as much Buggy stood up. 'Lads, I'm sorry,' he said. 'But I can guarantee that what happened on Sunday will never happen again.'

Sometimes these meetings can be disasters. You can waffle all you want, but deep down if you know the set-up is not right you're only fooling yourselves. This time we knew there was no more the management could have done for us.

I've heard that the Munster and Ireland rugby squads go to town on each other with brutal self-analysis but that's a professional game and I'm not sure if lads would always take it in the GAA. But with an old hand like Declan and a young lad like Buggy putting their hands up there was a rare honesty and a really positive vibe about this session.

It was nearing an end when Dr Murchan looked over at me: 'Larry, you're the only senior player not to speak. What have you to say for yourself?'

I suppose there are different types of leadership and when it comes to talking in front of a group I'm not your man. I would worry that what I had to say wasn't relevant. Would it make any difference in training or on match day? Would I just be talking for the sake of it? I'd be very conscious of that – but Peter had me nailed now; I had to say something.

I agreed I hadn't been doing the gym work either and admitted I hadn't helped the cause in Cork by missing three of their short puck-outs. 'I just didn't perform,' I said. 'But now I have stuff to work harder on in training and I promise I'll do that.'

I also told the boys to ignore the rubbish being written about us and the crazy rumours flying around – the county was alive with wild stories of what was happening behind the scenes but all we could do as players was to deal with the facts. We really are an awful county for that sort of stuff – you may as well have a stockpile of incendiary stories and just toss a few of them on the fire every couple of months to fuel the flames.

Wexford offered us the chance of redemption. We drew them in the qualifiers in Thurles. We just wanted a team we could get past and we had enough confidence that we could deal with Wexford. They had beaten us in the 2006 All-Ireland quarter-final but our set-up wasn't right back then. This time, even though we faltered against Cork, we knew things were different.

Liam and the lads just tweaked a few things, gave the likes of Bonner Maher a chance, but really they didn't panic and the overall shape of the team remained in place. The consensus was that if we wanted to win a title we would have to beat the likes of Wexford, get our confidence back and then prepare even harder for what would come down the line.

We got off to a good start and I don't think the result was ever in doubt. Declan Fanning's game was over almost before it started, however. He had to leave the field after an incident with an opponent. Dec's helmet was pulled off and his ear was torn almost in two. Peter Murchan had some serious work to attend to in the dressing-room and anyone who saw the injury was shocked by it.

Declan came back out and sat on the bench, shaken. He wouldn't play at full-back again that year, but fortunately for him and us he was just as capable at wing-back and that's where he slotted in for the rest of the season. Imagine if he was less versatile – what he would have missed out on!

One thing I would say about that episode. The GAA are great for their disciplinary groups – the CCC (Competitions Control Committee), the CAC (Central Appeals Committee) and the CHC (Central Hearings Committee) – but little was done about Declan's injury. I saw footage of the incident and to me it looked terrible.

I had a good day and bagged two goals and three points. We got our scores at the right time and pushed the wagon back on track.

We were fixated on the performance. At one stage Bonner went for his own score when a pass was the better option. Eoin and I came out roaring to let him know he had screwed up. I'm sure it looked way over the top from the terraces, but after losing to Cork we were now walking a tightrope and any slip could prove fatal. We simply had to take the right option every time and we wanted that message rammed home.

A few minutes later Bonner got the ball again and this time set up the score. He duly got the thumbs up from the two of us.

\*

We got through by fourteen points and after the crushing disappointment of Cork we were giddy. There was a two-week gap till our next qualifier so the lads reckoned they'd go for a few scoops. But Sheedy got wind of it ahead of time and wasn't at all happy.

I think Liam was concerned we could go soft again very easily. But one of his qualities as a manager is being able to use different means to achieve an end. If he drew a hard line and said pints were forbidden, one or two of the lads – maybe disillusioned subs who weren't getting game time – would have gone out regardless. Liam knew that, so he asked Declan Fanning to handle it.

Declan did that in a very low-key way: 'Well done, lads. We're after getting over today but we won't go out tonight now – we'll be back in training on Tuesday and we'll just drive it on.'

That was that. Every player looked at himself and said if Declan wasn't going out, no-one was. They wouldn't let him down. Not one player went out that night. And Sheedy achieved his target.

I'm sometimes asked by GAA reporters what makes a good manager. Well, there's just one example. Leaders don't create followers, they create more leaders.

We rolled on. Offaly were next up and we did enough to win by six points. An All-Ireland quarter-final against Galway beckoned just seven days later.

There was something special about that Galway game. I have already mentioned how as youngsters Pa and I used to puck the sliotar for hours and hours on end. You probably felt I was harping on about it a little – sure we all puck around as kids, you might say, even those who never go on to play the game. But I mentioned it for a reason.

We were in deep slurry – a point down, with time running out – when Pa, who had only just been recalled to the squad,

**Above**: Receiving close attention from Kilkenny's Brian Hogan and Michael Rice during the 2009 All-Ireland final.

**Below**: Brendan Cummins appeals against referee Diarmuid Kirwan's decision to award Kilkenny a penalty at a crucial stage in the 2009 final.

**Left**: From the start, there was no quarter given in the 2010 All-Ireland final.

**Below left**: About to catch the sliotar and turn away from Noel Hickey to strike the first goal of the day against the Cats.

**Below right**: Turning in celebration after scoring the first of three goals on the day.

**Below**: Striking for our second goal as John Tennyson's hurley comes flying towards me.

**Above**: Offering my hand to commiserate with Jackie Tyrrell after the game.

**Below**: Tipperary: 2010 All Ireland hurling champions!

**Above**: Pure joy: Eoin Kelly lifts the Liam McCarthy Cup.

**Left**: The 'dream team' in jubilant form: (*left to right*) selector Michael Ryan, manager Liam Sheedy, and coach Eamon O'Shea.

**Below**: With (*left to right*) Pa Bourke and Pádraic Maher at the 2010 homecoming party at The Dome at Semple Stadium.

**Left**: With Eddie O'Brien in New York: the last man to score three goals in an All-Ireland final when he played for Cork against Wexford in 1970.

With Elaine (**above left**) and Mam (**above right**) at the 2010 GPA awards.

**Centre**: With Katie Taylor and Bernard Brogan after receiving the Hurler of the Year award at the 2010 Texaco Sportstars awards.

Being introduced to HM Queen Elizabeth by GAA President Christy Cooney during her visit to Croke Park in 2011.

**Above**: Showing what it means to me. Celebrating a goal against Cork in the 2011 championship .

Dejected as I leave the pitch at the end of the 2011 All-Ireland final.

**Above**: Roaring encouragement from the sideline during the 2012 championship game against Limerick.

**Right**: Hand passing to Noel McGrath for the decisive goal in the 2012 Munster championship semi-final.

**Above**: Tommy Walsh and Pa Bourke tussling (*left*) while once again Jackie Tyrrell is on my case during the 2012 All-Ireland semi-final.

**Below**: Referee Cathal McAllister has a brief word with Jackie Tyrrell while checking to see if I require to be temporarily substituted.

came onto the field. Pa's first touch was to ping a ball back out to Gearóid Ryan, who shot straight over the bar to level the scores. A couple of minutes later, with neither team allowing an opponent to get a shot on goal, a ball broke to him again and off he took into the right corner of the field.

Instinctively, I knew that if Pa didn't shoot for the posts within three or four steps he was going to track back. Don't ask me how I knew that, I just did. It's what he does. I trailed him as he headed for the corner, didn't yell once and didn't feel the need to. Instead of flanking him I hung back and even retreated a bit. Sure enough Pa doubled back and saw me in situ. Tap. Straight into my hand. Just like when we were kids.

If I hit immediately off my left I knew I'd be blocked down, so I spun around, never looked at the posts and struck off the right. Over she went. That score was down to Pa. All those pucks and taps over the years. Not a word needed to be said between us. We just knew what was going to happen.

It was as well we won because I don't think we would ever have recovered from losing. Maybe the eight lads under the age of twenty-two would have coped but the likes of myself, Eoin and Brendan, I'm not so sure.

Also, it was the first time in my memory that Tipp came back from the dead in a championship match. Cyril Farrell called it a classic, an epic. Ger Loughnane went a step further and called it the 'epic of all epics'.

There were plenty of mistakes but I have to admit it was some game. I also have to accept that we really only came through when Ollie Canning limped off injured and space began to appear in their back line; our last two points were hit from his patch. It was Ollie's last game for the county. After such a great career it must have been a hugely disappointing way to bow out.

We were aware of what was on the line for the lads in charge as well. Again, who knows what would have happened had we lost? Perhaps we had got an insight at half-time when Eamon tried to address us before getting a little emotional. There were tears in his eyes and tears in mine as well. We couldn't let this go after all the boys had done for us. There was every possibility they would walk following a defeat and we'd be set back another three years.

They gave us the belief to stay going until the end and we started to pay them back. The Bonner played Eoin in for a goal and this time Eoin and I raced out to thump him on the back and congratulate him for taking the right option.

As a team we were closer to our goal. Progress. The subs played a massive role – Noel set up Séamus Callanan for a great goal; John O hit a fine score late on; Pa was on fire. It was end to end until the final whistle and then there was pure elation. I saw Sheedy running onto the field and I swear I almost saw the steam coming out of him.

Behind the scenes we had been working with Caroline Currid, a sports psychologist. I liked her from the start because I found out she was working with Paul O'Connell and yet she never mentioned it. That was a big plus for her in my book.

We'd had other people down through the years and you'd know all about their courses, qualifications and clients before you even introduced yourself. But put thirty Tipp hurlers in a room and they would know few of our names. Caroline got to know us all individually and every chat was informal.

She told me she was meeting the lads once a fortnight but I didn't need to attend that often. I suppose she reckoned she was wasting her time trying to figure me out. I objected, though.

'Hang on, Caroline, if the lads are on the bus talking about some new concept you have and I don't know about it I'll only lose out. I want to be at every session – just tell me the times and dates.'

Maybe all that visualisation and mental stuff was helping; I certainly got a lot from it anyway. Throughout the team you could see lads were stepping up to the mark. We were back in an All-Ireland semi-final against Waterford and we were thriving.

The same could not be said for the Déise. A few of their big names – Dan Shanahan, Ken McGrath, Séamus Prendergast and Eoin McGrath – were dropped and we concluded all was not well with them. We weren't far wrong.

On the day they never got their balance right – as usual they relied too much on John Mullane. Over the years I think that was the one thing that held Waterford back; sometimes they would click as a team and play the most beautiful hurling. Most of the time, though, they looked to individuals and John had been saving their bacon year in and year out. That over-dependence on one player will get you only so far, as we found out with our Eoin.

Leaving the likes of Ken on the bench was another tactical blunder – he hit three lovely points when he came in and as the third sailed over the bar I said to Pa, 'Thanks be to God they didn't start him!'

To further illustrate the fault lines in their squad, when Eoin Kelly, the Waterford version, was replaced after fifty-odd minutes he gave Davy Fitz an earful. We had the game almost wrapped up by then. We had taken the scenic route but we'd given the plain people of Ireland what they wanted – another Tipp v. Kilkenny All-Ireland final.

This time there was a different feeling in the build-up. In 2009 we didn't know what to expect, because it had been eight years since we were in a final and everything associated with it; the lead-in, the tension – it can all get to you. But now I knew we had a right good chance. Even though we had lost the year before not one of our lads doubted we could beat them. We had serious belief.

The Cats were going for the five-in-a-row and immortality beckoned. That always brings pressure. The media circus in Kilkenny was getting out of hand, and that suited us just fine. Brian Cody is a master of the low-key approach but this time even he was unable to keep the lid on it. All they were short of was the boys from Sky Sports taking over the Marble City to douse more hype on the whole thing.

We listened to them being heralded as the greatest team in history – which they probably were. Crowds of ten thousand were turning up to watch them train. We heard Kilkenny's traffic wardens and clampers were into bonus territory as gridlock prevailed around Nowlan Park.

By comparison, Thurles was a haven of peace and quiet. True, a couple of thousand turned up to cheer us off the field after our final session and that applause raised the hairs on the back of my neck. We didn't want the world and its mother stalking us, but the people who did show up let their feelings be known and as we went into the dressing-room I could feel the strength coursing through our team.

We knew, too, that Kilkenny were fretting over the fitness of Henry Shefflin and John Tennyson, both of them facing into the final nursing cruciate ligaments. I think they went to Ger Hartmann and both of them played in the final, which suited us fine because we wanted to beat them with every big name on that field.

Meanwhile, we had only ourselves to focus upon and the one downside was the disappointment of certain lads in the dressing-room when the team was announced the Tuesday before the final. None more so than Séamie Callanan, who had been pushing hard for a starting place.

Séamie could have sat down and sulked – only for his goal against Galway we wouldn't have been in the final – but when Liam asked him to give the team talk that night he put his personal disappointment aside, stood up and cleared his throat. You could see the passion in his eyes and his message was simple.

'Lads, I'll be ready to come in and drive the thing on. There are fourteen other lads ready too. We all have the work done so we'll be there when ye need us. We're ready.'

Eamon O'Shea was next to speak.

'Do you know the gas thing about teams playing Kilkenny? All this talk of hanging in there, keeping up with them until half-time and then hoping to drive on if the chance arises? That's nonsense and we're not going down that road.

'Instead, we're going to bring our intensity to a level they haven't yet seen. From the moment the ball is thrown in we're going to work harder than we've ever worked before. Every one of us. Movement, encouragement, we'll let them worry about who they mark. The forwards – don't have it in your head that you're playing in any defined position. A lot could change.

'We're going to attack five and seven (Tommy Walsh and JJ Delaney). That's where we'll attack. Those are the pillars of their team. When the pillars fall the whole thing will collapse. We're going to bring them to a place they've never been before!'

Eoin was next to stand up.

'Lads, are we going to drive at them? Are we going to drive this on?'

A roar. Fucking right we are!

I get up. For once I'm not worried if what I say makes any sense. I ask the boys to visualise the start of the game.

'Imagine that scoreboard after ten minutes. Tipperary one-four, Kilkenny a point. Imagine that, lads! And now imagine that we haven't even started hurling yet. Eamon and Eoin are right – we're going to bring them to places they won't like at all!'

Everything was kept simple. After the game, the media focused on how Bonner Maher had kept Tommy Walsh quiet, but I can tell you hand on heart I hadn't a clue about any plan to counteract Tommy – apart from driving at him.

Maybe Bonner and Eamon had something planned, but all I was told was to follow my instincts. Noel McGrath and I were to interchange between centre- and full-forward all day long and we were to be cute about it. As for the rest of the lads, I couldn't tell you what their jobs were.

The boys had a simple logic. There's the field, there's the posts and here's your hurley. Now go out and play.

A couple of funny stories.

With two weeks left to the final, Liam could sense that there was serious tension in the camp. After the disappointment of 2009 losing was just not an option this time. The mood in the camp was positive but with so much at stake you could tell some of our lads were wound up and edgy.

To lighten the mood a little Liam told us we would have a special guest waiting when we went to Carton House in Maynooth to fine-tune our preparations for the final. Sheedy wouldn't tell us who it was, but even speculating on who the mystery guest might be proved a bit of diversion and took our minds off the game.

And so, after we finished a training session at Carton House, about fifty of us crammed into a room, still wondering. We waited three or four minutes, and then Liam asked us to give a big welcome to the comedian Pat Shortt.

In walked Pat, a lad born and reared in Thurles, to a huge cheer, and the gas thing is he didn't even have to open his mouth to get a reaction. He shot an oul' look around the room with a sneer on him – whatever way he can twist and turn his face it's priceless – and soon everyone was shaking with laughter. I'd say it was the easiest gig Pat ever had; he even got giddy himself and started cracking up.

Pat hadn't uttered one word but already Sheedy's idea was a hit.

The next thing, Pat brought in this lad from outside in the corridor, put a Kilkenny jersey on him and left him at the top of the room.

He then went into his usual routine, going around embarrassing people in the audience. Every so often, without saying a word, Pat would mosey up to the fella with the Kilkenny jersey and kick him in the arse for no obvious reason. I'd say he was with us for an hour and your man in the black and amber shirt got a fair few boots for his troubles. You couldn't buy what we got off Pat Shortt that day. You could actually feel the energy in the room as we cheered him and clapped his antics.

At our last training session, just four days before we played the final, Eoin and I looked like two characters out of the movie *Grumpy Old Men*. Eoin had received a painkilling injection into his back and had a bit of a stoop about him as the anti-inflammatory went to work. We were all very wary of him aggravating it further.

Me? I was ambling around the place wearing a pair of runners. Two weeks earlier, at a training camp in Carton House, I had damaged a toe and the pain was tormenting me. I absolutely dread the sight of needles so Dr Murchan was kind enough not to insist on giving me an injection. Instead, he placed me on a course of tablets, but they were fierce slow to work. As the rest of the team went through a demanding last set of drills before the biggest game of our lives Eoin and I hobbled to a corner of Semple Stadium to puck a few balls at each other.

We were tipping away – Eoin wincing with every shot we took – when Eamon came running over wearing a worried frown.

'Mind his toe, Eoin! Larry, don't be hitting the ball to Eoin so low – we don't want him bending down, for God's sake!'

We just looked at each other and cracked up laughing. Both of us were in a heap, a dodgy back and a smashed toe. It was hard to believe we'd be flat to the boards a few days later. The miracles of modern science!

On the Friday before the match I popped down the road to Josie Collins and her husband, Bill, in Friar Street, to get a drop of holy water. Josie sprinkled it on my head, legs and arms and when she had finished dousing me she went out to the van and sprinkled the good stuff on that too.

I had been friends with her son Tommy in school, and when I started working at the Dew Valley factory, Josie insisted I call in for dinner every day at one o'clock – her house was handier than ours to the factory. That routine lasted for ten years and I loved every minute of it. If I wasn't down by five past one I'd get a phone call telling me my dinner was on the table.

She had ten in her own family, but she always had room for four or five other stragglers like myself, so dinner there was an experience and a half. Hurling was rarely discussed; Josie knew I'd be better off without listening to all that.

You'd go in, sit down and eat the best of meat, spuds and vegetables. Well, I would anyway. Her nearest and dearest would often be on spaghetti bolognese while I'd have a juicy big steak put in front of me with dessert, a few biscuits and a pot of tea to wash it all down. When the belly was full I'd hop off the chair and another of the hungry masses would sit down to be fed.

The Collinses were just one of those families. When Josie went to the local butcher's a steak would be thrown in with the sausages and rashers and mincemeat, and someone would say, 'That steak is for Larry. Tell him the best of luck on Sunday.'

My mother shopped in the same butcher's but the steak was given to Josie because they knew that was where I ate. She was my second mother. If match day arrived and I hadn't been sprinkled in holy water I'd have to drive down to her.

Before the final, I reminded myself that I was playing for the likes of Josie and Bill. She never said in words what it meant to her that I was hurling for Tipp. She never had to.

Can a life in sport be distilled into one day?

I blot out the crowd and walk into the middle of the field. I offer no handshakes. If someone puts his paw out I'll match the gesture but around 2004 I decided shaking hands with my marker only rubber-stamps his job specification for the day – a licence to follow me. These days I like to keep them guessing.

When the ball is thrown in I amble to centre-forward. Seven minutes have passed when Shane McGrath gathers the sliotar in the middle of the field. Immediately I know where it's going – with Shane it always lands on the edge of the square.

Noel Hickey is behind me on my right-hand side and straight away I sense there's a goal on. A defender will look to get a piece of your jersey and pull you back and once he checks you the ball will often trickle harmlessly to the keeper. The stakes are high. I know it's basically me against Hickey.

I run across Noel with my left hand on his shoulder so he can't get a clean grab of me and I catch the missile coming in with my right hand. If I went with my left he'd catch on to me and spoil it. Now he has no chance. He goes to grab me but he loses balance as there's nothing there – my body has stepped back into him and swerved across to the left of him. He falls to the ground as I catch at the last second. I'm in.

The flip side is I have to strike off my weaker left side as I turn. Thankfully, hurling is instinctive and I just make contact with the ball and hit it. It skims off PJ Ryan's back and into the net – a year ago he would have stopped it with a cheek of his arse, but not this time.

The stadium erupts and I feel a rare surge of energy. My heart pounds. For a second I put a finger in the air before Paul Curran's words from the year earlier sound an alarm in my head: 'Lads, for a second we allowed ourselves to think we had it won. Look what happened.'

I glance up at the scoreboard. Tipperary 1-4, Kilkenny 0-1. I blink. This is crazy! It's the exact scoreline I asked the lads to imagine in that training-ground huddle a few weeks back! Visualisation!

Again I check myself. Don't get carried away, Lar! The job only starts now. Let's drive on and bring these lads to those places they've never been!

Kilkenny lose Henry after fourteen minutes – he hobbles off with the cruciate – but we're probably as disappointed as they are; we want to beat them with their best players on the field.

At half-time Eoin speaks again. We're on top of them, but even after losing Shefflin they have gone ahead on the scoreboard.

'We're not leaving it behind!' Kelly shouts. Another roar. That's grand. Everyone is tuned in. We go back out and tear into them all over again.

Gearóid Ryan pings a ball off his left to Noel McGrath. When I see Noel running onto it, I take off from the halfway line. I don't need to shout at him because he knows I'm gone – it's my job. The handpass drops in front of me as I bear down on goal at full speed, without even putting the ball on my hurl. There's a risk of being blown for taking too many steps – but maybe not on All-Ireland final day.

The year before we had taken our shots from too far out so this time I'm going to look for the whites in PJ's eyes before I pull the trigger. Onto my right without breaking stride I unload. John Tennyson throws his hurley at me but it whizzes harmlessly past. Whenever I hit off my right I know there's only one place the ball is going.

*

After the game I bumped into John in the players' lounge.

'You're a gas man, firing the hurl at me.'

'Sure why not?' he replied.

'What do you mean?'

'If it worked I stopped you from scoring and we could still have beaten you. If it didn't – well, the worst I was going to get in an All-Ireland was a yellow card. Sure I wasn't going to be sent off. It was worth a shot.'

I shook his hand: 'John, you're dead right.'

Given what was at stake, he was right to give it a shot, even if it wasn't the most sporting thing to do.

The place goes bananas again as the ball whizzes to PJ's left, but again I don't celebrate; I won't get any bonus points for show-boating. As PJ gets up and dusts himself down I run back out looking for more work. Is there a hook or a block going?

I notice my teammates are all on message, pointing to their temples and urging each other to stayed tuned in. We're not going to sit back and invite the Cats back onto us this time. We're going for the kill.

Noel McGrath follows up with a scrappy goal of his own but they keep coming at us. They just don't know how to lie down. Still, I know we have them where we want them.

A year after being sent off in the last final Benny Dunne comes on and scores a terrific point. Redemption!

David Young is on too and he mishits a ball. It arrives in at a fair old pace and the Bonner goes up for it. I loiter nearby, know-ing he will feed me if there's half a chance. Sure enough he does. I tip it up on my hurl and it spins back toward my body, making a block less likely. I barely get the swing away but it's enough. The net shivers for a third time.

*

The feeling at the final whistle is unreal. The boys go spare but I keep cool. All I feel is inner satisfaction; I don't need to go haywire to express my happiness.

Remembering my little chat with Jackie Tyrrell the year before and subsequently at the All-Stars I pop straight over to him. He's down on one knee. I just look him in the eye and hold out a hand. We shake on it.

I look for the boys, then Eamon and Liam. We hug but say nothing. There's no need for words.

Off we go on a lap of honour but I can't keep up – I cut every corner like a lad shirking drills at training.

After the game I sit down on the bus and look across at Eamon. Everyone has been clapping me on the back and applauding me onto the bus, but Eamon has his own take on the day.

'You should have got four, you should have created another chance,' he says.

I feel like telling him where to put that remark – until I see the glint in his eye. All the same, it may be the biggest day of my life but he's already laying down another challenge to me.

That was one thing that stood out in the chaotic aftermath of that game. The other was when I met Maurice McCormack, Paudie Maher's uncle. He congratulated me, but added a caveat.

'Larry,' he said, 'be ready! Because your life will never be the same again.'

# 13

# The fame game

As the weeks passed and the hullaballoo died down I began to see what Maurice McCormack was talking about. Shortly after the final I came across an interview with Eddie O'Brien, the former Cork hurler and the last man before me to score three goals in an All-Ireland final – back in 1970 against Wexford. He seemed genuinely delighted I had taken his place in the record books but he had a warning for me.

'Lar's life is going to change and he won't even realise it,' Eddie said. 'People don't forget stuff like that, I've found over the years. They do remember that you're the guy who got the three goals. It never goes away, and anywhere he goes, in Tipperary or across Ireland, it will be the first thing they bring up. At least that's the way it is for me.'

I really couldn't see what all the fuss was about, though. Life changing? Sure, what will be different?

Even when an All-Star and the three Hurler-of-the-Year awards (Texaco, All-Stars and GPA) came my way in 2010 I didn't change – not that I was aware of anyway – and I certainly didn't get carried away. The cogs in my mind still turned like they always did, and I'd like to believe I treated everyone

I met with respect and a bit of courtesy. Sure I love meeting and talking to people anyway, so that aspect of it wasn't going to trouble me.

Still, as the weeks and months passed, I could see that while I hadn't changed, people's perception of me most definitely had. Especially people I was meeting for the first time – they would look at me as if they knew me, as if they had shared their closest secrets with me.

Some lads were quite cheeky about it – they'd come right up and stare. There were nights I went out and didn't have a second to myself. People were looking for photographs and autographs everywhere I went, and I wasn't used to that.

It wasn't just strangers. I hope I'm not sounding big-headed here, but even people I'd known all my life seemed to be looking at me a little differently. It was just weird.

But apart from people gawking at me, I can't say there was much wrong with the new-found attention. In fact, it opened plenty of doors.

In April 2011 I got a phone call from John Cunningham, a producer at RTÉ, asking if I would go on the *Late Late Show* and speak about being unemployed. I said I would but only if I could bring one or two teammates. Half the country knew I was out of work but there were six or seven lads on the Tipp team in the same boat and I thought going on the show would help them as well. The producer agreed and so I phoned Paudie Maher and Conor O'Mahony. They had no problem doing the gig.

I had been in Donnybrook before as part of the Micheál Ó Muircheartaigh tribute show, but then I was just a face in the crowd. This time I was sitting in the hot seat as the 2010 Hurler of the Year opposite Ryan Tubridy.

There was a hidden bonus to the gig. It was around this time that Kevin Coppinger and I were planning to go into business together by opening a bar with my name on it above his establishment in Parnell Street, and we recognised the slot on TV as a fantastic opportunity to advertise the venture.

I decided if the boys and I were going to do it we would do it right – we had to prepare for it. So the three of us hopped in the car early on Friday morning and drove straight to the Communications Clinic in Ballsbridge. I asked RTÉ to email a list of questions that might come up and enquired where the three of us would be sitting, and we got Eoghan McDermott, one of the Clinic directors, to put us through our paces. No way were we going on Ireland's biggest chat show stuttering and stammering, making complete eejits of ourselves.

Eoghan was brilliant – we knew him from courses he had given for the Gaelic Players Association. On this occasion he played the role of Tubridy and sat us in the same relative positions we would occupy that night. He asked us the first round of questions, then called us together and replayed the video. The camera doesn't lie and we were awful – the three of us.

Eoghan was nice about it: 'Lar, you need to interact more. Conor, you need to sit up straighter. Paudie, you look very tense – relax.'

We did the interview all over again. Eoghan was happier with this one but not totally satisfied. Back we went a third time. By the finish we were 90 per cent better than our first screening.

Leaving Eoghan's office I knew we were prepared. It was like facing into a match having all the work done. I was delighted.

We went from there to the Shelbourne Hotel, where we were to stay that night courtesy of RTÉ. They must have felt sorry for the lads off the dole queue, because we were each given a magnificent bedroom with a luxurious lounge en suite. Well, that's what I got anyway. Downstairs we went then to be served their finest steak dinner.

'Lads, why would you want to get a job at all?' I joked to the boys. 'The Shelbourne Hotel, a posh suite, a steak dinner and the *Late Late Show*. You wouldn't get this carry-on if you were working!'

Heading into Montrose I knew we would do ourselves justice, and we did. I think we came across well and, in fairness, Ryan was a great help. Before the show he came over, and though it was clear he was out of his comfort zone talking GAA, it didn't stop him putting us at ease.

'Don't worry about stumbling on a word or freezing for a second – I'll see it and jump in,' he said to us. 'Don't worry about doddering around a question either; I'll make sure you're looked after.'

People complimented us on how we came across in that show and we told them it was all off the cuff. Conor later got a job as sales manager with Irish Bobbles – the hurling figurines – and Paudie picked up a sales job with Evergreen, a tree company, before returning to college in Limerick.

By the way, Coppinger nearly blew a gasket in the audience because I was so wrapped up in the discussion I almost forgot to plug the bar. I think he was doing a jig trying to attract my attention. Fortunately I got my spoke in before the finish.

After the show we went to O'Donoghue's bar on Merrion Row and then on to Krystal nightclub on Harcourt Street. Tubridy came with us and he was a good sport. At one stage we were about to order more drinks and we started shaking our near-empty bottles at him.

'Hey, these are not going to fill themselves! Three lads on the dole, skint, and you won't even buy us a round. We only got the dole money yesterday and we have to make it last until next Thursday. In fact things were never as bad for us. And you're going to look on while we buy our own drink!'

He was laughing out loud and sure enough a while later he sent a round of drinks in our direction. The man gets lots of flak because of his position but I think he's a real gent.

Later we asked at the bar what Ryan was drinking and they told us he had moved to another floor of the club. We bought drinks and asked the staff to bring them to him with a message. They found him with a group of friends and conveyed the message: 'These are from the three Tipp lads on the dole.' The staff told us he enjoyed that.

While going on the *Late Late* was a great experience no doubt the biggest door that opened was the opportunity to meet Queen Elizabeth when she visited Ireland in May 2011. Eddie O'Donnell, a trusted adviser, phoned to ask if I would be interested in meeting the queen at Croke Park.

Seemingly a few hurlers and footballers had been approached by the GPA but were less than enthusiastic, not quite sure if they should turn up with all the historical baggage involved – especially the memory of Bloody Sunday, 1920. Personally I had no qualms.

'Eddie, if I have the opportunity to go and meet that woman I'll jump at it,' I told him. 'And what's more, if you want me to, I'll ask Paudie or one of the boys as well.'

To me it was simple. Obviously there is history and lots of it between Ireland and England and the queen is the figurehead for her country and is associated, for better or worse, with much of that history. But I just got the feeling that if she ever visited a second time people would be queuing up to meet her and I wanted to be in the first batch.

People in Ireland don't always trust change and they didn't know how to react to her visit but I could see no issue. Eddie rang back to say myself and Paudie were on the list and to be up at GAA HQ bright and early on 11 May.

About a month beforehand the security checks started. We were vetted by the Garda, had our passports checked and were eventually given the green light.

As the days counted down I suppose I became more aware of the emotional significance of a royal visit to Croke Park, especially as a Tipperary footballer, Michael Hogan, was one of the fourteen people killed on Bloody Sunday. An awful lot of sadness surrounded that atrocity, but I was honoured to represent the GAA and GPA for the present occasion.

Paudie and I also saw the whole royal visit as a positive thing for the country and a chance to build relations with England. Furthermore, we agreed this was one visit to Croke Park where we just couldn't lose. We're usually playing in matches and it's win or bust; this time we were just honoured to be there.

On the morning of 11 May the two of us drove to Dublin and parked on Clonliffe Road. From that point on the precautions were fierce. We had to carry our passports and go through big metal gates outside the stadium. There were gardaí and plain-clothes men everywhere.

We were told to go into the dressing-rooms and wait for herself. Another queue. Once we got inside, the doors were sealed with tape and no-one was allowed to leave. That was the drill all over the stadium. If any of the seals had been broken a red alert would be triggered.

We had been instructed to wear our official Tipp tracksuits and inside we met the Dublin footballer Kevin Nolan and Joe Sheridan from Meath. We had a grand chat and it was just as well because two hours had passed by the time we were told to assume our positions. The four of us lined up with the gifts we were to present; Paudie and I had a hurl each.

In she came with the entourage swarming around her and that's the first thing I noticed – the prison she lives in. Security came in ten minutes beforehand, then a pile of plain-clothes detectives, then armed police in front of her and more still behind her. There were all sorts of suits besides. She had a heap of people following her the whole time and it was like she was in a bubble and that bubble moves all over the world with her wherever she goes.

She stopped and shook hands with us.

'At what age did you take up the game?'

'We're playing it all our lives,' Paudie replied.

'And how many play on each team?'

I took this one. A nice easy one. 'Fifteen a side.'

'What is the game like?'

'Not too unlike shinty or hockey,' I added.

'And what is Croke Park like to play in?'

'Very big and wide,' Paudie grinned. She quizzed him further on the hurley he was holding in his hands, enquiring how it was made.

She was very well spoken, as you would expect. There was a definite aura about her, and even though she's a small woman she definitely left an impression as we chatted.

I was surprised at her genuine interest in the sport. She seemed amazed, visibly raising her eyebrows, when Christy Cooney, the GAA president at the time, told her that despite playing in front of huge crowds at weekends we were amateur sportsmen in the old-fashioned sense and worked day jobs all week.

She was a fair lady for eighty-five years of age. The main thing I took from her was the interest she showed in everyone she met.

After four or five minutes she was ushered out onto the field but we had to stay locked in the dressing-rooms. I think she visited four or five corners of the stadium that day and none of us could go anywhere until she had left the ground.

It was only when I got back to Thurles and watched the news that I saw Nickey Brennan, who served as GAA president before Christy, shaking the collarbone off her. Well, in fairness, all he did was put his arm on her but the secret service lads were getting the jitters. It was a purely instinctive gesture by Nickey and I could sympathise – I was given so many instructions in the lead-up to meeting her that I didn't blame him in the slightest. Random people were coming up to me telling me not to offer a handshake unless she extended her hand first; they were saying not to speak unless I was spoken to. Everyone in Thurles suddenly seemed to be an expert on meeting the queen!

On the way home we pulled into the Poitín Stil at Rathcoole for a bit of grub – we were starving. Any notions you had about yourself were soon dispelled. An hour earlier you were shaking hands with one of the most influential women in the world and now you were paying for shepherd's pie and drinking a glass of orange juice like all the other anonymous punters.

If there was ever any danger of a lad getting carried away with himself, though, the GAA can always be relied upon to drag him back down to earth. Six days after I scored those three goals against Kilkenny I got a phone call from Marty Morrissey asking if I would do an interview with Brian Carthy of RTÉ Radio before the 2010 All-Ireland under-21 final between Tipp and Galway at Semple Stadium.

'No bother. Do I need a ticket to get into the stadium, Marty?' I asked.

'Sure you won't need a ticket. If you can't get in, who can?' he replied.

'As far as I know everyone needs a ticket,' I said.

Our county secretary, Tim Floyd, had two tickets arranged for the senior panel but as I was going to be in the stadium two hours before the match I gave those tickets to my girlfriend, Elaine Gleeson, so she could bring her father, Paddy. I thought no more about it until I arrived at the ground and went to the press entrance.

'You have no ticket, you can't get in,' the bloke at the turnstile, not a local, I hasten to add, told me.

A few people had gathered around at this stage and were looking at me. Gordon Manning, a GAA journalist with the *Irish Sun*, approached your man and told him who I was. Sure the fella didn't give a shite; if I didn't have a ticket I wasn't getting past him and that was that.

I disappeared straight away because I didn't want to create a scene. I just slipped around the corner and rang Philly Butler, the groundsman, who brought me up to the RTÉ box.

The last thing I wanted was a fuss but of course it appeared in the newspapers two days later. I think your man on the gate was dead right – he's probably under pressure all the time to let in ex-hurlers and well-known people but you have to be thick about it. If a lad is everyone's friend how will he ever say no? He was only doing his job. He certainly brought me back down to earth!

I knocked a great bit of craic out of that episode and it was just one of several memorable days I had following on from that All-Ireland win – and maybe there were a few too many of those, truth be told. There were times when I went out for a pint and ended up going mad altogether. Drinks would be thrown in front of me and it's not so much that you'd be worried about consuming too many pints, it was a case of where you might end up.

# 14

# Everything changes

That buzz wasn't going to last for ever, though. In fact my bubble was burst on 5 October 2010, when Eoin Kelly's number flashed up on my mobile.

'Lar, I've something to tell you and it's serious.'

In all my years knowing Eoin, 'serious' was not a word I'd ever associated with him. No matter how bad the situation or how tight the corner, there was always an exit strategy or escape route. Nothing fazes him; that's just the type of lad he is. This time, though, he was worried.

'The lads are gone,' he blurted. 'Sheedy, Eamon O'Shea, Mick Ryan. It's done and dusted. They've already told the county board, done it all by the book and there's nothing we can do. They're finished.'

'Huh? You're joking!'

'I wish I was. Just got the call there now. Not a hope of getting them to reconsider. They'll be releasing a statement tomorrow.'

Shocked, I mumbled a few words – haven't a clue what they were – and put the phone down. Then I started crying. Crying! Out of nowhere the tears just welled up. It was like a family had broken up. Elaine was in the room and thought from my reaction that someone had just died. She asked what was wrong but I just sobbed quietly. She had never seen me cry before and I don't know what she made of it.

'They're gone – Liam, Eamon, Mick Ryan. They're after telling the county board,' I told her. 'A statement is being drafted. Fuck it anyway!'

Elaine knew how highly I regarded the three men in question and did her best to offer a positive spin. 'Sure they might be persuaded to come back. Or maybe Nicky will come in again.'

Nicky English. That would be something. But it was unlikely. I looked her in the eye and said it straight out: 'Elaine, that's me finished. That's me done.'

She knew I wasn't joking. I had often told Pa that I would see out my career with those three lads. It was just the connection we had, how I got on with them as a unit within the set-up. They had arrived into the job after years of confusion in the Tipp camp, taken over a broken team and led us up the steps of the Hogan Stand. They were like a tonic. Before they landed, managers were coming and going; key players would be dropped hours or minutes before championship matches; we had become a shambles. A laughing stock.

The thoughts of starting all over again with a new crowd absolutely sickened me. I had been in intercounty hurling nearly ten years and I just hadn't the stomach for building more connections with a new bunch of managers and selectors. I felt in my heart that I would never work under a better set-up than the one to which we were waving goodbye. They had raised the bar each year they were with us. And Kelly was right – it was pointless trying to talk them out of it.

I looked at Elaine again and asked her to go downtown with me for a drink. But my head was fried and I lasted only about twenty minutes. I was just too upset. On the way home I turned to her.

'Elaine, I'm almost sure I've played my last game for Tipp.'

The next few days were miserable for me. I felt left down and I know a few of the other boys did as well. I felt that way because I would never have easily become attached to anyone. Those who know me best know I don't latch on to others too quickly. While I'll chat away to anyone, on a deeper level I have kind of a stand-off personality until I really get to know someone.

I latched on to Liam and Eamon, though. I trusted everything they said, both on and off the field. The relationship went much deeper than hurling. Liam might ring me or I could buzz him with something that had been on my mind, a problem I needed to unravel. It was the same with Eamon.

The team was one close circle – it wasn't just the management team saying something from the top of a room, but not meaning it. Over the years other people would have stood up in dressing-rooms and talked the talk but I knew that when they were gone away they weren't thinking that way at all – they just said stuff because it sounded good at the time.

What Liam and Eamon said they meant. And I felt betrayed when they stepped aside. I felt that everything I believed in counted for nothing. They had their own circumstances and reasons for leaving and I get that now but I just didn't see it at the time.

In the days and weeks after they walked I couldn't understand it. I felt that although I was coming to the latter stages of my career we were going to go to a place that no Tipp team had gone before. And they would bring us there.

We had nearly beaten the best team of all time in 2009 – the whole country knew how close we were to winning that final – and we believed in those three lads even more because they had taken us to that position. Everything they said seemed to come to pass. They had come into the camp in 2008 and built us up from nothing like they had developed a company from scratch.

God, I was just so let down and I didn't know how to deal with it in my own mind.

The aggression levels built up inside me. One day I typed out a long text message and sent it to Sheedy:

*How many times did you mention the word "family" in front of us? You spoke about togetherness – that we were all taking this journey together, but really what you said to me was not true.*

He rang me back and I spent half an hour on the phone with him. In fairness, everything he told me about his reasons for leaving the job made sense from his point of view but back then I didn't see it. I was being selfish and looking at things only from my point of view.

As the winter of 2010 set in I wasn't a happy person. My mind was racing and when my mind is racing I'm almost impossible to deal with. When I ask myself a question I'll always get an answer that suits me. At the time I thought Liam was the one being selfish; I know now it was me.

The world doesn't stop for one man, however, and the county board set about the task of replacing the three lads. For two weeks solid there was only one name on the list: Nicky.

Everyone in the county has huge respect for Nicky English and what he's done for Tipp. He would be the closest thing we'd ever get to replacing the lads who were leaving. As well as that I owed him big time. To say he took a chance on me when he drafted me into the Tipp panel in 2001 would be a massive understatement; I was nothing before he took that gamble.

An informal agreement was struck: Eoin Kelly, John O'Brien and I were dispatched to go and doorstep him in Dublin. We were given a simple brief by a county board officer: 'Just go up and see what his situation is.'

We drove to Dublin, headed out the M50 to where our man lived, between Blackrock and Sandymount, and knocked on Nicky's door. His wife, Anne, opened it and burst out laughing.

'I think there are a few lads here to see you,' she called out.

He walked out to us. 'Ah Jesus, will ye go away,' he said jokingly before inviting us in.

We had a general chinwag over a cup of tea before Nicky asked if we would be partial to a beer. We said why not? He checked the fridge but came up empty-handed, so being the perfect host, he offered to scout his local for something to quench our thirst. And we decided it would be bad manners to have him going down there on his own. I can't recall the whole conversation that evening – but I do know there was feck-all talk about the Tipp job. We got that out of the way early on.

Nicky was interested in coming back – you could see that a mile away – but he was up to his eyes with work and needed to negotiate with his employers at the time, AIB, to see what was possible. He doubted there would be a good outcome and we had to respect that. It's all very well giving up time for something you love but you can't jeopardise livelihood and family.

We'd had a few pints when he got up to leave. But instead of going home the three of us agreed it would be a pity to waste a rare night in Dublin – so we headed to Flannery's Bar on Camden Street. Punters there kept asking what we were up to; we just said we were doing 'ambassadorial work' and they seemed happy with that.

It had been great to see Nicky again and we got the message across that everyone wanted him, but leaving Dublin we kind of knew he wouldn't be the next Tipp manager. Not because he didn't want to but because there was no way, especially in the middle of a recession, he could combine it with a demanding job in banking.

The hunt to replace Sheedy and the boys hadn't got off to a good start. I began having serious doubts that we'd ever properly replace them.

By the time Declan Ryan, Tommy Dunne and Michael Gleeson – or 'Glossy' as we call him – were appointed in November, however, I had talked myself out of quitting.

Even though I knew it would be impossible to form a bond like the one I had with the three boys just departed, I didn't want any regrets, so I went back training. I returned on the basis that, after the year I'd had, winning the All-Ireland and scoring for fun, my confidence would surely see me through the 2011 season.

But right from the start, things felt different under the new boys. That's not necessarily a reflection on them, because it usually feels weird for a while with a change of managers. In a way it's like starting a new job – you have to learn and see everything all over again, this time from their point of view. Looking back now – and it's only now I see it clearly – when I came in for the 2011 season I was still feeling hurt from the previous management resigning.

I tried to persuade myself to never mention Liam or Eamon again. As we tore into preparations for the new campaign Eoin Kelly spoke up and said we all had to move on.

'No point in looking back on what we used to do, lads – what will we do in the future?' he asked.

Eoin was right, of course, but he might as well have been talking to a brick wall as talking to me. As the 2011 season progressed I have no problem in saying that while I gave all I could in training and in matches, I probably didn't show the new management the respect they deserved because in my head I kept comparing everything to the old order.

At one stage Liam himself told me to drive on and not look back but the hostility I felt towards the lads for leaving only grew stronger and it was not healthy. Without knowing it I brought that anger with me into the new season. The seeds of a perceived betrayal were planted in my psyche and it wasn't a good thing.

One consolation, I suppose, was that most of the backroom team stayed in place: Cian O'Neill, our fitness trainer; John Casey, our physio; Hotpoint, aka John Hayes, our kitman; and people like Dr Peter Murchan and Mick Clohessy.

When the pre-season dawned I challenged myself to lift it again. As the weeks passed, though, I couldn't see anything like the movement game that had just carried us to All-Ireland glory. We had a slow start to the league and then began winning a few games, but behind it all we seemed to be losing our way. By the time the league finished and the championship loomed I was still looking for a game plan, still looking for the old ways.

But I clutched on to the positives.

We got through the Clare game and reached another Munster final, against Waterford. Anything I touched that day turned to gold and the sliotar just seemed to follow me around – hence my four goals. I ran from midfield for one of those and I think the ball ricocheted off two Waterford lads on the way before it finally trickled into my path. I suppose I had to make that run in the first place but it was a day where everything just clicked. For another goal I took a left-handed swipe at the ball and it whizzed into the net. It could just as easily have flown into the terrace.

I kept moving that afternoon. I could see too that Jerome Maher, the young lad I was marking, was a bag of nerves and I wouldn't blame him because for years I was nervous too.

The game was never in doubt and with another Munster title in the trophy cabinet and four goals in the bag I typed out a text to Eamon when I reached the dressing-room.

*Four goals. Well, are you happy now?*
For some reason I never sent it.

Dublin awaited us in the All-Ireland semi-final and they were all over us. We were lucky to get out alive. Against the run of play I managed a goal but even though I ended up with 1-3 my marker, Peter Kelly, was nominated for man of the match. I still have people saying he beat me up and down the field but I'll be honest – if I got a goal and three points every game I played I'd be delighted.

Dublin were physical and they were fast and we were all over the place, which didn't help matters. In the end we needed two points from Paudie from wing-back, a sideline cut from Noel and two sixty-fives from Eoin to get through.

Looking back, the writing was on the wall after that Dublin game. We were lucky boys to reach another All-Ireland final. But our good fortune was about to run out.

Hindsight is twenty-twenty vision. After we lost to Kilkenny in the All-Ireland final I heard it said that they were hungrier than us, that we weren't even looking sharp in the warm-up and that we relied too much on the long ball. I read an interview with Brian Cody after the game where he said he could 'almost smell' the hunger off his players.

I don't know about that sort of stuff. Who was hungrier in 2009? Were we all that much hungrier than them in 2010 when they pushed us to the last minute? It's easy to say these things after a game.

We hit thirty-two long balls into the full-forward line and won only ten of them. In the few days after the final every expert in the land laid bare our tactical deficiencies. They failed to recall that we managed 4-13 from long balls in the Munster final and that three of our goals had come from the direct ball in the 2010

All-Ireland. People just see things and go with it, but it's easy to be wise afterwards.

Along with several others I was slated for not showing up but I handled the ball three times and set up a goal and a point.

Tipp fans had a go at some of us for wearing our tracksuit tops in the warm-up, which they reckoned was not befitting an All-Ireland final. I was one of those wearing a warm-up top. I had also worn a warm-up top before the 2009 and 2010 finals, and I don't remember getting flak for it after those games.

There was a bit of drizzle before two of those All-Ireland finals and I don't see the point in being wet before the ball throws in. After all we're on the field at five past three and the game doesn't start until half past – or sometimes a minute or two after that.

On days like that I always wear a top warming up; the same way I always bring four hurleys with four new grips whenever rain is forecast for a match; the same way I always wear long studs in Croke Park.

Around 2006 I realised that multi-studs, comfortable as they are, just would not cut it on the sand-based Croke Park surface. I chanced them again for the 2010 All-Ireland quarter-final but had to take them off after twenty minutes in favour of the long stud. Had I still been wearing cogs there was no way I would have been able to turn without slipping near the end of that game and shoot the winning point.

So it's the same routine all the time: four broken-in hurleys with four new grips the morning of a game, long-stud boots and a top for the warm-up.

We went five points down in the opening ten minutes and we were still half asleep when Michael Fennelly ghosted through the middle of the field to fire a goal. From there on we were fighting for our survival.

John O'Keeffe had been preferred to the fit-again Brendan Maher, and Henry Shefflin went straight over on him and latched on to nearly every ball Tommy Walsh hit his way.

The lads in charge were crucified for starting John, but while many people in the county probably wanted the more experienced Brendan to start there wasn't much talk of the move in the dressing-room beforehand, because we knew how good John was. We also knew that Shefflin would go straight over on him but there wasn't much concern about that. Henry had done the same thing when Paudie Maher played his first final, in 2009, and he ended up going away from Paudie after twenty minutes.

This time, with Tommy Walsh buzzing around like a hornet and sending diagonal balls into Shefflin's paw, John had little or no chance of curtailing him. But it's not something that players can afford to worry about – we have enough on our minds. That's the job of management.

Throughout the game there were clear signs that Kilkenny's defence just would not be beaten on the day. We were winning plenty of puck-outs but they turned us over eighteen times after we had won possession.

At one stage I got the ball and was slow about hitting it, and Colin Fennelly stuck his head in and blocked me down. For the Kilkenny fans that was like Mel Gibson giving his *Braveheart* horseback speech on the Curragh plain. People said my head dropped after that but while I was slow in striking I did what I always do: I put it behind me and moved on to the next ball. Stuff like that doesn't worry me.

Cody later described the game as the best defensive display of his reign, but I'd look further up the field, where Paudie Maher was put under insane pressure by their forwards. Their plan was simple: cut off our best defender. With Paudie not being able to supply us up front it took sixteen minutes to get our first score – that's not good enough, I admit.

And yet we narrowed the gap to three points near the end. The problem was we never looked like scoring a second goal. If we were hitting points from all over the place it would have been something, but out of the six starting forwards we managed only three points from play.

We came to play a match but they came to Dublin to fight a war.

My head melted even more in the months after that loss. I should have spoken up beforehand. It was our third final in a row against them and a lad with my experience should have known they would have something up their sleeve to keep me quiet after my three goals a year earlier.

After two minutes it was clear as day that Jackie Tyrrell had been given the job of tailgating me and was going to be on my case even if I went to the jacks. I brought him on an amble around the field and when he sauntered out to midfield alongside me I knew for sure he was in it for the long haul. Usually, a defender might trot out to the half-back line before letting someone else take over but Tyrrell was sticking to me like a limpet in heat.

Twelve months earlier I'd been on fire but this time he pulled out of me, dragged me and used every trick in the book to keep me scoreless. Fair play to him, I didn't get a sniff.

At the break, I went to Glossy and Declan and asked for a plan to give Tyrrell the slip – something we should have had beforehand anyway. I told them I was out of the game. I proposed switching with Bonner Maher to mix things up. Glossy told me to try that and see how it went.

But going back out for the second half, even though we were still in sight, I felt we were fighting a losing battle. The structures that could have been in place to counteract Brian Cody's game plan simply weren't there. We had to start thinking outside the box if we were to come back at them. Instead, we just went out to play again.

I told Bonner I was going to roam around in his slot for a few minutes, but in front of 82,000 people I don't think he fully understood what I was saying or doing. My game is all about movement and freedom, but my wings had been clipped and I was limited to setting up John O and Pa for scores. I don't think I hit a ball with my hurley all day. We came back hard at them near the end but it was too little and too late.

The disappointment was absolutely cruel – not just because I didn't play well but because Tipp had been beaten. That hit me harder than anything. We had been forty-seven years trying to put titles back to back and the wait would continue.

My mood didn't improve at the banquet that night. Paudie Maher, a lad I have massive respect for, the best young hurler in the game, and someone I consider a close friend, came over for a chat.

'Larry, I looked over at you during the half-time break and I knew we were beat,' he said. 'The fight just wasn't in you.'

I was stopped in my tracks.

'Seriously, Paudie, did you get that vibe from me?'

'I did. I could tell by you – there was no fire in your eyes.'

It was like being hit by a train.

'Paudie, fair play to you. You're the most honest man I know and I respect that.'

The following day I was still digesting Paudie's words because they were lodged in my brain. It was laid in front of me nice and clear now – if this is all I can offer the backbone of Tipperary hurling, these young lads coming through, I'm in the wrong place.

At this level, sport is a jungle: only the fittest and the best survive. And if the lads in that dressing-room could read my thoughts so easily then I was letting them down. They were wasting energy worrying about me when they needed to be at their most ruthless out the field, where Kilkenny were all over us, hunting us down like ravenous wolves.

If Paudie noticed my body language was off, that I wasn't up for the fight on the day of an All-Ireland final, I had no place in the team. At thirty, I was supposed to be a leader. Yes, after Eamon left I had tried to motivate the younger lads just as he had done – always make sure when you've finished talking to them that they feel better about themselves. That was the aim. Instead, without realising it, I was giving them negative vibes. I was fast running out of reasons to stick around.

The next day we had the homecoming to face. It was lashing rain in the heartland of Tipperary and the inquests had begun well before we pulled into Semple Stadium to meet the supporters.

No-one wanted to be there. We had lost an All-Ireland final that we never even turned up for and I'd imagine the general reaction of Tipp people lay somewhere between crushing disappointment and downright anger. It wasn't all that different within the squad.

I felt it was mortifying having to go out and wave to the people we had just let down. To make matters worse most of us were drinking during the day, and speaking for myself I would rather have been anywhere else in the county.

The sky was leaking bucketloads and the turnout was dire. One of the boys reckoned there were only five thousand supporters on the field and someone else said it's amazing what losing a game would do because there were 45,000 this time last year. To be fair, one look outside partly explained the low turnout.

Still, the county board lads had a job to do: present the team to those who have made the effort to welcome us home. They steered us into The Dome, just behind the pitch, and we were told to hang tough for a while, that if the rain cleared a few more fans might arrive.

That only prolonged the agony. I can't think of anything worse than having to go out there as a bunch of losers. Especially after we hardly landed a blow on Kilkenny and I myself didn't puck a ball.

Pa saw I was struggling and twigged what was going through my mind. I suppose he's a bit guarded himself and maybe that's why we get on. We must have drilled ten thousand pucks at each other over the years and with each shot he probably got to know me better. We built up a right understanding.

Anyway, I needed to get out of there and although I tried hard not to let on, I might as well have had it tattooed in luminous ink across my face. Pa stepped in, reaching across me.

'Lar, if you try to bail out I'll pin you to the fucking floor. Just try me!'

'I can't face it, Pa. I just can't face it,' I replied.

'Try it, Lar, I'm telling you! We have to go out there. You have to go out there.'

I might have known he would read me like a book.

I got lucky. Someone came over for a chat and Pa took his eye off the ball. I threw a few shapes about going for another round of drinks, melted into the crowd and made my escape.

As I put distance between myself and The Dome I was so conspicuous that I might as well have been naked. The few pints on the train down from Dublin had kicked in and the legs were not the best; I felt like a newborn foal trying to run. The rain got heavier and I had no jacket, so the shirt and trousers stuck to me. I just wanted to get over the bridge beside the stadium and run, run, run. The fucking madness of it all.

Supporters passed on the pavement and shot surprised looks.

'Howya, Lar?'

'Where are you off to, Lar?'

'Where's the fire, Corbett?'

I lowered my head and rushed on for fear I'd blurt out something I might regret. I didn't stop running until The Dome and Semple were at a safe distance. Then I paused to gather my thoughts.

'Lar, you're absolutely one hundred per cent right here and everyone knows that. Get away up the town. Get out of here!'

I was talking to myself.

I headed for Liberty Square. There was no-one there so I made tracks for my bar. I popped in there and stayed out of the way. Waited for the lads on the squad to arrive up. Passed the night away.

Some of the panel came up for a drink later. I knew they were disappointed with me, though they didn't say much. Together we drowned the sorrows of another All-Ireland lost. A few of us were in the same boat – played four, won two, lost two.

'Next year,' we told each other, trying to put a brave face on it.

When I woke up on Tuesday morning the silence hit me hard. I knew I'd get serious slack for last night. What in the name of Jesus was I thinking? Even if I was 100 per cent right at the time it didn't make any sense when I awoke.

I dragged myself out of bed and looked around and I knew there was a fork coming in the road.

'You're almost finished here, Larry,' I muttered. 'Your glory days are done.'

The mood didn't lift, to be honest. For months afterwards I had to listen to people telling me I was in Jackie Tyrrell's pocket. Every night I went out his name was mentioned or came up in conversation, whether I was in Dublin or Thurles. I think Elaine was even more fed up hearing about Jackie than I was. You could be out for a meal and his name would crop up at some stage of the night.

The worst was at the 2011 ploughing championships. The previous year I had been at a stall with the former Tipp hurler Michael 'Skippy' Cleary, who was involved with the hurling rebounder net, a useful product for players to practise their skills and touch. People were coming over clapping me on the back, getting their photos taken. Not that I take any of that stuff seriously, but you were the hero if you wanted to be.

Twelve months on it was a much different story. I was back at the stall, close enough to Skippy again, and this time I was a sitting target. One oul' fella came over and made a big deal of taking something out of his pocket. I knew straight away there was a dig coming because he made sure there was a crowd around him. Next thing he handed me an A4 sheet with Jackie's picture on it. He thought he was a great yoke as he walked off without saying a word and everyone around him laughing. I said nothing. What could I say?

It got worse. I would say four or five fathers sent their young lads over to me to ask how Jackie Tyrrell was. I would see them stooping down, whispering in the young lads' ears, shaking with the laughter as if they were the first people to think of slagging me. Brave as lions they were, sending kids to make a smart comment. Look, if that's what gives these fellas a kick, fair enough. But there was a bit of needle in it too. It wasn't done in a laid-back, dry-wit sort of way. I got it in my face that day, with crowds around all the time.

I got a couple of abusive letters from so-called Tipperary supporters. The handwriting was cat in both instances. The person who wrote them accused me and others on the team of going on the beer the Thursday before the final and said I was a disgrace because of how I played. I could go on, but you probably get the point.

You'd imagine I would be safe enough in my own pub but that wasn't the case either. I was working one evening when a lad came up the stairs and made a beeline for me.

'I'm a Kilkenny man,' he said to me.

'Fair play to you,' I replied.

'Would Noel Hickey ever drink in here?' he enquired.

'God, I've no idea. I haven't seen him here,' I said. 'But that's not to say he hasn't been here when I've been off.'

'And would JJ Delaney drink in here?'

'Well, the same thing, I suppose. He might have been here once or twice but I haven't come across him.'

'And would Jackie Tyrrell ever drink here?'

'The same answer as I've given you – maybe but I haven't seen him,' I replied again, waiting for the punchline. But there was no punchline. Your man just thought this was hilarious and cracked up, delighted with himself.

Next thing, and you couldn't make this up, he handed me his business card as if expecting me to keep him in mind if our paths ever crossed down the line. Jesus, I'm only learning about business but surely there's a better way to make a sales pitch.

And on it went for the winter. I dealt with it well enough, I suppose. Each time someone came up and threw Tyrrell's name at me I issued a standard reply.

'Yeah, Jackie is some player, isn't he? Serious.'

# 15

# No easy way to say goodbye

We had reached an All-Ireland final and lorded it in Munster, and in another year that might have been acceptable. To me, though, we weren't really going anywhere. We seemed to be living and dying by the high ball – and I wasn't forgetting it had been good to us in many a tight game – but as a result the movement off the ball was almost non-existent. We had stopped talking among ourselves as well.

We used to have one-on-one meetings with Liam and they were brilliant, but now the channels of communication had dried up and I could sense the confidence of senior players slipping. I included myself in that.

In fairness to Declan and Tommy, they both made efforts to speak to me after we lost to Kilkenny. Declan rang in November of 2011 and suggested we meet. He mentioned that his wife, Olive, suspected I was taking the Kilkenny defeat very badly and was wondering had anyone spoken to me about it.

I replied that I wasn't taking it badly on a personal level but that I was extremely upset for the hurling people of Tipperary. The final hadn't gone well for me but it wasn't just about Lar Corbett.

I didn't know how the conversation might go, Declan and I hadn't had many heart-to-heart conversations, but I agreed to meet him anyway.

When we met, I brought up Kilkenny's game plan and Jackie's role in man-marking me out of the final and wondered what we should have done to counter it. I tried to get stuff off my chest.

I wasn't devastated at being held by Tyrrell; I can't control how other people mark me – all I can do is accept it and try to fight back. Same way if a supporter has a pop at me, I don't take any of that on board. Everyone was making out that I was crushed at being taken out of the game but they were missing the point. Nobody can make you feel inferior without your consent. The point is we should have been able to respond to Kilkenny's tactics.

'God almighty, you're thinking a lot about it!' Declan said.

'Of course I am, Declan!' I replied. 'What's next? Have we a plan? Let's go out and find one!'

We spent two hours sitting there thrashing things out but, although he had the best of intentions, when I went back training a few weeks later there was no sign of anything different. We were back out doing the same things.

Tommy contacted me too. He was going around meeting a few players to see what they could do to drive it on. It was clear that he wanted only the best for us too. But again it didn't seem to produce any great change in our approach.

In between the final and the return to training I went back to my club, Thurles Sarsfields, and scored two goals against Upperchurch at The Ragg. It was a shot in the arm and I was never as glad to get a couple of scores; I felt a bit more confidence seep through the body each time the green flag was raised.

But the spark didn't last long – it went out again when I was sent off in the county semi-final against Clonoulty. I was marking the same lad all day and he did what he could to rile me – digging, dragging and mouthing non-stop. I never really took the bait, bar giving a few digs back, but I got a second yellow card late on and got my marching orders. Worse still, I was held scoreless again.

It was only my second time ever to be sent off. And funny enough, it was the same ref that flashed the red card both times.

The Clonoulty lads didn't spare me.

'Where were you on All-Ireland final day, you useless prick?'

And another dig: 'You couldn't even face the homecoming.'

The papers got their headline and Clonoulty had what they wanted.

Anyway, I wasn't around for the handshakes at the end of the game but had I been I still would have stuck out the paw. You win some and you lose some, but no matter how bad it gets you never let your man on the other side see that he got inside your head.

Later on that night I replayed the game in my mind and wondered what a ten-year-old boy looking on would think of it all. Would he want to be like me, an intercounty hurler being singled out by a club defender, having to take all that sledging – and then actually getting sent off?

Or would he feel that by copying what the Clonoulty man had done he might some day play at the top himself? Would he hear people say, 'Sure that lad held Lar scoreless. Give him a shot!' Would he grow up thinking the smart way to stop lads is to roar in their faces, pull and drag out of them and shout in their ears for seventy minutes?

In terms of my hurling life I was going further down a road I didn't like. I had won another All-Star, my third on the trot, and that was fair cause for celebration. But I was again losing motivation and, worse still, I was less and less optimistic about the road ahead for the Tipp team. I was going soft. I needed to stand back and take a breather.

Before I got a chance to do that, though, the call to arms sounded once more. It felt like the 2011 season had hardly ended when we were preparing for 2012. I went along with it, mostly because I didn't want to finish my career on a negative note.

Every pre-season starts with a gym programme and by God that's one thing I hate. I'm useless at weights and very limited in what I achieve in there. I love ball alley and pucking the sliotar around with the likes of Pa, but horsing barbells and all that is not my scene. It didn't help that our fitness coach, Cian O'Neill, the best I ever worked with, moved on and linked up with the Mayo football team. It was just another sign that the old family was breaking up all the time.

We had an early meeting at the Horse and Jockey hotel and our schedule was set out. Fieldwork and stamina runs on Tuesdays and Thursdays. Gym on Mondays and Wednesdays. Fridays were on the cards too. All of this before Christmas.

Paul Curran was appointed captain and Paudie was his deputy, and as usual Paudie said it straight out: 'Lads, just do the weights – don't be saying halfway through the league that we didn't put it in.'

When Paudie talks people listen so I decided I'd better raise my game. I turned to Pa: 'Do me one favour, Pa – please just call to the house for me and we'll drive to the gym together. I'm right good at coming up with excuses but if you'll call to my door then I have to go.'

Religiously, Pa called to my house for the next few weeks. If we were in the gym at six o'clock he'd be outside my door at ten to six.

He'd text during the day to remind me, and I needed his encouragement, because if I was supposed to lift a weight ten times in the gym I'd lift it only nine if I thought no-one was looking. Then I'd go to the ball alley and flog myself with work I felt was more suited to my game.

This time around we had a personal trainer on board, Keith Hennessy, who supervised us as we worked out. Keith was excellent at his job. He showed me how to do press-ups properly and lift weights with correct technique. But that sort of stuff meant little to me.

I broke away for the All-Stars tour in San Francisco – and the nagging feeling throughout that trip was that it would be my last – spent five nights in New York and looked forward to heading for Australia after Christmas.

The journey down under was a landmark in my life. We went out for the wedding of Elaine's brother, John, and while out there I proposed to Elaine. I also arranged with Setanta Ó hAilpín and Nicholas Walsh – we communicated via Twitter – to visit their AFL club, Greater Western Sydney Giants, and take in a training session.

I was to be there at eight o'clock in the morning, but on the morning in question I arrived with Elaine's father, Paddy, fifteen minutes early. I wanted to see the players arriving for training, observe how they walked in and study their body language. I sat back in the shadows and was happy to watch the whole thing unfold, but I think Paddy began to imagine a career in Aussie Rules for himself – he nearly got stuck into the session and looked like he was getting ready to knock lumps out of people.

Nicholas, who played senior football for Cavan and had worked at Croke Park, introduced himself, and the first thing he demonstrated was the GPS system they use to track the distances players cover in training and games. One of the coaches was concerned that a player was way down on his personal stats so they took him aside and, after a brief but precise assessment, they detected a minor injury, just in time to prevent it becoming a major one. I was impressed by that.

Another thing I spotted was an injured player in a cast doing nothing but throwing an oval ball at a rebounder. I watched him for twenty minutes before I started getting dizzy with the repetition of it all, but he was only getting going; I think he spent the whole morning at it.

The injured lads hit the gym and trained much harder than their teammates on the field because the field was where they wanted to be and I could relate to that. In different pockets of the pitch the forwards trained as a group, doing their own thing, the midfielders assembled together, and the backs worked in tandem too.

Throughout the morning a camera hovered over the pitch capturing every aspect of the session. The squad were then called in to watch the video analysis, and just before they switched on the monitors and screens, the manager, Mark 'Choco' Williams, who in 2004 coached Port Adelaide to their only premiership, called on 'Nick's friends from Ireland' to say a word.

I could tell Paddy was raring to get up and recount his life story – and I'm sure they would have lapped it up – but I hid behind a locker and just thanked them for giving us access to their training. They weren't having it. Mark called me again and told his team they could see my sport and some of my scores on YouTube. I was mortified.

'No, lads, you're grand but thanks, really.'

'Lar, everyone who comes into this room has to tell us about himself,' Williams said bluntly. 'We want to know about you and see if there's anything we can apply to our sport.'

I just shot up and stood with them, said I wouldn't talk about myself but would say how impressed I was with their set-up. I looked across at Setanta as I told them that although GAA players prided themselves on being professional we weren't in the same ballpark as them.

Nicholas invited me in and we walked into a room with long, soft couches and about three lads sitting on each one. Again Paddy hopped straight into one group, determined to soak up all he could, while I looked around and saw the man I wanted to quiz. His name was Stewart Edge and he was a forwards coach. He reminded me a little of Eamon O'Shea – no laptop, no gimmicks, just short answers and players leaving him with a smile on their faces. Eventually I got the chance to approach him. Maybe it's sad, but here I was on holidays, still half tormented by the events of the previous September.

'Stewart, can I give you a scenario?' I asked. 'Maybe you could give me your opinion and I'll translate that back into my own terms.'

'Sure,' he replied.

'2010,' I began. 'A major final in my sport. Two teams and 82,000 people. I have the freedom of the park, the run of the house. If I was walking across the square with my back to the play a ball would have gone in off my arse.

'2011. The same venue and the same teams. Everything is the same only the guy that's marking me this time dogs me for seventy minutes. If I went to the takeaway at half-time he'd be there beside me grabbing my chips. I don't get a score. I don't get a sniff.'

He cut me short. 'Ah, you were being tagged,' he said, grasping the gist of my story.

He seemed interested and immediately explained how they would plan for this situation.

'Your man was given a job by his manager but you don't necessarily have to go with that,' Stewart insisted. 'There should be a couple of back-up options. You can play a role for the team; try and roam and find space. Take the defender out of his comfort zone into a position he is most uncomfortable with. The movement you create will open room for others.

Even though you're out of the game you can open doors for others.

'For example, the opposition would have changed their defensive set-up to match your attack, therefore there should be opportunities for some of your other forwards if you can get the right match-ups in the right positions. Your original marker will follow you regardless but you can do a job for the team even with him down your neck.'

I paused to take it all in. You couldn't but be impressed by the thought process and level of detail that went into their planning for every situation. But Stewart wasn't finished.

'The opposition is intent on keeping you out of the action – but other forwards can run into space and make a serious impact while this is going on. Their coaches might get doubts and they could decide to alter their game plan – one they thought was foolproof.'

I felt a load being lifted off my mind there and then. I had been killing myself, wondering was there anything I could have done to make more of an impact on All-Ireland final day. It seemed we had just let Kilkenny do what they wanted but deep down I felt we could have counteracted their system.

Stewart then proceeded to talk about different ways he has to look at a game if things aren't working. He seemed to have a plan B and even a plan C for every game if his first theory didn't work. I was blown away by his analysis.

Before we parted company he put it in perspective: 'Look, Lar, this is sport. There are no guarantees that any of these templates would have worked for you. If there was a guarantee there would be no such thing as sport. But I'll tell you one thing – having systems like these are food for thought.'

I got back to our house in Manly and, like a child with a shiny new toy, struggled to keep my findings to myself. On my return home I spoke to one of the senior lads on the team about them.

I was after being challenged and felt I could bring home some of this stuff to the Tipp team. I came home with an open mind and I was already planning to meet Declan and Tommy and run them past them. Looking back I can see that I probably lost the run of myself.

The grunt from my teammate at the other end of the line was certainly less than encouraging.

'For God's sake, Larry, will you let it go! Eamon and the boys might have used stuff like that but they're gone. Will you ever get that into your head!'

Maybe he was right but I was disappointed at the reaction. The frustration from losing the All-Ireland final was building up inside and I didn't know where to go. I wondered if the problem was only in my head, and I didn't want to step on anyone's toes by talking any more about the final. Instead, I just bottled it all up.

I returned to training with Tipp on 3 January 2012, but I soon felt I was only delaying the inevitable. Even though we were training harder and doing more work I still couldn't see progress. Communication had hardly improved, and we were not being challenged any more than before.

I'm not saying the coaches were not putting it in – they were giving it everything – but I don't know if we were confident of reaching that next level. That was just the way I saw things.

I could do press-ups properly and lift weights without slipping a disc, but so what? What was our game plan for 2012? What direction were we going in?

I also had to look at myself. I was definitely going soft. Maybe I didn't want to struggle any more. People were doing their living best for me but still I wasn't happy.

Matters didn't improve when I trained with Tipp at Dr Morris Park on the last Monday in January. That was when a routine injury and the reaction – or lack of reaction – to it led me to make up my mind for once and for all.

During training I took an awful knock to my knee. I hit the ground straight away in agony. It was a dead leg, the likes of which happen every day in contact sports, so it was no big deal – but this time the pain was just killing me.

I was lying on the pitch for about a minute when I looked around and saw Declan and Glossy about thirty metres away. Neither of them was rushing over. I felt like letting a roar: I'm fucking injured here, lads, any chance ye'd like to give me a hand? I didn't want to be there. No-one else was showing any interest in coming over either. For those few seconds I felt isolated but then I thought, Grand, they have thirty-five players to look after. I'm not the only one here on the field.

I lay on the ground for a while, unable to get up, until Dr Kevin Delargy came over, helped me to his car, and drove me back to The Dome.

'I'll tell you one thing,' I moaned. 'You wouldn't want to be having a heart attack on that field.'

I couldn't take off my tracksuit bottoms. Our physio, John Casey, gave me a hand, examined me and said it was a real beauty of a dead leg – I'd be out for maybe four weeks.

There was no way I could drive home so Pa dropped me off while Paul Curran and Eoin Kelly brought the van back to my house. I was thoroughly pissed off, and my mood didn't really lift when Tuesday passed without any contact from Declan, Tommy or Glossy. The same on Wednesday. By the time Thursday arrived my head was melting. Still nothing on Friday.

Tipp were playing University of Limerick in the Waterford Crystal tournament on the Saturday. When I didn't go to that match one of the lads on the team texted me asking what was the story. I replied that there hadn't been a word from anyone since I got the injury on Monday night.

I don't for a second think that Declan and the lads were questioning the fact I was injured, but I felt they should have contacted me in case it was more serious, or at least spoken to me.

Those few days of communications blackout proved the straw that broke the camel's back. I had reached the 100 per cent mark in my decision. I rang my mother and told her I was calling it a day. I also told Elaine. No-one else.

Mam said to do whatever I was most comfortable with, and Elaine knew by the look on my face that I wasn't for turning.

I felt a rush of adrenaline, a weight lifted from my shoulders. I was still walking on air when, a couple of days later, I reached for the phone and rang Declan, and I could tell he was a little taken aback when I asked to meet him.

'Is it something serious, Lar?'

I wasn't going to do it over the phone. Elaine wouldn't let me in any case. 'Look, we'll have a chat. I'll be out to you in a few minutes.'

I headed to Clonoulty and knocked on his door. He welcomed me and led me out to the shed for a chat. This was a man I had started off with on the Tipp team as a player, a teammate who had looked out for me on my debut in 2001 when we played Clare. He came to my aid then when Brian Quinn was all over me, trying to shake me up. Now I had to tell him I was quitting. It wasn't simple.

'Dec, there's something on my mind and it's been there for the last few weeks – I won't be able to give the full commitment and I'm taking a step back from the whole lot. Making a go of the bar is getting on top of me. I can't go full steam ahead on that and play hurling to this level at the same time. I can't give Monday to Friday training with a game at the weekend because I'm never in the pub and that has to change.'

I could tell he wasn't fully convinced I was stepping aside.

'Well, that's a relief,' he said after a few seconds. 'I thought you were going to tell me you were off to Australia or something.'

There had been rumours since my trip down under and some people chose not to believe it was simply a three-week holiday to take in John's wedding; it had to be that I was checking the lie of the land with a view to emigrating.

'No, I have an opportunity to try making a go of it in Ireland with the bar and I'm going to have to make the most of it,' I responded.

I had decided there was no real point in bitching any further about my thoughts on the set-up. At that stage I reckoned there was no turning back and I wanted to make the break as cleanly as possible without getting into pros and cons about training methods or team tactics. I had no intention of hurting Declan's feelings.

Anyway, I really don't think it's my job as a player to tell the manager how to do his job – I'm well aware I'm only passing through here. Whatever my personal preferences I wasn't entitled to cast aspersions on those running the team.

Declan asked me straight out if I had problems with the set-up, but I sidestepped by saying the difficulties were mostly on my side of the fence and it was all about not being able to make a full commitment any more.

I think he appreciated that work was coming more and more into the equation but he probably sensed I wasn't overly happy with various things and was not for turning at that time. The last thing he needed from me was a rant on what I thought was wrong with the squad. Taking potshots at people is not my style anyway.

It was important that I left Declan's house with my conscience clear and our relationship intact. I had no problems personally with Declan, Tommy, Glossy or my teammates, and I didn't want that to change. Since 2010, I had half wanted out and, win or lose, I had been edging closer to the exit door all the time. I only regretted that I didn't retire in 2010 when we reached the summit.

Declan is a good man. He continued to try talking me around.

'Is there anything we can do to help you out? God, you'll be a huge loss.'

'No, I'm not here to negotiate, Dec. My mind's made up for the moment. I hope the lads can drive it on for you.'

Still he didn't give up. He surveyed his shed and came up with a suggestion: 'You don't have to do all the gym work, Lar. We can put structures in place with the instructors. We'll work out a different scenario.'

He said to take six weeks off and then make the call. Again, I said thanks, but no. He eventually realised I wasn't having a moan or making an empty threat. Thinking about it a little further, he looked me in the eye.

'You're after having three unreal years,' he said.

It may sound pathetic that someone who has been at or near the top for eleven years and won a bit might need to be boosted but that's how it is and I probably needed to hear such encouragement a bit earlier. We all need to hear nice stuff about ourselves, because I think we're all built on confidence. And mine had been knocked. It was part of the reason I was here in Clonoulty.

We both knew leaving the panel wouldn't look good for anyone so I insisted I was going to deal only with the here and now and not be prolonging the agony by leaving a question mark hanging.

We had been there about half an hour when the conversation wrapped up. We shook hands. I just looked at him and said, 'Declan, I started off with you and here I am leaving with you now. I hope there are no hard feelings.'

And I meant it. I wanted no cheap dig. I was only saying honestly what I was feeling. I kept thinking back to a great picture taken of the two of us and Eoin Kelly on my debut over a decade earlier. He was a hero of ours and there he was standing in the centre like a protective father with a wide arm around each of us as the national anthem sounded – just like that photo of big Mick Galwey 'minding' Peter Stringer and Ronan O'Gara as they lined up together in 2000 for their first Ireland rugby cap.

I went home and rang Paul Curran and Paudie Maher. Paudie thinks a bit like me and he knew my decision was made so he didn't even bother trying to talk me out of it. He was taken aback, though: 'Okay, right. Fuck. I appreciate the phone call, Larry.'

Paul asked if I was certain of what I was doing and wondered if I should think it over a bit further. He warned that there would be a big media storm headed our way. I reassured him I'd be grand and would handle all that.

'Paul, I'm only here to deal directly with you as captain. I don't want to lose any relationship I've built up with a Tipp player. I want to be able to go to matches in years to come, meet for a pint or whatever, and have a chat.'

I gave Ger Ryan, our PRO, a heads-up too because we had an excellent relationship and I felt he needed notice of this before the reporters got on his trail. After that it was down to telling the lads on the panel.

I typed out a text and showed it to Elaine but it was basic enough and she wasn't impressed. She reckoned that after spending the best part of twelve years with most of those lads I owed them a more thought-out message. She was right. The text to teammates was every bit as important as giving Declan the news face to face.

I struggled, though, as I tried to put my thoughts down on paper – English composition was never my strong point in school – so I turned to Elaine for help.

Elaine is a schoolteacher and is great with words. I might hold my own against her in a bit of verbal banter, but if it comes to text or email and, say, thrashing out something we disagree on, she wins the argument every time. I told her what I wanted to get across and she scribbled a few lines and read it back to me. After a few changes we sent it off.

*Well lads, I'm sorry to say that I have withdrawn from the Tipp panel. I know this may come as a shock but, after careful consideration, I know that I cannot give the 100 per cent commitment that is required. I did not want to give this news by text but I could not ring everyone. I hope my decision will not affect the friendships I have made over the years.*

*This decision was one of the hardest yet. I do not have all of the panel members' numbers so can you please pass this on as I want you, the players, to be the first to know. I look forward to the second Sunday in September when I will be shouting on the players and the team I love. Larry.*

In hindsight it was just as well that I put a bit of thought into my farewell – and got Elaine to compose it – because the message ended up in all the national newspapers and on TV. I was pretty disappointed with that, saddened for the panel that some lad had decided to break ranks and throw the message out into the public domain. We always strove to be a close family and I still wonder how it ended up in the papers.

When I sat down to watch the *Six One* news the night after I stepped away I saw my text appear on screen. 'Mother of God,' I thought. 'I didn't mean for the entire population of Ireland to read it.'

As soon as word got out on 7 February my phone started hopping so I just switched it off, watched TV for a while and went to bed, feeling a huge burden had been eased from my mind.

People say I should have expected what was coming next but

I genuinely didn't. I woke up the following morning and there were sixty or seventy text and phone messages from players and friends, and as many again from journalists and producers of TV and radio shows. The mobile just hopped so I turned it off again. I didn't like hitting the off button – it's my phone and I should be able to answer it when anyone rings – but I reckoned every media caller would be on for at least three minutes. And since I wouldn't be making any comment for the media just yet, it would be the bones of 210 minutes wasted saying nothing.

I had been dealing with the media for years and learned a bit as I went along. From 2008 the public interest had really picked up because things were obviously going better for me on the pitch. I knew the reporters had jobs to do and had editors on their backs, and I also remembered they had been extremely good to me when I opened my bar, helping to spread the news.

Friends suggested I should hold a press conference but I'm an amateur sportsman and I feel I don't necessarily have the same obligations as a professional. Yes, journalists had been good to me, but I had been good to them too, and I felt in the present situation I didn't owe them anything. Out of courtesy I did speak to a few of them a couple of days after making the announcement but my message was always the same: 'Thanks for everything, lads, but I'm saying nothing on this occasion.'

People asked if I was stressed by the whole media circus but it didn't take a peep out of me. The same cannot be said for others around me. The day after the news became public I went about my business downtown and managed to get into the pub without being seen. Kevin came out looking like he'd seen a ghost.

'Reporters,' he said, trying to catch his breath. 'They're everywhere. Down in the car park, out around the square – they're in and out of the pub. Feckin' cameras and tripods everywhere. It's cruel.'

I took refuge in the upstairs office and lay low for a couple of hours until Kevin came up again.

'Larry, they're going nowhere,' he warned. 'They're after spotting your van and now they're camped out beside it. We're after getting a call from one of the lads at the Horse and Jockey – there's more of them on the way over to you.'

My white van was sponsored by Barlo Motors and the logo on the side actually incorporated my name, but it was so subtle it was barely visible. Fair play to the reporters, though, they're good at their jobs because they spotted it and duly dug in and waited for my parking ticket to expire.

What they didn't suspect, though, is that the local traffic wardens are sound men and Coppinger and I get on well with them – we knew that in the circumstances they wouldn't kill us with parking fines. Eventually the hacks regrouped in the pub and asked my barman where they might find me.

'Not a clue,' my man said, as innocent as he could manage, two floors below me.

Undeterred, the posse ordered teas and coffees.

By now I myself was starving, so I texted the barman below to fetch me up a bite to eat. He was just about to fill my order when one of the regulars asked for a pint. Without thinking, my man guarding the pass called out, 'Hang on, Jim, I'm just bringing a sandwich up to Larry.'

My cover was blown and the hacks rolled around laughing. They stayed put for a fair while longer, hoping I'd eventually come down to them. I was made to wait for that sandwich, I can tell you.

The press corps got more than they bargained for when they rang my mother, Breda. When the *Late Late Show* phoned her she did a bit of horse-trading by telling them she would try persuading me to do the show if they sent her four audience tickets. She knew well there was no point even asking me, but the tickets arrived in the post two days later.

Marty Morrissey of RTÉ also met his match when he got through to her. He asked her to have a word with me, persuade me that it would be better to get my real story across and confound the rumour mongers. She said she would do what she could.

'And before I let you go, Marty, now that Larry has left the squad, I'm going to need someone to help me get tickets for Croke Park. What's your number again?'

It did get crazy, though. The cameras eventually left Thurles but the phone calls didn't stop. I woke up on Wednesday to see my mush on the front page of the *Irish Independent* and I was there on the back page too with a big banner headline: 'WAS THERE A BUST-UP?'

There were two full pages in the news section as well. All of the papers carried the story, front and back pages, and apart from the *Late Late*, I got calls from *Primetime*, the *John Murray Show*, *TV3*, *Newstalk* and anyone else you can think of. I was almost waiting for *Loose Women* from Channel 4 to give me a buzz. Come to think of it, I might have given them a shot.

Rumours were flying around that I had had a slagging match with Tommy Dunne and a war of words with Declan. With hand on heart I can tell you there were no rows. I'm just not into confrontation and never have been. In fact, the only heated arguments I've had in the recent past were probably with Liam Sheedy when he pulled me up on a few things during his stint in charge. But even then there are good ways to have a confrontation. This time I had no argument with anyone, good, bad or indifferent.

There were other stories. I was supposedly pissed off at not being appointed captain. Then Elaine was supposed to be calling the shots now we had become engaged.

*

Just as the whole thing started to die down, the name M Morrissey popped up on my mobile again. Marty is a gas ticket. This time he rang looking for a big interview, for my benefit. It seemed there was sensationalist stuff about to break in the Sunday papers – he reckoned it would be in my best interests to nip it all in the bud.

'I'll come down to Thurles and we'll do an interview,' he reassured me. 'We'll sort it out and, bang, everything will be squashed before the Sunday papers get at it.'

I responded politely: 'Ah, I'm happy enough with the way things are at the moment, Marty. Sure I'm under no pressure at all – the media have been dead sound.'

His number appeared on my phone once more the next day.

'Lar, I'll be coming through Thurles at some stage on the way to Clare. As a friend I think this is the angle you need to come at. A lot of rumours were about the place over the past few years but one interview always nipped them in the bud.'

'Look, I appreciate the call, Marty, but no thanks.'

'There need be no cameras, no audio, nothing,' he persisted. 'I just want to meet one-on-one for a chat. You know as well as I do that there's an undercurrent in the camp and it's not as settled as it was.'

I knew if I gave any response whatsoever to that last statement I was leaving myself open to being quoted, so I put on my best number-ten rugby shirt and kicked for touch. Like an answering machine I just kept repeating the same message.

'Ah sure I'm happy enough at the minute, Marty. But sure if you want to drop by as a friend I'll meet you for a coffee anytime.'

And that was it.

The Sunday papers came out and I actually enjoyed reading them because I was fascinated by how they perceived my decision. The Sunday papers have to take a distinctive line and I had suspected they would try to read my mind and reach similar conclusions. That's exactly what happened and some of the articles were close enough to the facts. At times it was like reading my own first-hand account of how the past couple of seasons had panned out.

I didn't mind what was written anyway, whether it was pretty accurate or way off the mark. It was interesting to see the different takes on it. I enjoyed talking to Marty too, witnessing how a seasoned TV journalist works and learning something about the efforts he makes to get the story. We never did meet for that coffee.

After a couple of days the circus left town, as I knew it would, and life soon returned almost to normal. I kept my head high – I kept reminding myself I had as much right as anyone else to walk up and down the town. People in Thurles were asking questions but they were well entitled to after the media invasion and the support they had given me, and I have to say the neighbours around the town backed me to the hilt.

I was treated very well by everyone. The newspaper lads wrote some grand things and once the rumours of a falling-out died down everything was fine.

I couldn't understand, though, when Ben O'Connor retired a few weeks later, why there was barely a mention of it in the media. I was out of the country at the time and first saw the news on Twitter, but the lads back home told me there was nothing like the hype that had followed my decision.

Ben was one of the best forwards in the game over ten years and captained Cork to the 2004 All-Ireland title. He was possibly the most consistent of them all in terms of the way he played and the big scores he got. Compare that to my career and the four or five years I hardly struck a ball in anger. I still can't make it out.

I faced into the spring of 2012 happy that I'd made the right call. Sometimes, though, peace of mind follows a decision even when it's the wrong one.

# 16

# Pay cheque or professionalism?

Very few people bought my line about 'business commitments' to explain walking away from the team and they weren't slow in telling me.

One guy stopped me in the street: 'Larry, I heard you had it out with the boys over the team. I'm just lettin' you know I don't for a second believe this crap about not having the time. And no-one else does either.'

He was right: people were throwing their eyes to heaven when they heard my story; most of them reckoned that if I had really wanted to stay with Tipp I'd have found a way. They're entitled to their opinion, but then not many of them would have a clue what was going on behind the scenes.

I'm the sort of bloke who will sit down in front of the TV of an evening and maybe throw on the National Geographic channel – I love their wildlife documentaries. But while I'm looking at the programme and taking it in, other thoughts will be running through my mind and bugging me, especially if there is a big game on the horizon. My eyes might be focused on the TV but

I'll actually be thinking about the game next weekend. I used to place massive emphasis on visualisation, picturing myself fielding the sliotar and rounding lads and scoring goals and all that. If I'm into something I'm into it 150 per cent.

As a child I was out banging a sliotar non-stop against the neighbours' walls but it only got worse as I grew up; there were times I'd have to hop off the couch and go puck a ball, just to try and work out some move or tactic that was going through my head. The next-door wall was roughly the same size as a hurling goal-frame, so I'd think of the opposing keeper waiting for me that weekend and I'd be placing balls to his weak side.

In recent years, no matter what I did, I found I was always thinking of hurling. I'd go and get a sandwich for lunch and would eat all the right sort of stuff – not because it was the food I liked best but because the nutritionist had recommended it. I tried to do everything right.

I had worked from the moment I left school, and after I had done my apprenticeship the ten years I spent with my electrician bosses, Ray Corbet and Tom McDonald, were brilliant. A wage packet was waiting for me every Friday. I didn't know where the money came from and to be honest I didn't care; once the cheque was in my hand I was grand.

Life was fine until the recession kicked in. Soon I was working part-time – a week on and a week off. Then it got worse, a week on and two weeks off, and eventually three weeks off. It was brutal having no work to go to and I hated it, but the lads had no choice; everything had dried up in the building game.

Eventually, after much deliberation, I had no choice but to head to the Social Welfare office and sign on for dole, or job-seekers' allowance as they politely label it these days. I signed on for the first time in my life on 24 January 2009 and stayed on the register until 13 April 2011. Those are dates that will stay with me for ever.

After the welfare people took my details they posted out a form that I immediately called the Xs and Os sheet because of the number of multiple-choice questions you had to answer and the number of boxes you had to tick.

There was an upside to claiming social welfare: the free time allowed me to prepare better than ever for matches. And so my time on the dole coincided with the most prolific spell of my hurling career. But it also left me in the biggest quandary of my life. Through hurling I had a higher profile than I had ever bargained for, and to an extent I was public property around Thurles. I'm not saying I am any better than, or different from, my neighbours, but through sport I was on a pedestal, and I can tell you that for as long as it lasted signing on was the most difficult thing I did all week; I felt really uneasy about it.

Tipp were on course to ultimately winning the 2010 All-Ireland and otherwise I was in good form. I started picking up man-of-the-match awards and there was hardly a GAA sports programme on TV that didn't open up with a goal either a teammate or I had conjured up.

Most analysts didn't really think to stop and credit the likes of Noel McGrath and Bonner Maher for setting me up, but everyone inside our dressing-room knew they were the chief suppliers. Instead, the TV lads liked to show clips of me gliding into space and setting the net rippling. The edited footage looked great and made me appear better than I was. The result being that even people with only a passing interest in hurling were becoming aware of my name.

There was a flip-side, however. I was getting recognised in a lot of places and meeting people from different walks of life – people I should have had no bother chatting to – but because I didn't have a job I felt I really had no substance when dealing face-to-face with those who were successful in their own professions.

Up in Dublin, mixing with the great and good at all these banquets, it was forever at the back of my mind that I'd be at home drawing the dole the following Tuesday. When the crowds had exited, the lights had dimmed and the tuxedos were put away I'd be back to reality with a bang.

Winning a second Celtic Cross was the reward for nine years of suffering, but in the real world, with the economy in freefall and my own money problems worsening with every passing day, it meant sweet fanny all – in that sense one of the highest honours in the game was a worthless currency.

People probably imagined I'd be able to dine out for the rest of my life on the back of those three goals in September 2010. And they probably looked on nine months later, saw me shaking hands with Queen Elizabeth and her husband, Prince Philip, and imagined I was one of society's elite, rubbing shoulders with the movers and shakers. They didn't realise I had to stop off at the Poitín Stil and buy my dinner on the way home from meeting the queen. I was in that woman's bubble for only two minutes. A few days later I'd be signing on again.

That got to me. I was so embarrassed to be seen drawing the dole that I actually sent Mam down with the necessary forms and after that I would ask her to go down whenever another piece of paperwork was required. She arranged that the money would come to our house in the form of a cheque so I wouldn't have to worry about going down and collecting it myself, but I would have been mortified to have even cashed that cheque, so Mam would put it in her account and give me cash instead.

In Thurles some people probably felt I was 'someone', an intercounty hurler right at the top of his game, and they may have imagined I was raking it in. There were a few sponsorship deals and the van from Barlo Motors, I went on the *Late Late Show* and met the royals, but I didn't necessarily want to be 'someone', and, let me tell you, when you're playing Xs and Os with those

Social Welfare forms you don't forget where you came from.

As I write this, thousands of GAA players are looking for work; that's just the way it is and we have to accept it. In 2011, as far as I know, 256 international club transfers were approved in just one month by Croke Park, and that says it all. It's no country for young players any more and that's why so many are heading away to Boston or New York or Sydney, no matter what stage of the season they're at.

In any part of the world, if you meet an Irish person, the conversation will soon turn to two subjects – the weather and 'what do you do yourself?'

When folk who were genuinely interested to know what I worked at asked me that question, I was actually ashamed to say I did nothing. The truth is I was unemployed for over two full years, with benefits dropping into my account every Tuesday for twenty-seven months, and it took a lot out of me.

I was especially mortified to admit I wasn't working so soon after winning the All-Ireland and enjoying all the trappings that go with it. The endorsements that rolled in were grand but they were temporary. I had a deal with Lidl to promote hurleys, for instance, but that lasted only a short while and was hardly going to see me through to retirement. So while scoring those goals in the final did wonders for my profile and my confidence, they weren't going to pay all the bills.

People saw me quoted in the papers and on TV every week, and yet I was drawing €188 a week in dole, couldn't really support myself and was living at home with my mother. I wouldn't go hungry there!

At that stage I'd been going out with Elaine for three years and we had been talking about getting a house and getting engaged, but after losing so much work I couldn't see it happening. I had saved a small few bob over the years but that wouldn't last long, and she was getting only part-time teaching hours.

'Elaine, we can't do this,' I said. 'I'm on a couple of hundred quid a week, you're subbing, and we're talking about getting a house and paying for a wedding. It's not a runner.'

Deep down, my biggest fear was that Elaine would meet someone who had more to offer; someone who might have been useless at sport but had a good job, drove a nice car and maybe moved in the right circles. I definitely feared I might get left behind because I had little or nothing going on bar hurling. And it undermined me.

Not long after the All-Ireland final, when the hoopla and hype died down, a young lad approached me one night and started talking about how he would love to be in my shoes. The lad was only being nice but I kind of snapped at him.

'You want to be in my shoes? Fucking mighty. No bother. I'll take off my shoes right now and I'll follow you. Where will we go? What will we do? I'll follow you.'

I was being ignorant – and I regret it to this day – but I was pure frustrated and it was starting to come out. Everyone wants to be comfortable and have a decent standard of living. I just wanted a reason to get up in the morning, a proper job, a routine and a decent wage. You can get sucked into a lazy way of life very quickly and I could see myself heading down that road.

Compared to others I knew I was lucky enough – there were families losing their homes and struggling to feed their kids, whereas I had team and All-Star holidays to look forward to and I was unlikely to starve. But my outlook was pessimistic enough, no doubt there. Hurling and sport in general are built on confidence and what you're doing off the field comes into it as well. After two years and more out of work – and despite my All-Ireland medals – I found my self-belief had been severely dented.

All I could do was approach hurling with the mindset of a professional athlete and that's exactly what I did. I pretended

I was being paid to play hurling full-time, told myself I was getting €188 a week to play for Tipperary and filled in my days accordingly. I'd take myself up to the Anner Hotel on the day after a match, stretch out at my leisure and use the jacuzzi. I'd even go to the gym two or three times a week, which for me is beyond the call of duty.

There would be a few pucks here and there, visits to the ball alley, a bit of visualisation and maybe a swim in the hotel pool. A few of my teammates were in the same boat. We kept ourselves busy and made sure we were always up to something.

Gradually I stopped worrying about the stigma of being unemployed and actually began to enjoy the spare time. Elaine and I ended up renting a house together and I soon got another introduction to the real world when the rent, gas, TV and electricity bills started piling in. This time I couldn't hand the bills to Mam and beat a retreat. It was time to man up; I decided the uncertainty couldn't go on. I wanted to drive on with my life. I was hitting thirty and wondered what I'd be at ten years down the line when my hurling days were only a golden memory.

I met Elaine in Kevin Coppinger's bar one night and after a while Kevin approached us. We started talking about the premises upstairs, which had been used for food before the dinner trade eased off but was now idle. One suggestion led to another, and after we had tossed the ball back and forward for a few weeks Kevin offered me the opportunity to put my name on the upstairs bar. There was no massive risk, because the premises were already there, above the main bar, so I didn't have all the usual start-up costs or overheads.

It was a watershed moment. Elaine and I were on the path to getting engaged and I needed to have ambition; I didn't want to look back and regret not seizing the moment. I had a choice: play on with Tipp for another three years or so and see what turned up – or take the plunge now.

It was the first time in ages that I felt someone was giving me an opportunity from which Elaine and I could benefit in the long run. It was the opposite to what I was used to when a company would come in, use your name to promote their product, and move on quickly once they hit their sales target.

The electrical work had been grand – I could go and put a socket in a wall without thinking – but I wanted the challenge of drumming up business and establishing a regular bar clientele. That was a massive test.

It looked like a good team on paper – Kevin was top class on the commercial side while I had a profile and was full of ideas. We didn't waste much time joining forces but we didn't get the start we wanted either. In fact, our first collaboration bombed, though I could see no way it would fail.

My theory was simple: the country is bleeding people and most of those who have stayed put are drinking and socialising at home because they have no money. That's the truth of it – young men and women are relaxing in their homes rather than heading out to bars and nightclubs. I needed some of them to come and visit my new bar.

So I came up with a scheme. Punters would pay €35 on the door and for that they would get eleven drink vouchers for the night. On top of that, they would get food. And music would be laid on too. They'd have €6 taken off their nightclub admission fee, so they could meet friends and neighbours for a reasonable price instead of being stuck at home watching the *X-Factor* or some other reality show.

We had books of vouchers on sale at the bar but the plan just didn't work. Rather than buying the vouchers, which would have given them a better deal, people continued going to the till and forking out hard cash for each round. We had three thousand vouchers printed but sure they might as well have wallpapered my room because they're still behind the bar. We had advertised heavily but to no avail. I wasn't going to make the *Sunday Times* rich list just yet.

Still, I loved putting that idea together and while it didn't work I knew I couldn't have done any more. Never mind that the idea failed – did I do it to the best of my ability? Yes, I did.

After that experiment bombed I was happy enough to sit back, lash my name over the door of the bar, take a small cut if there was one and let everything take care of itself. I signed off social welfare and immediately felt better. Then, almost as quickly, I dropped the ball.

They say in business that the fear of failure will kill anyone but fear wasn't the problem. It was my attitude. After starting out in the pub business with a burst of energy I soon lost a bit of interest as hurling took over my life again. It took an awful long time to get to grips with what was expected of me in that bar. In fact I would say it took the bones of a year.

Kevin was under pressure to organise bands and entertainment but I would leave it all up to him and at five o'clock, when we should have been sitting down making decisions, I'd be running out the door to pick up my gear for training. That put serious pressure on him and it was part of the reason why I withdrew from Tipp.

Saturday night was the busiest night and our only real opportunity to make money because, let's be honest, you're not going to balance the books on a Tuesday or Wednesday. But if a match loomed the following morning I'd have to be gone by ten on the Saturday night.

People would come in looking for me behind the bar but I wouldn't be there. Then there were Fridays and Sundays when I'd be walking into the bar at nine o'clock at night and folk around town would be speculating that I was on the beer. It was crazy.

For the bones of twelve months I was carrying on like that, leaving Kevin to pick up the slack, until one day he sat me down for a serious talk. The bottom line was that if I kept going the way I was, the project would be dead and buried within six months and it would be back to the dole for yours truly.

We needed busy premises every week for the bar to break even and there was one Tuesday when our entire takings were a miserable €86. You'd make more money selling cheese to dairy farmers. So whether people believed me, or chose to laugh at the reason I gave for walking away, the fact is that business commitments did play a major role at the time in my decision to quit hurling for Tipperary.

Even though I later returned to the Tipp squad I still take those obligations seriously.

It would have been easier to have thrown myself into the venture ten years back when we trained only twice a week with the odd game at weekends, but under Declan and Tommy it was shaping up like five or six meetings a week, and long term I didn't feel it was sustainable to run the business properly and meet those demands as well.

In the few months I was away from the Tipp camp, I was way more visible in the pub. I was there behind the bar at weekends and not scurrying off to train or play a match when I was most needed on the premises.

If there's not a match the next day I'll be there ready for a chat with customers. I have as many faults and weaknesses as the next person – and I don't make lifetime friendships at the drop of a hat – but the one thing I have is the ability to be friendly and talk to anyone, and I think people appreciate that.

Thank God the venture is starting to take off a little. We've put a massive effort into planning parties and offering sun holidays to those who make bookings. But you have to work hard to get anything. There are always people who start socialising in their own homes and only head out about ten o'clock or even later. If they can buy a bottle of beer for eighty-five cents in SuperValu we have to offer them a lot extra to get them in the door and have them pay €4.40 for the same bottle. We have to provide good entertainment, and with so many pubs and ten off-licences in the town of Thurles we have to give customers something back for walking through our doors.

Most nights at the weekend we'll be looking at paying between €500 and €1,000 for a band or an entertainment act, so we have to clear €3,000 in staff and security costs before we start seeing any semblance of a profit. With eight to ten staff working on a busy night, overheads are high.

It costs €400 a day just to open the doors of the pub and the banks are brutal to deal with – you'd get money quicker out of a stone. We have to paddle our own canoe but you can't sit back and wallow.

We're going against the grain in many ways, I suppose. We opened up a bar when everyone else was closing them down. That's pressure in itself; it means we have to be better than any-one else.

I'm just happy that I've finally got to grips with the whole thing. In the past I'd pop in after big matches and the place would be mobbed – but you'd hardly ever see me in there at other times. I'm ashamed to say that for the first ten months I didn't even know how to work the till. I was mortified having to ask one of the barmen to show me.

Kevin was doing orders, doing wages, doing everything, and while Lar Corbett's name was on the door the truth is Lar Corbett was not putting any effort in and anyone who came into the pub knew that.

When I stepped away from the Tipp squad I got the chance to put structures in place for the bar. We've turned it around a fair bit and since my return to hurling everything is more balanced. Kevin is fine with the arrangement and we're six weeks to two months ahead of ourselves in terms of booking entertainment and stock control. We're using any promotion that's going and advertising everything on social media. Twitter and Facebook are where it's all happening. And through competitions and other offers we've collected a massive amount of mobile numbers, so there's a huge database of customers to text whenever we have big news to announce or updates.

You just have to be proactive, but sometimes we've been accused of being over-eager. I don't think the 2011 Munster final was even three-quarters through when one of the bar lads was Facebooking on behalf of the place, advertising a gig for later that night. The lad obviously got a little bit excited and forgot the match had twenty minutes to run when he posted the message, in my name, on five thousand walls. But in my view it would be worse if he wasn't trying to drum up trade. Anyway, I took a fair bit of flak for that, even though I had nothing to do with it. When people brought it up I just cut them off: 'Hey, lads, do ye think I had a mobile phone in my sock or something?'

Please God, there's more to come for the business. We've built a new stage and earned a reputation as a 'live' music venue, there's a new cocktail bar and we've completely redesigned the entrance. Kevin is looking at setting up another bar in Tipp, possibly Clonmel or Carrick-on-Suir, but I'd really like everything to be 100 per cent in Thurles before we start to expand. That's for the future, though.

# 17

# Change of course

The break away from hurling gave me a new lease of life. Although I was working hard on the business I felt pretty free to come and go as I pleased without having to worry about training five nights a week.

We had a lot of gigs booked and secured for the St Patrick's Day 2012 celebrations at the bar so when the possibility of taking off to New York to watch Matthew Macklin fight was mooted I didn't need to think twice about it.

Matthew is a friend of mine with massive Tipperary connections and he was fighting Sergio Martinez for the world middleweight championship belt. Kevin came with me and the night before the bout a group of us, including Eoin Kelly and the retired Munster and Ireland rugby player Alan Quinlan, gathered for a chat. Matthew dropped by as well with Amir Khan, the former world light-welterweight and international lightweight champion, and introduced us.

Pointing to me, he told Khan, 'This chap here plays hurling, an Irish game. He plays in front of eighty thousand people. And he doesn't get paid.'

Khan seemed fascinated. 'He doesn't get paid? And how much are tickets for these games?'

'Ah, you could pay up to eighty euro,' I replied.

'What? Eighty euro! Who runs this show? Where does all this money go?' he persisted.

'The game is run by a group called the GAA,' I continued. 'They look after all that.'

'All the money goes to these GAA guys?' he exclaimed. 'Who are these people? Are they run by Don King too?' he asked, making reference to the controversial promoter who has dominated the world of professional boxing for decades.

I enjoyed that trip so much. I hardly took a drink and instead soaked up every bit of knowledge and advice I could get from people like the Irish boxing promoter and bar owner Brian Peters and other Irish bar owners that had set up in Manhattan and elsewhere.

But when pictures of Eoin and me appeared in the media back home I suppose it was the first time I really noticed criticism of my decision to step away from Tipp hurling. Many supporters couldn't understand how I could be out there enjoying myself when I should be with the team getting ready for another championship.

At first I didn't mind that reaction and I had no problem putting it to the back of my mind. Most of my close friends and family seemed to take my decision as final and it was the same with the majority of my teammates, Sars as well as Tipp. Even though they'd still occasionally touch base – either by phone or by dropping into the bar – they soon stopped talking hurling to me.

Not everyone accepted the situation, though.

From the moment I stepped aside others were on the blower asking me to reconsider. Most of them had the same message: 'Lar, you'll only regret this in years to come.'

I didn't close my ears to all the advice. About six weeks after I came back from New York I met Declan for a chat at the Horse and Jockey hotel. He asked if I had given any thought to coming back. I hadn't really. My first concert promotion was arriving down the track just a few days later and it was a big one. I was bringing the musician Bressie to the Premier Hall in Thurles and had taken on the bar licence. I needed to sell eight hundred tickets to break even and I told Declan my entire focus was on that.

'The lads would love to have you back, Larry. We all would,' he said.

'Declan, I'll get back to you, but at the minute I'm just up the walls with work and I don't know what I'd offer to the set-up,' I replied.

We chatted away for forty minutes but there wasn't much more to be said.

Organising the Bressie gig was some challenge but I learned a lot from it. The Premier Hall hadn't really been used for such occasions in years and it took a lot of work to turn it into a concert venue, secure it, insure it, and then get the doors open for business. We had a lot of work to do to fill the place, but we did it.

I suppose the biggest thing we had going for us was Bressie himself. The guy is a phenomenon; not only was he a top-class sportsman – it's not long since he played senior football for Westmeath and rugby for Leinster – but after his appearance as the winning coach on RTÉ's *The Voice of Ireland* he had become every woman's fancy and was selling out all over the country.

Organising that gig was demanding but enjoyable, and the truth is I had no time to think about hurling. Even when I popped up home, a place I'd hardly ever leave without banging a few balls off the wall, I had no interest.

Some years back Mam had installed a kitchen cabinet that

included a special, built-in slot for my hurleys. Usually I'd come in the door, have a cup of tea and a chat, grab a hurl and hit a few balls, but ever since my withdrawal from the Tipp panel those sticks had remained untouched. I didn't want to puck around because I knew I'd enjoy it and I was half afraid that even beating a sliotar against the gable end would only set my mind wandering again. For the bones of three months those hurls just gathered dust in the kitchen unit. Still, I always knew they were there. And I'd often throw them a glance on my way out the door.

As I say, after the initial madness most hurling people let me off about my business, but when Cork beat us in the league semi-final I started to notice a big change in the air. The kickback definitely went up a notch. Championship was approaching – the time of year I usually come to life – but now the only thing stirring was people's frustration at me. They reminded me of my responsibilities and asked hard questions. I gave the same answers a hundred times a week. But truth be told, my head melted a little with every passing day.

With the Munster championship opener against Limerick looming, the pressure ramped up even further. I was taking more and more flak, even from customers. I'd get it in the neck at night – lads would have a few jars and give it to me straight: I should still be hurling. And sure the customer is always right. What could I say?

I'll be totally frank: it was as if every mark I achieved in a Tipp jersey over eleven seasons was in danger of being wiped from the record.

Even schoolchildren were giving me pangs of conscience. Paul Curran's pupils at St Mary's NS in Irishtown sat down at their computers and typed out a bunch of letters asking me to rejoin the team. It was a lovely touch. I phoned Paul and asked him to thank the kids and tell them how much I valued their support.

Mind you, I always got a good many letters and postcards. They had usually arrived after I scored a few goals, won a medal or got an All-Star. But when I retired they came in sackloads. Almost every one was positive and I appreciated them, even if the writing was sometimes hard to read. It's gas the addresses they would scribble: 'Lar Corbett, Tipperary hurler, Tipperary', or 'Lar Corbett, he owns a bar, Thurles'. Most would include a stamped, addressed envelope and I always replied. If they take the time and trouble to write to me I can at least make the effort to get back to them.

Now, however, the pressure was mounting. One night my head was so strained I headed off for a run. I got the iPhone, plugged in the headphones and off I went. It was only five kilometres but it was the first bit of exercise I had taken since October and it helped clear the head.

A few days later I looked at the hurls in the kitchen cabinet and this time I picked one of them up. Immediately, I texted Pa asking did he fancy a few pucks? Within two minutes he was at the door. It was like old times.

'Jaysus, I was surprised to get the text from you,' Pa said when we finished.

'Look, it's just something to fill the time,' I replied.

Still, those few pucks put me at peace. It had been a while since I had felt that way.


On 7 May I got a phone call from John O'Brien. He was attending a Škoda sponsorship gig at Semple Stadium, had finished earlier than expected and had time to kill before training: 'Larry, I haven't seen you for ages. Are you around for a cup of tea?'

I was struggling with a serious dose of man flu but any time you meet John O is a good time and an hour later we hooked up at the Anner Hotel. We had a right oul' chat too, about everything and anything. He didn't mention hurling at first and didn't push me in the slightest but naturally the conversation drifted to the Tipp camp. Among other things, he told me to ignore any negative talk going around the county about supposed tensions within the squad – as is the norm in Tipp when the team struggle, the vibes about the place had been less than heartwarming. But John O had the inside track and it told a different story.

'We're going well, Larry. We're working fierce hard and the atmosphere is positive. Bonner and Séamie Callanan are back in full training. They'll be some addition. There's togetherness about us, no matter what's being said.'

Then he came straight out with it: 'Would you not meet Tommy Dunne?'

I thought about it for a second and then gave my answer: 'I'll meet him no problem.'

John O was happy with that. Then he lobbed a small grenade: 'Larry, I didn't come over here to talk hurling but it's only fourteen weeks to the end of the championship. That's not a lot in the grand scheme of things.'

I hadn't thought of it like that. Trust John O to find an angle! We left the hurling talk there and went back to discussing how I might hunt the cursed flu. He headed off training then. Later that evening he texted, asking if I would meet Tommy the next day.

I had no problem with that.

The following morning I met Tommy for ninety minutes, again at the Horse and Jockey – the scene of all my summit talks! We got straight to the point.

'Lar, I didn't know what way to approach it when you left,' Tommy said. 'I didn't know whether I should ring you or leave you alone.'

I told Tommy I didn't know what to do myself and we got on with it. I have to say, meeting him was one of the best things I ever did, because I laid it on the line for him and he was totally honest with me.

'Tommy,' I said, 'I hurled with you for years but I don't really know what way you think. And in a way that stops me doing my job to the best of my ability.'

We had an intense, private discussion. I got a bit emotional as he chatted about what he stood for and what Tipperary hurling meant to him. I could actually see the fire burning in his eyes as he spoke and it drilled home the message to me – you just could not doubt his passion for the county.

'Like, what happened against Kilkenny in the 2011 final – we had nothing arranged for something like that happening,' I added, trying to free myself of the burden I had carried through the previous winter. 'The whole thing wrecked my head for six months and I felt I couldn't talk to any of ye. As far as I could see, my mindset was different from everyone else's.'

Tommy took it on board: 'Maybe what they came up with caught us by surprise, Lar, but we can work together for solutions if it happens again.'

I pressed a bit further.

'Honest to God, Tommy, if I went back I wouldn't care if I didn't touch a ball for the rest of the year but surely I could be used to open up space for someone else. I'm not going back over old ground, it's not my job as a player, but we'll have to look at things going forward if changes are needed.'

Then I stopped. Whatever reasons I had for walking away, there was nothing to be gained from an interrogation or raking over the coals of the 2011 championship. Even if I catalogued the reasons I had for walking Tommy might well have said, 'Yeah, you're right, Larry.'

What would I have gained from that?

Our meeting was an absolute godsend. It felt like I could finally purge my mind of the waste of the 2011 All-Ireland. After months of searching for answers I felt it was at last time to move on.

It was also the first time I got an insight into Tommy's personality. Before that I just didn't fully understand him.

He reiterated that everyone would love to have me back, and gradually the notion of giving it another crack took shape in my head. I said I'd have a look at the business again and see if I could find a way back to hurling – and we parted on terms better than ever before. I had definitely seen a warmer side to Tommy and that helped. I need to be able to figure people out and trust them – maybe that's one of my flaws – but if you have to work with a person I think you need that.

The evening after I met Tommy I phoned Eamon O'Shea, looking for advice. Typically, he never once mentioned the words 'return' or 'coming back'. He just took out a blank canvas and painted the scenario that faced me. And by God did he frame it well!

'Larry, you only get a few years to really express yourself in life,' he said. 'The older you get, the fewer chances you have to express yourself, be it with work, business or family. You're lucky enough you can express yourself in packed houses around the country but as you get older that starts to diminish. You should just express yourself. Feel free about what you want to do because you have only a few years left.'

Upon hanging up I went to Kevin Coppinger and floated the idea of going back to hurling and we discussed what that would mean for the pub – late nights behind the counter would once again be out, for instance.

Not for the first time Kevin was completely understanding. In light of my earlier commitment to concentrate solely on the business, he could easily have baulked at this latest U-turn and told me to get lost, but he was happy with the way things were panning out and he offered his full support.

Another friend came to see me with a sheet of paper and a line down the middle, the pros for returning on one side and the cons on the other. My head was in a spin.

For two days I went around in a half-daze and with the pressure building inside me. I discussed it with a few close friends and everyone seemed to have a different opinion. Maybe I discussed it with too many.

Eventually, on 12 May, I more or less made up my mind to give it another shot. I was restless from lack of physical exercise. I missed having a hurl in my hands. It seemed the whole county had been on my back at one time or another and there was no let-up in sight.

I slept on it and rang Tommy the next morning to tell him my decision. Only this time I was going back to do whatever specific job I was given. I suppose I had to accept it wasn't my job to compose game plans and dictate tactics.

'Tommy, I've been thinking about it. As and from now I'm there to give ye one hundred per cent commitment.'

'That's great, Larry. When can you come back to training?

'As and from this moment I'll do whatever it takes. I'll do all in my power to get back,' I replied.

I hold my hands up. I thought the spark had been snuffed out. I was fairly sure I would spend the rest of my life away from the game. Deep down, though, the fire must have been smouldering away.

I turned my thoughts to the club.

When Thurles Sarsfields submitted to the Mid-Tipperary board a list of thirty players eligible for the 2012 championship they had to leave my name off it because I had withdrawn from all levels of hurling at the start of the year.

My decision disappointed a few of the locals but I had no problem sticking to my guns; I just felt that if I played for the

Sars I'd have to play for Tipp and it was best to cut all ties.

By early summer the Sars had three championship games under their belt – games I had taken no part in – but in fairness the players invited me to attend a team meeting at the club's social centre when they heard I was making a comeback. Those meetings are held every year and are useful in giving a platform for lads to air grievances that can be addressed before molehills are turned into mountains.

I sat in the circle, a small bit uncomfortable if I'm being entirely honest, because I knew some of the lads felt I should have stayed hurling away with the club no matter what happened with Tipp. At the end of the meeting Paudie Maher asked if I had anything to say.

'Can someone give me directions home? I was barely able to find my way up here,' I said, tongue in cheek. It was all I could think of but thankfully it broke the ice and I think the boys took it in the spirit in which it was meant.

I rang the Sars manager, Séamus Quinn, and told him I was ready to give him 100 per cent. Two weeks later I played a Cahill Cup game against Moycarkey-Borris. It was my first start since getting sent off against Clonoulty in the 2011 county semi-final and while I didn't score I loved being back and getting on the ball.

There's no doubt that there was a bit of soreness about the place because I hadn't kept going with the club but it wasn't all bad feeling – there was a bit of banter as well. Lenny Phillips, our junior B manager, wasn't slow in telling me I was firmly in his plans.

'Larry, you're eligible for intermediate now but don't tog at all this year. Then you'll be able to come down two grades next year. I'm over the juniors – we'll have some craic.'

\*

I went back with Tipp on 15 May and from there it was full steam ahead. A six-week programme with our trainer, Ross Dunphy, was drawn up, and I got off to a great start when I hopped up on the scales the first night back – 83.5 kilos, the exact same weight as I had been for the 2011 All-Ireland final. Thank God for the Corbett family genes!

'Jesus, you're in great nick,' Ross said. 'You must have been working away on your own.'

'Ah, doing a bit,' I replied, thinking of that solitary five-kilometre run and those few pucks with Pa. If that constituted 'doing a bit' we were all in trouble. The truth is I'm just blessed that I don't put on weight.

In the dressing-room the boys gave me a merciless slagging.

'Hey, John O, who's the new kid?'

'Feck this, lads, some strange fella is after takin' my seat!'

I let them away with it for a few minutes and once the messing died down I asked if we could get on with the business of training.

From that night the relationship between Tommy and me grew. We did six one-on-one sessions between my first night back and the start of June. We met at Dúrlas Óg, using either the hurling wall or the astroturf pitch. We stood just a few feet apart and absolutely leathered the ball off each other. They were all full-on sessions and lasted about ninety minutes. Tommy would tog out, lean as a greyhound, and tear into the drills. His speed, touch, class are unreal. At one stage I leaned on the hurley, guzzled some air and looked over at him, not a bead of sweat on his brow.

'Hey, Tommy, are these sessions for you or for me?' I asked.

I got an entirely new insight into the man. He's pure driven; he just doesn't want to be beaten at anything. I've had it easier marking fellas playing championship hurling than training with him and I sincerely mean that.

Whenever Tommy's schedule allowed, we met – half eight or nine o'clock in the morning or maybe six o'clock in the evening. I respected Tommy for giving his time to bring me back up to speed. I finally got to see what he's about.

It's not that we chattered away non-stop, more that I got the chance to communicate with him in the first place. You can do that with sliotars and hurleys just as well as by talking. Now at training I can read his mind without him having to stop and talk to me. That allows me to get on with my business because I know what he wants from me. If meeting him was a positive thing, those one-on-one sessions just lifted the relationship to a different level.

I had no problem being left out of the squad for the Limerick match on 27 May. On the Tuesday before the game Declan told me I wouldn't be on the panel. I replied that it was fine, I would do whatever they wanted. On the morning of the match Tommy asked me to look after the water and I told him I'd be the best water-boy in Semple Stadium. I meant it – if I could only drive the boys on I'd offer something at least.

At two o'clock on 27 May 2012, the Tipperary team bus snaked its way through Liberty Square and as I looked down at the bar a shiver went up my spine. I looked out the bus window and saw customers going inside.

'I could so easily be in there pulling pints, but sure I can do that for the rest of my life,' I thought to myself.

I was with my teammates, on the way to play Limerick in the Munster championship. While I wasn't part of the official squad I was satisfied that I wanted to be nowhere else.

The game was tight and we very nearly got caught. After sitting patiently through the first half I got a bit excited in the second, running in and out with the bottle, roaring lads on. Paudie

Maher said later he thought I was going to pull hard on one ball that dropped beside him. Pa told me I was giving him a great lift so I kept doing what I was doing.

Pa is fair cool by the way. After he scored what turned out to be a crucial goal in the first half I ran to him with the bottle.

'Hey, I'm going to get a second one!' he said. 'I'm going to get a second one, I'm telling you!'

He didn't, but he did play his best ever game for Tipperary.

Afterwards people told me I was wired on the line. I got a few texts from friends saying they hadn't seen me run so much even when I was playing. The thing is, when you're out there on the field you can go and make things happen, get on the ball, throw an old pass or score a point – but on the sideline you're just like everyone else, looking on, unable to influence what's happening, and you feel the need to let off steam.

I enjoyed that job and in some ways I actually enjoyed it more than playing. That probably sounds strange, but there was none of the usual pressure on me. I was just happy I could give Pa, Noel, Bonner and the boys some sort of a lift.

Unfortunately, my repeated pitch invasions had a downside. It was a baking hot day and I was on and off the field with the water bottle like a hare on speed – and that resulted in a series of fines for the county board.

We were behind at half-time in that game but there was no major panic. We knew we hadn't played well and the forwards hadn't worked hard enough. When the bench was emptied we eventually ground them down.

I was delighted for Buggy O'Meara, in particular, who got a goal and two points from play. And Bonner Maher was just unbelievable when he came on; I think he was responsible for setting up 1-3 in the half-hour or so he featured. He's developed into a machine, the ultimate athlete. I've never seen anyone like him for physique or work-rate – no-one comes near. He has the whole package, doesn't drink or smoke, is ripped like a *Baywatch* extra and would die on his hurl if he thought it would help the team.

For most of the game, however, it was the Limerick boys who produced that Bonner-like intensity. Eoin threw the ball in the air at one stage and was blocked; Noel McGrath raced in and was blocked too; then Gearóid Ryan tried to grab the sliotar and was put on his arse – that drew the biggest roar of the day.

Limerick were serious underdogs – 6-1 against with the bookies – and had very little to lose, but you knew from their body language after the first few scores that their young side also possessed great belief. They ran out of steam on a warm day, that's all.

But our lads deserved credit for a great comeback. I think we got serious confidence out of that. Limerick seemed on the way to a famous win but we had the strength on the bench to get by and the experience and composure to dig ourselves out of a hole. It was tight but it usually is against them.

That night I went up to the bar and it was hopping. Straight away I noticed a difference. People were coming over, tapping me on the back, the vibe was positive and there and then I made a decision: the next – and final – time I draw the curtain on my days in the blue and gold I'll be a physical wreck, two stone overweight with a pair of banjaxed knees. People will be saying, 'Sure that lad is bollixed – he has nothing more to offer.' I know now that leaving the way I did was wrong. Of course I felt at the time it was right, but I didn't handle it the best.

I immediately felt at peace being back in the set-up. There was a weight taken off my shoulders, a heaviness I didn't even fully realise was there in the first place. After three months of soul-searching I finally gave up looking for answers as to why it didn't happen for me in the 2011 final. Thank God for that!

\*

On Tuesday morning, 5 June, I forced my eyes open and peered at the alarm clock. Ten past five! Jesus! The last time I was up this early I was getting into the bed, not crawling out of it.

Making sure not to disturb Elaine, I threw on a tracksuit, headed out to the van and tipped down to Semple Stadium for training at the ungodly hour of six o'clock.

It's exactly nine days since we beat Limerick and while nothing has been said officially it's clear this session is payback for a few of the boys prolonging the celebrations after our dramatic escape. The management had said there was no problem with fellas heading out for a pint the evening of the Limerick match but they were drawing the line after that.

But judging by how Declan gathered us in the dressing-room two days after that win and ate us alive it was clear he felt too many players were still caught up in the merriment of winning a championship game. He spoke for fifteen minutes with a burning passion. The gist was that we had to represent the people of Tipperary and he seemed bemused that we could be so happy after just winning one game. I can't speak for the rest of the lads, but I had never seen him talk with such fire and anger. I thought it was brilliant.

The good thing was that once Declan had finished, Tommy got up and said the slate would now be wiped clean. We would start afresh and move forward, and he would put together three weeks of training that would knock us into serious shape for the meeting with Cork.

The dawn session is the first real test for us but sure I don't mind whether we train at five in the morning or ten at night because early-morning sessions are good for the soul and I need all the preparation I can get.

I told myself it was 100 per cent or nothing and set my mind on featuring in the Munster semi-final against Cork which was pencilled in for 24 June. I went back eating like a draught horse too. I start off the day with a good breakfast – cereal, toast and tea; I'll have a healthy chicken sandwich or roll at ten o'clock; a full dinner at one o'clock and if I'm not training another dinner at six; and maybe something later, before I go to bed.

On training nights I'll have a second dinner in the catering room at Semple Stadium afterwards. Because I'm back in full training – and coming from so far off the pace – everything has to be done right and I'm manic about it. This is probably an accurate reflection of my personality – I make a decision and then back myself 100 per cent on it. But if I then decide to switch back I'll be just as committed. I can understand why people wouldn't get that, but that's just the way I'm set up.

Once I returned to hurling mode I went back into the zone almost immediately, breaking in hurleys, tightening studs, guzzling my three litres of water a day.

I set about building myself right back up and homed in on the Cork game. Tommy was delighted that my touch was still there and Ross worked hard with me on 200-metre sprints and the like. I knew myself I wasn't going too badly but I played it down, kept it low-key.

I told the lads if they wanted me just to haul water for the year I'd be happy to do it. Still, you don't get up at five in the morning with only that in mind. If the embers had been gently smouldering, the competitive flame was now fully ablaze.

At the start of June I went back playing for Sars in that Cahill Cup match against Moycarkey, my first game in that competition in ten years. It was also my first start for the club since I had copped that red card against Clonoulty the previous October.

I was still off the pace against Moycarkey – probably trying too hard to make things happen instead of going with the flow of the game – but I was happy to be back in the thick of the action.

During that game one of the hamstrings tightened, not surprising after such a long absence, so immediately I sought treatment from John Casey and then went out to Mick Clohessy's house at Borrisoleigh for an hour-long rub. Meanwhile, Tommy and I kept up our routine, meeting twice a week, while I trained with the team and did separate fitness work with Ross and prehab work with John.

I ran on against Boherlahan in the Mid-Tipperary championship on the second weekend of June, scored a goal and made a goal. A few days later Tipp picked me against Galway in a challenge match in the middle of June and I hit three points, but the main thing was I was all over the field and right up to the pace of the game. I felt as fresh as I had done in years.

I know I'm something of a rare breed in that I don't put on weight – and when I think of these three- to four-month reconditioning programmes inflicted on GAA players I count my blessings that just four weeks after going back training I felt capable of playing championship hurling again.

The weather gods may have decreed that June 2012 was a washout but I felt as upbeat as I have ever done. My mind was burden-free. It was great to be back in harness.

# 18

# Rucksacks and sandbags

Before we left Thurles to head for Páirc Uí Chaoimh and Cork in the Munster semi-final, Elaine said she had some advice for me.

Though I wasn't starting, the indications were I would be brought into the game at some stage. I didn't think it would be in the first half but with just thirty minutes gone Declan turned around and told me to warm up.

Was I ready? I was ready from when I decided to go back training.

Cork were ahead by a couple of points but we were well in the game and as Gearóid Ryan made his way off the field, unluckily in my opinion, I thought of Elaine.

Earlier at home she had started chatting about the match and in all honesty I was probably a little crusty with her. I felt the world and its mother were trying to tell me how to prepare for getting back on the field and that was enough.

'I hope to God you're not going to tell me how to play the game,' I said. I was full sure she was going to tell me to go out, score a goal and keep everyone happy. I had enough people telling me that.

'Relax,' she laughed. 'You don't even know what I'm going to say yet . . . All I'll say is that when you come on the field your only job is to win the first ball. If you do that everything else will look after itself.'

It was the best advice I had received from anyone all week long.

As the half drew to a close, Declan called me over to the sideline, my number flashed up on the board and I heard an almighty roar. I tried to stop a shiver from surging up my spine as the Tipperary supporters rose to their feet. But the rush I felt at wearing that jersey, representing those people, it was something else. The pride just pumped out of me.

'No! Put that out of your mind,' I warned myself. 'You've a game to play.'

Running onto the field I knew the roar was getting louder, and while I've had my ups and downs in a Tipp shirt I realised there and then that I belonged. For good or bad.

I went on and did what Elaine wanted. I won the first ball. That's down to Brendan Cummins, who sent a good clean possession my way from a low puck-out. I was fouled and Pa came out and put the free over the bar.

My first breath was gone as quickly as I'd drawn it and to be honest I was glad of the half-time break to gather my thoughts.

As usual the dressing-room was packed and we tried to make sure it was players and management only. Over the years I have always changed my jersey, togs and socks at the break. Sometimes I'd even have a shower or change my boots. I like the feeling of running out for the restart with fresh gear. It's like a new start. I've done it for club and county over the past ten years; it's a habit I like. I'd feel like a new man running back onto the pitch.

This time, though, I had only been on the field a few minutes and although I was already soaked in sweat there was just no room in there to change. As I had already mentioned, the dressing-rooms here are like sweat boxes. Instead I sat down and listened to the boys, Tommy and Declan, talking.

They told me to keep making runs and that's what I did in the second half.

Once or twice I thought I was in on goal but in the end I had to be content with winning two frees and setting up a goal for Noel McGrath after John O'Brien had played me in. I was happy enough with Noel's goal – it was like a reverse of the 2010 final when he had set me up.

We were lucky enough to get past them in the end. Cian McCarthy had a goal chance near the death but it sizzled over the bar. He wasn't the only Cork player who missed an opportunity.

When we lost John O'Brien to a second yellow card we could have panicked but ultimately it spurred us on. We actually looked like we had the extra man. We quickly reshaped as a forward unit and the five of us just kept moving around. Essentially they had no spare man. Well, they didn't even know who the spare man was, I'd say.

Once John O went every player automatically lifted his game by an extra 10 per cent – isn't that always the way?

We looked to the bench. Shane Bourke came on and made a huge difference once more with his high-tempo style, while Eoin came on to another massive cheer at the very end, which gave us a lift too.

It was a major win and at the final whistle we huddled together. Winning in Cork is always a serious achievement – it was only the second time I'd managed it in the championship – and you'd always remember the older Tipp generation talking about any time they'd gone to Cork they'd usually come home after a beating.

Before we headed to the Maryborough Hotel for food and to meet our partners and family, Ger Ryan asked me to do some media interviews.

'Ah, I might leave it, Ger,' I said.

'No, you'll be grand, go on,' he replied.

One of the messages I got across was how the team was now starting to come from behind to win games. In the past we were better known for losing big leads but we had reversed the scores against both Limerick and now Cork. We were driving it on and we had lads fighting for every position. It was the first time in all my years with Tipp that we had such quality competition in the squad. I actually felt the panel was the strongest I'd ever seen it. The management had started to make changes before half-time and, while that's rough on the fellas being taken off, the truth was Kilkenny had been injecting new blood into their set-up for nearly two decades now without anyone hardly noticing. We were only playing catch-up.

For three weeks I worked hard in training and was picked to start the Munster final. Coming into that game my main focus was on creating space for others and if that meant being stationed out at midfield I didn't mind if it was for the good of the team. If the rest of the boys were getting goals at the other end I was happy.

Not everyone saw it like that, though. After the final – despite the fact that we won – lots of people came up to me, asking what I was at.

Maybe it's the way hurling is gone, I don't know, but I feel you have to keep on the move now and keep opponents guessing. I probably had four or five chances of going for a score but each time I decided to pass to others because I felt they were in better positions.

Did I feel a bit of pressure? Yeah, maybe I had a few doubts about myself and my ability to get back scoring goals.

I know that for the first goal chance I definitely lacked a little bit of confidence to pull the trigger and so I passed it out to Pa.

Maybe I should have gone myself but I felt I had to change tack. I put myself through hell after the 2011 All-Ireland final and I couldn't continue my life like that. Blaming myself for not being in a game achieves nothing; I'm only part of a team at the end of the day.

I decided to forget about what I'd done in the past and leave behind all that pressure of performing or not performing. I had walked away from the team for my own reasons and I had to deal with that. Now my job was to play a greater team role. I found that attitude relaxed me a little and I said I'd stop wondering if I'd scored lots or played well. I had to look at the 'team aspect' a little more and it took a bit of getting used to.

I remember Eoin Kelly saying at a team meeting three years ago that if you were nervous about your own game it was a selfish thing. Any day I play for Tipp I'm expected to score 1-3 but maybe signing up for more dirty work and running to create space for others and doing the right things for the team was just as important. That was my mindset going out to play Waterford in the final – I had to try and strike a balance between working hard out the pitch and coming off someone's shoulder for a pop pass at the other end.

I approached the final with a slight touch of nerves. Two or three chances came my way and in the past they would have been buried. This time, though, there was a little hesitation in my own mind and I didn't get a strike away. On a different day I might have left Cork with 2-3 but that didn't happen.

Still, we won with a bit to spare and I felt I played my part, especially in the second half. Waterford were good, Tony Browne particularly, but we didn't expect anything else. A lot of their lads had won four Munster titles, and the likes of John Mullane and Tony just produce it every day they go out.

Another Munster medal meant a lot to me. It's only when you flick through old match programmes and see where legends like

Jimmy Barry-Murphy won ten that you realise the importance of the provincial championship. Class players like Ollie Moran in Limerick never won a Munster medal and I'd imagine they'd love to have one. It's still the second-best championship in the GAA behind the All-Ireland series.

At the same time I was glad to see that the cup was brought into the dressing-room and quickly stowed away in the corner. The bottom line was that we had other business to attend to. Croke Park was beckoning and that's where it all starts.

I suppose the happiness I got from winning that final was tempered a little by rumours that started flying around the place and ultimately ended up on *The Sunday Game*.

By the time we went to a military training camp at Bere Island in Cork on the last weekend of July the whole country had it that I'd put a bet on myself not to score in the Munster final. Apparently that was the reason I didn't go for any scores myself. I heard the rumours a day after the Waterford game and laughed them off.

The word on the street was that a few of my mates had put the bet on as well and the dividends were rich. There were odds of 33-1 on offer, or something like that, for me not to raise a flag. And we had creamed the bookies, don't you know!

It would have been funny only the rumours progressed to such a level that they were brought up at a team meeting.

We arrived at Bere Island on a Friday evening and ended up running fifteen kilometres over hills and dunes with a rucksack strapped to our back. We ran carrying sandbags on other occasions.

Well, most of us had rucksacks. When I got the itinerary for the trip I knew trouble was ahead so I packed a big army rucksack with runners, socks, togs and T-shirts. I tried it on, fastened it as tightly as I could and knew that I'd be somewhat comfortable running with the bag on my back as my years of experience had led me to believe that's what lay ahead.

For all his years, though, Eoin was caught on the hop. He arrived at the foot of the hill for our first run with a bag you'd pack for your holiday – a big Adidas thing with wheels on it that you'd pull behind you at an airport. I might have looked like a cabin crew member giving a safety instruction before a flight with my yoke strapped to me but at least it was practical. Eoin was screwed and he knew it.

The rest of the lads tore off up the hill but Eoin just grimaced. He looked at the bag and the bag looked back at him before he picked it up, wrapped his arms around it and ploughed up the hill, with the wheels of the bag hanging out at the bottom.

The tears were rolling out of my eyes as I told him to give me one of the straps. We heaved it up the hill for a bit and, while I didn't think he would make it, he got there in the end. Kelly always does.

That night at our meeting we held one of those chats where lads speak about their teammates. We each got to talk about one other player and had to mention something good – and not so good – about them. It's all part of it. I had to discuss John O'Neill and I spoke about what a serious prospect he was and how well he was going at training. I added that he had a serious eye for goal in about the danger zone.

John then had to offer a few words about me and after saying something nice he highlighted my poor communication skills as a weakness. The rest of the lads looked a little startled at that and I shot him a look myself.

'Well, Larry, the next time you get a great tip for the Munster final you might let the rest of us know,' he said.

The room broke into laughter. It was only a bit of banter and I had no problem with John mentioning it at all. I put up with that stuff because I'm listening to it for the past ten or eleven years and it genuinely doesn't bother me. Rumours follow me all around the place.

But later that weekend on RTE's *Sunday Game* Tomás Mulcahy made reference to the rumour. Des Cahill jumped in straight away and made it clear that it was only a joke, not a rumour, but to me I could have done without either being mentioned. God knows how many people watched the programme that night and heard it.

The next day Paul Byrnes, the editor of the *Sunday Game*, rang me to apologise. He's a very decent fella and I accepted his apology even though the whole thing didn't sit right with me. Soon after, Tomás Mulcahy rang to do likewise and I spoke to him about making loose comments. He said sorry and I accepted that he was genuine.

Others told me that I should look at the whole thing a bit more closely but I told Tomás that I knew going on live TV wasn't easy and that sometimes things get away from you. We left it at that. It was a short enough phone call.

I've been thinking about it since. Thousands of people heard those comments and yet only one man heard an apology. All I can say to anyone who doubts me, apart from the fact that the rumours are totally slanderous, is where are these bookies that took the bets?

Can I see a slip? And if there is a slip, I had nothing to do with it.

Do people think I have nothing else to be thinking of? And do people seriously think that a bookmaker – or bookmakers – would not have come forward and screamed publicly if something like that went down?

I set out to play the Munster final, to make space for others and create goals. I think a lot of folk forget that I almost scored a goal with a high ball that I went for in the twenty-fourth minute when Kevin Moran and I went up for it. I got there first, flicked the hurley at the sliotar and sent it goalwards. I thought it was in the back of the net but it flashed just wide. A pity. There'd be none of this messing.

As for the training camp, well, lads went down there in the peak shape of their lives, but we didn't know what sort of a session awaited us. When we hopped off the ferry we knew.

The session from hell!

You can automatically come up with excuses as to why a weekend like this is wrong, or you can try to get something out of it. I did my best, ran about twelve or thirteen kilometres before my knee started to give way. I never had a pain in my knee before and it worried me so I had to tell Hotpoint to go back and get into his car which I sat into. I wasn't the only one who struggled. Tom Stapleton hurt his groin and so too did Eoin Kelly. That weekend effectively finished Eoin's season.

It was heavy stuff. The squad ran fifteen kilometres on the Friday, right up to the top of this huge hill, and along the way we were handed sandbags by three or four army lads who were driving it on. After our meeting and some food we hit the hay at half one in the morning. Four hours later we were up again for more running. It was a tough, tough twenty-four hours.

The clubs back home were not happy with what went on.

There was a round of divisional championship games that weekend and a lot of us had to leave Cork at lunchtime on Saturday to go and play in them. Now, evidently it didn't do some lads any harm – Pa scored six goals for us in the Mid-Tipperary final against Loughmore on the Sunday and it was the perfect response to being taken off early in the Munster final against Waterford. Paudie Maher and Michael Cahill played stormers too. Meanwhile, Brendan Maher practically beat Kilruane MacDonaghs on his own, scoring 0-11 against them.

So although the clubs were raging and injuries were picked up, the other side of the coin is that any coach or manager involved with intercounty has to be selfish. They have to make sure that the regime is right for the team that they're looking after.

For better or worse we went to the well that weekend. Whether it would build our character or come back to haunt us remained to be seen.

# 19

# Quantum of solace

I always knew the chance for redemption against Kilkenny would eventually come along. And I was fairly sure my old friend Jackie Tyrrell wouldn't be far away when it did.

But redemption never came. In fact, it was the opposite. We collapsed and got a hiding. You can call it sour grapes, you can say I bottled it or you can call me a shirker – I don't really mind, but this is my view on what went down.

I was certain Tyrrell would attach himself to me like a leech and try to replicate what he did in the 2011 final. The hurley was going to be a mere accessory because he had little or no interest in playing the game. That's my opinion anyway.

At the time of writing, Jackie has five All-Ireland medals and four All-Stars; he is a serious hurler. He doesn't really go in for verbals on the field; you don't hear much shouting or roaring out of him. That's actually a pity because I can easily ignore all that stuff. Instead, when we hooked up in the 2011 final he found plenty of other ways to keep me out of the game and fair play to him. He did what he had to do and it worked a treat.

I knew the template wouldn't be a whole lot different this time around – Kilkenny would want me marked absent again and would use every trick to stop me hurling. So once our Croke Park date was booked, we – players and management – began to discuss strategies and tactics, and high on the agenda was how I would deal with my old pal.

Tommy and Declan were considering playing me at centre-forward. It was also suggested I could roam way out the field and bring Jackie on a tour of Croke Park. But because I was playing much deeper now, almost as a third midfielder, not all the lads were convinced that Tyrrell would be on my case this time.

'Ye could be right,' I argued. 'But surely we can't forget what happened last year – we can't go out and just hurl away without any contingency plan.'

On 7 August, twelve days before the semi-final, Tommy Dunne, John O, Eoin and I met at the Horse and Jockey hotel and spoke about what the six forwards would do as a unit.

The meeting lasted two hours and the lines of communication were brilliant. We spoke about everything; every possible scenario Kilkenny could throw at us. Tommy seemed delighted we were giving so much thought to tactics, and everything was positive.

We decided as a group that if they were going to focus on stopping me from hurling we would fight fire with fire. We agreed that the idea of me marking Tommy Walsh could upset them.

Our plan was simple enough. Jackie would go looking for me as usual and Tommy Walsh would look to mark Pa. But I would roam across the field to Tommy's wing – which is where I was picked to play anyway. It might mean the four of us were going to be bunched together – and Pa would be given the job of dictating where we ran to – but it could free up space for our other forwards.

The goal was simple – if I was going to be hounded out of the game, we would do likewise to Tommy. The intention was to confuse them – throw a spanner in the works – and hope the rest of the Tipp team would benefit.

Now if you're shaking your head and wondering what in the name of God this is all about, I can understand. And let me say straight out that I would rather have gone on the field and played hurling. But I wasn't going to be let. So we had to try something. I just couldn't handle another 2011 scenario of being scragged and dragged and jostled, even when the sliotar was the far end of Croke Park, with no referee, umpire or linesman doing anything about it. There's no getting away from it – the back man nearly always wins when he takes a forward out of it.

If I come across as a whinger, I don't mean to.

I was scoring free and easy for years. My game is to go out and hurl and always has been. The ball and the stick are all I'm interested in.

In 2009 I was the top scorer from play in the championship. The same again in 2010. In 2011 I was in line for Hurler of the Year and played well in every game right up to the final.

What happened, then?

I answer that by asking a question of my own. Will the game of hurling be just a pulling and dragging fest in five years' time?

Because I was pretty sure that's what was facing me eleven months later, going into the 2012 All-Ireland semi-final. With that in mind we tried to do something different.

Did the other players know what we were about?

Management didn't feel the whole team needed that kind of tactical detail – lads had their own patches to worry about – but most of our forwards were on message. We knew Tommy would want to get onto as much ball as possible and feed it diagonally into his forwards, as he had done the year before. Getting onto loose ball is their first form of attack. So we reasoned that with me stuck to Tommy and Jackie breathing down my neck we might just upset their patterns.

Eoin, John O and Noel McGrath were fully aware of the plan too but Bonner Maher had his own concerns – to go in full-forward – and we didn't want any extra pressure on him. We would look to make space, and the boys would try to get the ball into Bonner in the hope he could break it to supporting team-mates.

About ten days before the semi-final, we got the chance to put the tactic to the test in an A-versus-B game. Tommy and Declan said nothing to the boys on the other team (Kilkenny, if you like) – except one; they called Michael Cahill aside and told him to tail me wherever I went. But I went over and marked Tom Stapleton while Michael played the Jackie Tyrrell role following me. The 'Kilkenny' boys hadn't a clue what was happening – they were all over the place – and that was the confirmation we needed that the system could work.

By the time match day arrived we were all aware of our roles.

Sure enough, Jackie came over on me, but I switched to Tommy's wing. The four of us ran around, almost in our own mini-game, and while I fully accept it might have looked bizarre, I would have done thirty laps of the field if it helped us win.

After about fifteen minutes I got a poke in the eye from the butt of Jackie's hurley. Even allowing for the fact that it happened in the heat of the moment I am never convinced these things are an accident but I am sure Jackie would see it differently. The referee, Cathal McAllister from Cork, came over to see what was going on. I showed him the cut under my eye and asked, 'Hey, where do you think this came from?'

Sure I don't think he had any interest – after seeing if I needed to be temporarily substituted and a quick word with Jackie he just ran off. Maybe he hadn't seen anything, but then again maybe it was the job of his umpires or linesmen to lend a hand.

Throughout the first half I was flaked left, right and centre.

Several times I looked back to see the umpires point at the boys and tell them to stop what they were at. The Kilkenny lads loved that. It seems to me that the officials had given them the freedom of Croke Park.

In that first half, while Pa and I kept the two boys occupied, other Tipp players got onto plenty of ball and were creating chances.

McAllister booked Tommy. I was pumped up and I suppose that's where this stuff came from, that I was trying to get Tommy sent off. I never, ever in my life went out to get anyone sent off, and apart from one or two pundits and commentators I think most people, including my opponents, will accept that. The hop and skip in the air mightn't have looked great but I was revved up. I wasn't celebrating him getting a booking, just the fact we might be getting to them. That's the unvarnished truth. Celebrating cards of any colour is just not me.

By the end of the first half we were ahead by a point. I had set up a goal and been on the ball three times. For one of the possessions I thought I had sent Pa in for a goal but his strike was blocked. On another occasion I got a ball on the Cusack Stand side and shot for a point but it trailed wide. I thought things were working well enough. We had shot five bad wides, though, and they would prove to be vital misses.

We had also missed a goal chance while Pa had a 21-yard free saved. I may not have been scoring but I definitely felt I was contributing. Tommy's diagonal passes had killed us in 2011 but this time he cleared only one ball in the first half and I don't think Jackie hit a ball at all.

So yeah, despite all the flak and the abuse that has since been hurled at me, I thought we were doing okay.

Tommy Dunne ran onto the field during the first half and I went straight over to him and asked, 'Well, Tommy, are you happy?'

'Yeah, it's going well,' he replied.

At half-time I again asked Tommy if he was happy, or if there was anything that needed to be worked on.

'Look, Larry, it's working. We'll keep going with it.'

I also went to Eoin at the break. Eoin was out of the squad with a groin injury he had picked up on Bere Island and aggravated two days later playing for his club in the South Tipp final.

'Eoin, where do you stand on this now?'

'It's working,' he said. 'Kilkenny are rattled – their backs are rattled – they're not getting clean possession.'

I asked if there was anything we could do to bring it to the next level.

'No, I don't think so.'

You need that reassurance. I'm only part of a team. There's absolutely no point in me saying something is working fine if everyone else is saying no, it's not

I had no difficulty changing the system if it wasn't working. I was open to any scenario. I had carried water against Limerick and was happy to do that.

After the game, aside from getting the heat for our tactics, I was met with a barrage of rumours that there had been a big half-time bust-up with the management. Depending on who you listened to, I went toe to toe with Declan or Tommy and it took Eoin Kelly to get me back on the field.

Complete rubbish. In fact, the mood could hardly have been more positive.

We went in a point ahead; we knew we were in contention and I'm glad to put a few things to rest here. I was involved in no row. No-one in the Tipp camp was involved in any row.

The only problem I had at the interval was my breathing. I was out of puff with all the extra running and Pa was in the same boat. We'd never covered so much of the park. So we sat down to get our breath for a few moments.

Then the backs and forwards gathered in their own little groups, with Tommy and Declan driving it on. Before the forwards spoke, someone noticed the subs weren't in the dressing-room.

There was no point in discussing tactics without them, because the boys who came off the bench, the likes of Eoin, Shane Bourke, Séamie Callanan and Gearóid Ryan, usually made an impact. They could win games on their own, and we were confident their fresh legs would take us through to the final.

Anyway, we had to wait for them to arrive and that delayed things for a few minutes. Then, with the clock ticking, I tried to go to the toilet but, probably a bit dehydrated after all the running, failed to get a result.

When I got back to the dressing-room I looked for Hotpoint and my customary change of boots, shorts and jersey. With the lads now shaping to go back out, and worried that I still had to use the toilet, I got in a bit of a muddle changing my gear. Between struggling with the fresh gear and finally managing to pass water I lagged a little behind.

I tore out after the lads and arrived on the field thirty-seven seconds late. In my absence the game had started, Kilkenny had won a free and converted. I put my hands up – it was clumsy. I'm always one of the last out of a dressing-room but never has a game restarted as quickly as that one. It shouldn't have happened.

Along with the half-time bust-up theory came the story that I was too afraid to meet Jackie at the tunnel, where he had met me at the exact same juncture in the 2011 final.

I'm not afraid to mark him or anyone else for that matter.

There was a team system we believed in and we genuinely felt this was the route to the All-Ireland final. If Tommy and Declan wanted me to stand on the edge of the square and go toe to toe with Jackie I would have done that too.

People reckon that I should have gone straight to Jackie. I think I've already explained what would have happened if I'd done that.

I've also been asked if I lost my head in all the commotion – the tactics, the late entrance and all that. But I saw no problems. We had created opportunities but just hadn't converted them all. Things were going okay.

That frame of mind soon changed, though. They got the first couple of scores and you could feel the momentum shifting in their favour.

Richie Power got a free and pointed it while Tommy, Jackie, Pa and myself were in the corner by the Davin Stand doing our own thing. It was then I sensed a kind of resentment in the crowd – the fans were losing patience with our antics.

Kilkenny went a few points up and it was clear that we'd soon have to change tack. The plan had worked up to half-time but once you go behind you have to re-evaluate. When one team gets a head of steam, the energy shifts and the scoreboard dictates tactics.

Within fifteen minutes of the restart we had fallen three points behind and as I ran past Pa I suggested we'd have to abandon the script and revert to our normal system. I went into full forward, with Jackie in hot pursuit. Pa was back on the wing with Tommy keeping him company.

What happened then?

The Kilkenny defenders started lording possession and won ball after ball.

We resumed our normal set-up and they grabbed two goals in ten minutes. Tommy and Brian Hogan saw so much ball they looked like men returning tennis volleys. We changed tack and they were let go back to what they're best at.

We were slaughtered.

Suddenly, it was hard to see a way out. Once Kilkenny get a run on you that's usually it. They went from being three points ahead to all of a shot steaming ten points in front. Croke Park then becomes the loneliest place in the world.

With seven minutes to go we were twelve points down. I looked around at my team-mates and saw everyone deflated. The lads at the back had been turned once or twice and smelling blood the Cats went in for the kill.

The theory that we were overtrained, that we were flogged too heavily on Bere Island, circulated in the days after the game. We weren't. Those goals sapped the energy from our legs and our minds. It had nothing to do with training.

The final whistle sounded and I turned towards the tunnel. I glanced back briefly to shake hands with Jackie but I wanted off that field as soon as I could. An eighteen-point hammering. Our biggest defeat since 1897.

I headed for the dressing-room with the intention of staying there as long as possible in the hope that everyone else would have left the stadium before me. I was never as low.

After a match people have boxes to tick and speeches to make. As we slumped exhausted in the dressing-room, Declan spoke and thanked us. He mentioned that the club championships would resume and we had to go back and put pride into our clubs. Paul Curran spoke.

'Lads, I'd just like to thank ye for the huge effort that every-one has made all year,' he said. 'It was a huge honour for me to captain Tipperary and . . .'

With that he got emotional and struggled to continue, and seeing him so upset, our captain, well, that had an awful effect on me and the rest of the lads. That's when it really hit home that we were out.

All I wanted was time to pass so I could get home.

Pa, sitting beside me as usual, offered words of comfort.

'Larry, it was working for us,' he insisted. 'The whole thing – we were getting on top. Don't be taking the hit for this on your own; we're all in it together.'

I got another lift from a text sent by someone who is very close to me and sensed I'd be getting all the flak: 'The people who believe in you still believe in you – that's all any of us need to know.'

I mucked about with my gear, had a shower and slowly got dressed. When I exited the dressing-room I thought the coast would be clear. But just as I was putting my gear into the bus I was approached by Oisin Langan from *Newstalk* asking for a few words. Oisin is a sound fella and even though I was at an all-time low I couldn't refuse him – the same lad had helped me promote the pub when I opened it. He was glad to help in the good times and now I felt I couldn't hide from him in the bad times. But no sooner had he stopped me than twenty other reporters came from nowhere, armed with their Dictaphones.

I was rock bottom in my career as a Tipperary hurler, drained physically and mentally, and I was taken aback by this media scrum. Some of the questioning seemed to be about my supposed efforts to get Tommy Walsh sent off and I couldn't get my head around that. To be honest, I hardly knew what I was saying.

People had obviously got it into their heads that I deliberately went out to get Tommy a second yellow, and as I stood there trying to answer their questions I think I got a feeling of what purgatory must be like. God knows what I said to the reporters but I can only repeat that I didn't go out to get anyone sent off. I'm 100 per cent sorry if any Tipperary or Kilkenny supporter thinks that of me. It's just not the case.

Anyway, I babbled on for a couple of minutes, but inside

there was pure silence in my head. I knew I was a beaten docket. Eventually, I got up to the players' lounge, met the others and we all headed for home. Michael Cahill, Paudie, Elaine and I got off the team bus at Portlaoise and travelled to Thurles together. We made for our house, got some food in, had a few drinks and spoke about the game.

About 11 p.m. we tipped in as far as the bar. I felt I had to show my face and it wasn't too bad in fairness. While there were plenty of brave lads with made-up names hiding behind computer screens abusing me, most of the ordinary people of Tipp were okay.

After a few hours we got a taxi home. The bed beckoned, and despite all the turmoil of the day I soon drifted off, and never was sleep a more blessed relief.

When I woke up the next morning, there was no escaping the sulphur that hung in the atmosphere. The towns and villages of Tipperary were alive with anger.

I thought it would calm down after a few days but I think it only got worse. I write a column from time to time for the *Irish Independent* and on Wednesday the sports editor, Dave Courtney, rang me and said that even though the Cork and Donegal All-Ireland football semi-final was only four days away scarcely a word had been written about it. Tipperary hurling was the only story in town and the 'Lar Corbett issue' was not going away.

I felt I had to come out and apologise in the newspaper. It was an apology to the genuine Tipperary supporters who don't know me as an individual but know me as a hurler. They are proud people who go to matches all year long. When they were younger they would have gone to games with their fathers and mothers and now they are the ones bringing their kids. I just wanted to offer them an explanation of what happened against Kilkenny. I wanted to say that, collectively, the team was sorry and bitterly disappointed. There was no point papering over cracks or trotting out excuses. I just made the point how much we regretted that things didn't work.

I was getting it in the neck but my thoughts were mostly with John O'Brien. On the Tuesday before the semi-final we were pucking around before training when news came through that his elder brother, Thomas, had died suddenly. We couldn't believe it. John O got word of it in the afternoon but he still joined us at training that night.

I'd like to think we were all there for him. On Thursday, Declan and Tommy decided that as a squad we would all to go to the funeral, wearing our Tipp tracksuits, and try to support John O, his brother Paddy, who won an All-Ireland with Tipp in 2001, and the family. I don't know where his strength came from. All I can say is that John O knew that every one of us was, and is, with him in his loss.

And looking back, about the only positive I can take from that semi-final is the reception he got from both sets of fans as he left the pitch. It was a credit to the GAA.

The other stuff? The abuse aimed at me? Well, none of that compared to what John O and his family faced. But I still had to deal with it.

People started ringing, saying this is what's out there, this is what Babs has said, and so on. Dave Courtney said he had never seen so much negativity toward one player.

One name kept coming at me, though.

'Michael Duignan – did you hear what he said about you?'

Every second person I met: 'Jesus, Duignan must have something against you. Called you a disgrace. Seemed to think you wanted Tommy Walsh sent off. Said you should have been taken off.'

A few days later I replayed the match commentary and while I have to admit our tactics ultimately failed and we collapsed in the second half, I have no doubt Duignan also set the tone for some of the reaction and the vile abuse I got. I doubt he set out to do that; it's just the power of TV. A massive audience tuned in for that game and by the end of it they were looking for someone to blame for what happened. Michael Duignan's comments have to be seen in that context.

I didn't think there was any balance. Michael's job is to comment on the game but how can you call anyone a disgrace? That's an awful thing to say about anyone in any walk of life, never mind an amateur player. I found his comments really personal and beyond the bounds of sports punditry.

The floodgates opened. Jokes, cartoons and the video clips were photoshopped and manipulated to show me chasing after Tommy in various scenarios. A few of them were pretty funny, I have to say. I could whine on about just how bad it all got, but thank God I'm designed in such a way I can handle it.

Within two weeks of the hammering, Declan, Tommy and Glossy stepped down. They took serious flak too but they'll all stay involved with the game because they are hurling men and they'll come back to different teams in their own time.

Since the game people have asked if I've been scarred with the way the season ended but I just have to get on with it. I don't want to hang up the blue and gold jersey in these circumstances, and so, like everyone on the team, I'll just wait and see what the new manager Eamon O'Shea thinks, see how I feel and if I'm wanted, before I make a call on going back. Everyone knows how highly I regard Eamon. He was the best man for the job and it's massive for the county that he's involved again.

I'd just love to go back and focus completely on hurling without any sideshows. Maybe I didn't help my own cause this season but for better or worse I was only staying true to myself. The season that has just passed will not define me. Not as a hurler, not as a man. It is just part of my story.

If you grow up in Tipperary, hurling is at the centre of everything and it gradually consumed me too. People may have questioned my heart when I walked away but I definitely feel proud to wear that shirt. I'm playing a sport in Tipperary that's number one on every patch of grass or street corner, in every village and town in the county.

There have been plenty of downs but when I see passion in peoples' faces during or after a match, or when I lift my head in a dressing-room and see Eoin Kelly or Tommy Dunne deliver a speech without missing a beat, that's really when it hits me that I'm in a lucky position in life.

I have a habit of looking at things through the eyes of others to find out exactly what it means to me – as you'll know by now, that's just the way I work. I spoke to a man in his eighties at the Anner Hotel recently and when he spoke of how Tipp would rise from the ashes in 2013 I saw the fire still blazing brightly in his eyes. That gave me a huge lift.

When we won the 2010 All-Ireland final one of Thurles Sars' – and Tipp's – greatest ever hurlers, Mickey 'The Rattler' Byrne, came into our dressing-room and cried. All these lads have one thing in common – passion.

I may have different ways of expressing my own emotions but that's what hurling for Tipp also means to me. That's why I spent months of soul-searching, trying desperately to investigate why I didn't fire in the 2011 All-Ireland final. That's why I spent years driving around the country like a lost sheep hoping to get my own hammers right. I have the same passion as these guys even if I'm not always as extrovert in showing it.

\*

Near the end of the 2010 final, after I got my third goal, I set about running back into position. The contest was over but I was programmed to get back to base. Before I did I took a second to look into the crowd. They were going nuts. For five or six seconds I focused on one small section of the stand and took a freeze frame of four or five seats, occupied by people of various shapes and sizes, young and old, all wearing the blue and gold.

I wondered if they knew each other and I tried to picture them the next day at work. One lad may be a CEO of a big company, the other running a newsagent's and the tall fella on the right drawing the dole maybe. The young fella beside them may be starting school the next morning, possibly hoping some day he'll get to play in an All-Ireland final.

And then it hit me. No matter if you're a managing director, keeping a small shop or filling out forms at the labour exchange, these lads are bound together, for seventy minutes and nine or ten times a year, by the same thing – Tipperary hurling.

Our jersey breaks down all barriers, what wages you get, the lifestyle you lead, the social circles you move in. It's about the only thing in our county that brings people together and lets them operate on the same level. That means more to me than anything.

As the roar at that third goal reverberated around the stadium, those four or five lads turned around and celebrated wildly with folk they had never met and were quickly sucked into that joyful sea of blue and gold.

Happy enough, I ran back out the field and allowed myself a little smile.

I want to get that feeling back.

# Acknowledgements

This seems as good a time as any to say thanks to a few people for everything they have done for me over the course of my life and hurling career.

My fiancée, Elaine Gleeson, is first on the list. We're getting married in December 2012, and I'm really looking forward to that day. She is the first person I turn to in every aspect of my life. Thanks, Elaine, for everything.

Back in 2001, having made no impression with county under-age teams, I first got the call to play hurling for Tipperary and it sent me on a different road. By then, though, a lot of people had already helped to shape my life.

Thanks to my mother, Breda, for all she has done for me throughout my childhood, youth and adult life. Anything I wanted growing up – a new hurley or boots – I only had to ask. She has always been there for me and I just want to remind her here how much I appreciate everything. Thanks, Mam!

I also hope I made my father, Eddie, proud over the years.

To my sister, Helen, for all she has done for me. I wish her the very best in her future.

Anyone who knows me or lives around Thurles will be aware that two of my closest friends are Tommy Maher and Ger 'Redser' O'Grady. The two lads want the best for me and are always there to watch my back. I have asked them to sit alongside me at the top table at my wedding reception – I couldn't think of better men to join me there.

Speaking of sitting at tables, I spent a lot of time in the kitchen of Josie and Bill Collins. They looked after me so well over the years and treated me like another son. I enjoyed all the chats and I'll never forget how nice you and your family were to me.

Eddie O'Donnell has been a close friend and trusted mentor in recent years – great to offer advice and always a fascinating man to chat to. I know he has my best interests at heart, so thanks, Eddie, for your friendship, steady hand and wisdom!

Eoin McHugh of Transworld has been a gentleman to deal with from start to finish, and his feedback and suggestions have kept everyone on track during the writing of my life story.

I'd like to say thanks to Sportsfile and Inpho for use of their pictures.

To the players, management teams and backroom staff members with both Thurles Sarsfields and Tipperary. The Sars gave me the platform to wear the blue and gold shirt and playing for Tipp I witnessed days I never thought were possible. I've formed lifelong friendships with people from both camps through the last two decades.

Thanks also to Damian Lawlor, another Tipperary man, who helped me put my story together.

The 2012 season was a tough one, no point in saying otherwise, but a single year doesn't classify a career, much less an entire life.

As I look back I can acknowledge that it's been some roller-coaster of a journey so far. I only hope you enjoyed my take on the highs and lows and switchbacks that I met along the road.

Hopefully there is yet more to come.

*Lar Corbett*

## ACKNOWLEDGEMENTS

Thanks a million, Larry, for entrusting me with the job of writing your story. I hope I've helped do you justice and I wish you every success wherever your career and life take you from here.

To my wife, Ruth, for her love, encouragement and understanding. And to Mam and Dad for exactly the same. Dad brought me to the hurling field in Cloughjordan when I was a small child and I cannot wait to bring my own little lad, Jamie, there for the first time. I just hope he's more skilful than his father – even at eighteen months old he probably already is.

Thanks to Eoin McHugh and Brian Langan at Transworld Ireland for their brilliant guidance; both thorough gentlemen and a pleasure to deal with.

I also want to acknowledge Eddie O'Donnell for his constant support and counsel.

In other areas of my life and work I owe a debt of gratitude to loyal and trusted colleagues – in particular Pat Nolan, Jackie Cahill, Cian Murphy, Christy O'Connor, Kieran Shannon, Peter Sweeney, Gordon Manning and Richard Gallagher. Also to John Greene, sports editor of the *Sunday Independent* for his understanding.

Finally, to two hurling fanatics who have gone to their eternal reward. My late uncle Paddy Lawlor and the man who opened the door to my journalism career, Gerry Slevin, former editor of the *Nenagh Guardian*. I will never forget either of you.

*Damian Lawlor*

# Picture Acknowledgements

Every effort has been made to contact copyright holders. Those who have not been acknowledged are invited to get in touch with the publishers.

Photos not credited have kindly been supplied by Lar Corbett.

*First section*
Pages 6/7: Tipperary manager Nicky English has a word with Lar Corbett before the 2001 All-Ireland hurling championship semi-final, Croke Park, Dublin: © Damien Eagers, Sportsfile, 069790; Munster hurling championship 3/6/2001 – Eoin Kelly, Declan Ryan, Lar Corbett: © INPHO/Patrick Bolger, INPHO 00050275; Tipperary captain Tommy Dunne lifts the Liam McCarthy Cup 9/9/2001: © INPHO/Lorraine O'Sullivan, INPHO 00055726.

Page 8: Lar Corbett receives treatment from (L–R) Jim Kilty and John Hayes during the All-Ireland senior hurling championship quarter final 27/7/2003: © INPHO/Morgan Treacy, INPHO 00098720; Lar Corbett and Eoin Kelly celebrate after the 2008 Allianz National Hurling League, Division 1 Final, at the Gaelic Grounds, Limerick: © Pat Murphy, Sportsfile, 292103.

*Second section*
Page 9: (L–R) Kilkenny's Brian Hogan and Michael Rice (No. 9) surround Lar Corbett during the 2009 All-Ireland senior hurling championship final, Croke Park, Dublin: © Ray McManus, Sportsfile, 377468; Tipperary goalkeeper Brendan Cummins reacts to referee Diarmuid Kirwan's decision to award a penalty in the second half of the 2009 All-Ireland senior hurling championship final, Croke Park, Dublin: © Daire Brennan, Sportsfile, 377529.

Page 10/11: Jackie Tyrrell, Kilkenny, and Patrick Maher, Tipperary, tussle during the 2010 All-Ireland senior hurling championship final, Croke Park, Dublin: © Matt Browne, Sportsfile, 457125; Lar Corbett catches the sliotar ahead of Noel Hickey of Kilkenny, 2010 All-Ireland senior hurling championship final, Croke Park, Dublin: © INPHO/Lorraine O'Sullivan, INPHO 00455679; Lar Corbett celebrates after scoring his side's first goal in the All-Ireland senior hurling championship final 5/9/2010: © David Maher, Sportsfile, 457044; Lar

Corbett scores Tipperary's second goal in the 2010 All-Ireland senior hurling championship final despite a hurley thrown in his direction: © INPHO/Donall Farmer, INPHO 00455773; Lar Corbett commiserates with Jackie Tyrrell, Kilkenny, after the 2010 All-Ireland senior hurling championship final: © Daire Brennan, Sportsfile, 457077; the Tipperary team celebrate with the Liam McCarthy Cup after the Kilkenny v Tipperary 2010 All-Ireland senior hurling championship final: © Paul Mohan, Sportsfile, 457085.

Page 12/13: Tipperary captain Eoin Kelly lifts the Liam McCarthy Cup, 2010 All-Ireland senior hurling championship final, Kilkenny v Tipperary, Croke Park, Dublin: © Daire Brennan, Sportsfile, 457048; Tipperary manager Liam Sheedy celebrates with the Liam McCarthy Cup alongside selector Michael Ryan, left, and coach Eamon O'Shea, right, after the 2010 All-Ireland senior hurling championship final: © Paul Mohan, Sportsfile, 457103; Lar Corbett and Elaine Gleeson at the 2010 Opel Gaelic Players Association Gala Awards, Citywest Hotel, Saggart, Co. Dublin: © Alan Place, Sportsfile, 470981; Texaco Sportstars Awards, Four Seasons Hotel, Dublin, 18/11/2010 – award winners (L-R) Lar Corbett, Hurler of the Year, Bernard Brogan of Dublin, Footballer of the Year, and Katie Taylor, Boxer of the Year: © INPHO/Cathal Noonan, INPHO 00472952; Lar Corbett is introduced to HM Queen Elizabeth II by President of the GAA Christy Cooney during her tour of Croke Park, 18/5/2011: © Ray McManus, Sportsfile, 516622.

Page 14/15: Lar Corbett celebrates scoring a goal against Cork in the Munster senior hurling championship quarter final, Semple Stadium, Thurles, 29/5/2011: © INPHO/Cathal Noonan, INPHO 00516397; Lar Corbett disappointed at the end of the 2011 All-Ireland senior hurling championship final, Croke Park, Dublin: © INPHO/Lorraine O'Sullivan, INPHO 00539123; Lar Corbett gives instructions to his teammates during the Munster senior hurling championship game between Tipperary and Limerick, Semple Stadium, Thurles, 27/5/2012: © Barry Cregg, Sportsfile, 625565; Lar Corbett makes a hand pass to Noel McGrath during the Munster senior hurling championship semi-final against Cork, 24/6/2012: © INPHO/Cathal Noonan, INPHO 00610976.

Page 16: (L-R) Pa Bourke, Tipperary, and Tommy Walsh, Kilkenny, and Lar Corbett, Tipperary, and Jackie Tyrrell, Kilkenny, tussle in the corner of the canal end and Cusack Stand during the 2012 All-Ireland senior hurling championship semi-final, Croke Park, Dublin: © INPHO/Donall Farmer, INPHO 00623147; referee Cathal McAllister speaks to Lar Corbett and Kilkenny's Jackie Tyrrell during the All-Ireland senior hurling championship semi-final, Croke Park, Dublin, 19/8/2012: © Ray McManus, Sportsfile, 675564.

# Index

# ABOUT THE AUTHORS

**Lar Corbett,** from the Thurles Sarsfields club, is renowned as one of the most exciting forwards the game of hurling has seen. A three-time All-Star and former Hurler of the Year, he has won two All-Ireland senior medals with Tipperary and will be for ever remembered for his three-goal haul in the 2010 All-Ireland final. Since his intercounty debut in 2001, Corbett has established himself as one of the game's greatest exponents.

**Damian Lawlor,** from Kilruane in County Tipperary, is an award-winning journalist and GAA Correspondent for the *Sunday Independent*. He also presented *Take Your Point* on RTE Radio One for two years. This, his third book, follows the best-selling *I Crossed the Line – the Liam Dunne Story* and *Working On a Dream – a Year on the Road with the Waterford Footballers*, which was runner-up in the 2009 William Hill Sports Book awards.